THE ROSE
IN FASHION

FOR MY MOTHER, JULIA

First published by Yale University Press 2020
302 Temple Street, P.O. Box 209040,
New Haven CT 06520-9040

47 Bedford Square, London WC1B 3DP
yalebooks.com | yalebooks.co.uk

To accompany the exhibition *Ravishing: The Rose in Fashion*
at The Museum at the Fashion Institute of Technology, New York

ISBN 978-0-300-250084-0 HB
Library of Congress Control Number: 2020931942

10 9 8 7 6 5 4 3 2 1
2024 2023 2022 2021 2020

Designed by Charlie Smith Design
Copy edited by Faye Robson
Printed in Italy

Front cover:
Noir Kei Ninomiya,
Rose ensemble with headdress,
Paris, Autumn/Winter 2019.
FirstView

Back cover:
Nick Knight
Sunday 8th July, 2018.
Hand-coated pigment print,
printed 2019, 77.4 x 63.5cm
Edition of 10, with 3 Artist Proofs
Courtesy of Nick Knight

THE ROSE
IN FASHION

...

AMY DE LA HAYE

...

YALE UNIVERSITY PRESS,
LONDON AND NEW HAVEN

CONTENTS

CONTENTS

'FASHION IS A LITTLE LIKE RADIUM...

[1] Couturier Charles James, notes for a speech given at the Chicago fashion guild dinner, Sherman Hotel, 3 June 1958.

OR LIKE ESSENCE OF ROSES, WHICH IF UNDILUTED WOULD ASPHYXIATE'

CHARLES JAMES, 1958[1]

It has been a joy to collaborate with Amy de la Haye on *Ravishing: The Rose in Fashion*. Her book and exhibition exploring the rose in fashion make an original and important contribution to fashion studies, while also presenting a beautiful and dramatic story that is sure to appeal to readers and museum visitors. The rose is not only beautiful and fragrant, its symbolism is powerful and multifaceted. As a result, when designers are inspired by the rose, their work draws on powerful emotions and ideas about love, sex and death. *Ravishing: The Rose in Fashion* draws on a wealth of scholarship across the disciplines, but it wears its learning accessibly. Each chapter of the book is an invitation to make a voyage of discovery, beginning with Amy's conversation with the brilliant image-maker, Nick Knight.

The Museum at the Fashion Institute of Technology seldom works with outside curators, but Amy's depth of experience as a curator and as professor of fashion curation at the London College of Fashion puts her in a category of her own. Colleen Hill, Curator of Costume and Accessories at The Museum at FIT, has worked closely with Amy on co-curating the exhibition, and their multiple collaborations have strengthened the relationship between the London College of Fashion and The Museum at FIT.

Valerie Steele
Director and Chief Curator, The Museum at FIT, New York

THE ROSE

...

'FLOWERS THAT ARE LOOKED AT'

AMY DE LA HAYE

...

... for the roses
Had the look of flowers that are looked at.

...

T. S. Eliot, 'Burnt Norton', 1936[1]

The rose – the most ravishingly beautiful and fragrant of flowers – is inextricably entwined with fashion and dressed appearances (the latter embraces perfume, grooming, jewellery, body adornment and gesture.) Roses, like fashion, are a luxury and they are ephemeral. Both are 'shown' (on catwalks and at flower shows); their appeal is multisensory; they are avidly collected and incite passion and obsession (a scarlet-red floribunda, bred by Stanley George Marciel in 1990, has this very name). In her seminal book *The Symbolic Rose* (1954), Barbara Seward wrote, 'Not only do its roots extend at least to the beginnings of recorded time, but its petals embrace the deepest positive values ever held by man. Although the flower is equalled in age and profundity by such fundamental symbols as sea, sun, bird, star and cross, it would be difficult to prove that it has been surpassed by any.'[2] It is worth noting that responses are entirely personal and partly culturally determined; not everyone has approved of, or subscribed to, such interpretations.

Not surprisingly, the rose and its savage, deterrent thorns (technically, they are prickles) – a conjunction of opposites – have provided a fertile source of inspiration for designers, artists and writers, who have drawn out allusions to love, beauty, sexuality, sin, gendered identities, rites of passage, transgression, degradation and death. *Ravishing: The Rose in Fashion* demonstrates visually and evaluates critically how the rose has inspired the ways we look, dress, feel and fantasise. It foregrounds innovative, refined and challenging fashion design dating from *c*.1700 to the latest global collections, while recognising that

almost everyone can wear, and feel transformed by wearing or holding, one or more fresh rose. As the author of the immensely popular nineteenth-century book *Le Langage des Fleurs* (1819, first translated into English 1820; see p.122) made explicit, while the rose is undoubtedly queen of flowers, it is also the 'commonest'.[3]

My written and curated projects are usually ignited by the desire to interpret a single or group of dress items, or archival documents. *Ravishing: The Rose in Fashion* evolved from the combination of three different sources: Nick Knight's sublime photographs of 'Roses from my Garden'; my mother's lovely, rose-filled walled garden; and the quote that opens this chapter by T. S. Eliot. This introduction takes up from there and reflects upon some historical, conceptual and terminological relationships between roses, fashion and dressed appearances before introducing the contributors, contents and broader rationale of this fashion-focused book.

The genus *Rosa* is believed to date back some 35–40 million years.[4] It is resilient, promiscuous and rambunctious, which accounts for its longevity, mutability and broad geographic territory. Roses flourish in China (where they were cultivated from at least 500 BCE), Korea, Japan, Siberia, northern and central Asia, India, the Caucasus, the Arabian Peninsula, Europe, North Africa, and North and Latin America. Roses, like fashion, are bound up with stories of travel, migration, international trade and cross-cultural influences.

Opposite above right
4. Isaac Oliver, *Portrait of a Lady Masqued as Flora*, c.1605.
Miniature, pigment on vellum,
5.3 x 4.1cm
Rijksmuseum, Amsterdam
The English court of James I enjoyed lavish masqued entertainments, often with allegorical and Classical subjects. Here, a fashionable woman is costumed as Flora, with roses in her hair.
Artokoloro Quint Lox Limited/ Alamy Stock Photo

Opposite below right
5. Alexander Roslin,
Flora of the Opera, c.1750.
Oil on canvas, 91.5 x 72.5cm
Musée des beaux-arts de Bordeaux
Roslin was a society portrait painter, noted for his fine depiction of fashionable dress and jewellery. His Rococo-style Flora wears a flower wreath, armlet and holds a garland in which roses feature prominently.
© Mairie de Bordeaux, Musée des beaux-arts

Right
6. V Buso, 'Rose' shoe, USA, c.1960.
Suede and metal
The Museum at FIT, New York
This gorgeous shoe might be interpreted within the contexts of Surrealism's preoccupations: the illusion of nature, displacement and improbability (a rose supports a person).
The Museum at FIT, P90.78.2.
Museum purchase

Bottom left
7. *Rosa* 'Christian Dior', a double hybrid tea rose introduced by Meilland, 1958.
Christian Dior was mid-twentieth-century fashion's floriculturist. Although the haute couturier's signature flower was lily of the valley, he adored and grew roses; this fragrant double hybrid tea rose was named after him following his premature death.
Yellow Cat/Shutterstock.com

Bottom right
8. Jeff Bark, Comme des Garçons, 'Roses and Blood' collection, *Dazed* magazine, spring 2015.
Stylist Robbie Spencer has placed petals in model Molly Blair's open mouth, symbolising uncontrollable passion or sublime suffocation by roses.
Courtesy of Jeff Bark

Fresh roses have been worn since at least the times of the ancient Egyptians. Because flowers are seasonal, their absence is strongly felt: when the earth no longer yielded natural blooms, these were supplanted by 'permanent botanicals', the name given to the first artificial flowers, which were crafted from stained horn. Roses were to become revered within cuisine and wine-craft, were used to beautify (the Egyptians used charred rose petals to colour their eyebrows) and as fragrance, while rose water and vitamin-rich rose hips were valued medicinally.

In ancient Greece, the poetess Sappho, who has become a cultural icon of female homosexuality, lyrically described the moon as 'rose fingered'.[5] She is reputed to have planted roses among the apple trees in the sanctuary of Aphrodite, goddess of love and human sexuality.[6] But, as erudite cultural and botanical historian Jennifer Potter reveals, she did not, as is commonly believed, crown the rose the 'queen of flowers'. It was the second-century Greek writer Achilles Tatius, in his prose romance *Leucippe* and *Clitophon*, who awarded the title.[7] Potter's *The Rose* (2010) has provided a core contextual reference for this book.

In ancient Rome, the rose came to be so adored that a lavish annual festival – Rosalia, also known as *rosatio*, meaning

'rose adornment' – was staged in its honour, and rose festivals
have been held by rose-growing nations ever since.[8] Long before
flowers were gendered feminine, rose wreaths or chaplets (circlets,
worn on the head; fig.12) and garlands (longer, strung) played
a vital role in economic, domestic, religious and ceremonial
life. They were awarded to men for great acts and virtues, and
on occasions, when Rome was warring, came to be subject to
sumptuary legislation. And it was men who wore perfume made
from roses (women preferred stronger oils such as myrrh and
sweet marjoram).

An examination of rose anatomy provides a terminology using
which it is possible to draw comparisons and further analogies
with dress. A rosebud is encased by five protective and supportive
sepals, which open when the flower is ready to bloom. Together,
these elements form the calyx – a term derived from the ancient
Greek word *kálux*, meaning 'husk or envelope', a protective outer
layer. The sum of petals is called the corolla, a diminutive from
the Latin *corona*, meaning 'little crown'. Stamen are the pollen-
producing reproductive organs of the flower; the term is Latin
for 'warp thread', the form and lengthwise arrangement of which
they share. The stem of the stamen is called a filament, its pollen-
containing sack the anther.

Rosaceae.

Rosa centifolia L.

UNE ROSE PARMI LES ROSES
Robe de Garden-party de Redfern

Opposite
13. Botanical diagram showing the anatomy of a cabbage rose, or *Rosa x centifolia*, nineteenth century. The name of this rose means '100 leaves' (before Carl Linnaeus's introduction of taxonomy in the late eighteenth century, botanists did not distinguish between petals and leaves). Native to Iran and grown since at least the sixteenth century, this species was historically traded as one of two roses used to make perfume (*Rosa x damascena* is the other) and for medicine (to treat inflammation and as an aphrodisiac). Bildagentur-online/Contributor/ Getty Images

Above left
14. J. Gosé, 'Robe de Garden-party de Redfern', illustration for *Gazette du Bon Ton*, April 1913. Pochoir print
A fashionable garden-party dress by British firm Redfern is portrayed in an Art Deco-styled rose garden setting. Image courtesy of Fashion Institute of Technology | SUNY, FIT Library Unit of Special Collections and College Archives

Above right
15. Waistcoat, France, c.1780. Silk brocade with gold metal embroidery
The Museum at FIT, New York
Flower-decorated waistcoats were highly fashionable in this period; this silk features a woven design of clusters of stemmed pink roses and buds. The Museum at FIT, 93.132.4. Gift of Thomas Oechsler

The gynoecium – from the Greek *gynaeceum*, meaning 'women's apartments' – lies in the centre of the rose and is a clumped mass of greenish-yellow organs called carpels, which include the ovary. Taxonomically, the rose is classified as hermaphrodite, rendering its ornamental application within twenty-first-century gender-neutral fashion all the more poignant.

Sexuality lies at the core of a flower's existence. More than any other flower, the rose has been personified, with analogies drawn between the rose and the human body, sexuality and female fertility. The origin of the term 'de-flower' to describe sexual penetration followed from the seventeenth-century herbalist Nicholas Culpeper's likening of the fleshy knobs around the hymen to a half-blown rose (this, in a directory for midwives).[9] From the eighteenth century, naturalists interpreted the stamen as male, the flower as womb-like and feminine, while the rosebud has become a near-universal metaphor for lips, nipples and clitoris. In the privately printed book *Vocabula Amatoria* of 1895 – listing words, phrases and allusions referenced by leading French writers – the entry for 'Rose' is indexed in relation to the female pudendum and 'Rosée' (dew) to semen.[10] Roses are also often named after people, including fashion designers Christian Dior (fig.7), Valentino (a dark-red 'sweetheart' rose, popular for cutting) and Vivienne Westwood (a light pink/apricot-coloured hybrid tea rose).

Right
16. Nick Knight, visual artist Maren
Bailey's mouth for *CHAOS 69*
magazine, 2017.
When Katie Lyall and Charlotte
Stockdale invited Nick Knight to
create a project for the first issue
of *CHAOS* magazine, he contacted
talented people who pushed the
boundaries of beauty on Instagram.
Bailey's dressmaker-pinned lips might
be likened to a twenty-first-century
rose with thorns.
Courtesy of Nick Knight

Opposite
17. Woman personified as a rose, set
in a card with printed rose graphic,
early 1920s.
Studio postcard
Private collection

Fine dress fabrics are often likened to the flower's semi-sheer, silken petals; the term 'petal' itself derives from the Latin *petalum*, meaning metal plate or blade, which feeds into our sense of the flower's compelling duality. Roses have prickles that comprise extensions of the cortex and epidermis, whereas thorns, strictly speaking, are modified branches or stems. However, as 'thorns' are so embedded within the literature and mythologising of the rose, the misuse is here deliberately perpetuated. Biblically, in the Garden of Eden, roses were said to be thorn-less before Adam and Eve succumbed to temptation and ate the forbidden fruit from the tree of knowledge of good and evil. The introduction of thorns was interpreted as God's curse on creation, the punishment for human sin. Thorns (not just rose thorns) were subsequently interpreted in the context of repentance: in the early sixth century, Saint Benedict of Nursia – considered the father of Western monasticism – threw himself upon a bush of thorns for having unchaste thoughts.

In many cultures, the garden is interpreted as a spiritual haven or paradise on earth, the adoration of flowers cast as the worship of a divinity. Vishnu, a principle Hindu deity, is said to have fashioned his wife Lakshmi – goddess of wealth, good fortune and beauty – from 108 large and 1,008 small rose petals. (An investigation of roses within mythology and world clothing would provide fascinating further study.) Charles Darwin's groundbreaking theory of biological evolution, published as *The Origin of Species by Means of Natural Selection* (1859), changed the way nature was viewed scientifically in the West, and introduced a new sense of nature's more ruthless, or at least pragmatic-seeming, traits to cultural output. Darwin's work made a deep impact upon Émile Zola – novelist, playwright, political activist and progenitor of the Naturalist movement in literature, which explored the influence of environment on the personalities and biographies of its characters. Zola's narratives brim with floral analogies and are referenced within this book

comedian Max Miller's use of rose double entendres, he closes with a photograph of a black wool suit with dramatic, crimson-red silk, rose-petal-like sleeves, designed by Sarah Burton for Alexander McQueen.

In Chapter III, 'The Eighteenth Century: Perennial Reign', Colleen Hill, Curator of Costume and Accessories at The Museum of FIT, New York, explores how innovations in textile production and advancements in botanical knowledge were deeply entwined in this century, resulting in increasingly naturalistic depictions of roses (and other flowers) on silk dress fabrics. A late-eighteenth-century dress silk, hand-painted with a meandering design of pink roses against blue stripes, provides the focus study. Hill highlights how women were some of the most significant contributors to fashion during this era: Maria Sibylla Merian's detailed and scientifically accurate botanical drawings were used as designs for embroidery; Anna Maria Garthwaite was the most prolific and renowned designer of Spitalfields silks; and the elaborately constructed *pouf* hairstyles popularised by Marie Antoinette at the court of Louis XVI sometimes employed fresh roses, combining nature and artifice in a way that helped to characterise the fashionable appearance of the eighteenth century.

It is important to recognise that luxury fashion garments are often designed in plain fabrics, which provide the perfect foil for magnificent jewellery. As many galleries do not have the security arrangements required to display intrinsically valuable jewellery, this critical component of fashionable appearance is all too often omitted from the discussion, as well as the exhibition. In Chapter IV, the jewellery specialist, television presenter and writer Geoffrey Munn has drawn upon his vast knowledge and undertaken exciting new research to reveal a trove of exquisitely arresting rose-themed jewellery, crafted from the most precious materials known to humanity. These include a funerary treasure from the tomb of Philip ll of Macedon; a suite of jewellery made from the rarest coloured diamonds during the reign of the Russian Empress Anna, which features bees 'bumbling around' the open roses; and exquisite pieces by René Lalique and Cartier. The author explores fascinating biographical narratives and analyses jewellery design and symbolism, highlighting the emphases placed upon love, its pleasures and pains, magic and power.

in relation to the cultural context of roses, artificial flower makers and flower culture more generally in the nineteenth century.

To twin roses with fashion requires contemplation of roses, as well as fashion. The first chapter of this book comprises a conversation 'On Roses' with internationally regarded image-maker Nick Knight, who has, since the 1980s, created visionary fashion images that convey the look and feeling of flowers. Here, he reveals the first time he really looked at roses; how he captures, portrays and communicates their likeness; and the technologies and craft practices he has harnessed to develop the ethereal, sensuous and unruly 'Roses from my Garden' iPhone photos that he posts on Instagram and from which he creates large-scale artworks. He stresses that, 'I am interested in photographing all the stages in the life of the rose: the bud, the bloom, the rosehip, the leaves and thorns – everything' and places on the record his unwavering loyalty to the flower.[11]

Jonathan Faiers, Professor of Fashion Thinking at Winchester School of Art, is author of 'Ravishing: The Rose in Context'. He appoints Zola's protagonist in *La Faute de l'Abbé Mouret* ('The Abbé Mouret's Sin', 1875) as one of his 'literary gardeners' and explores our emotional, cultural and political encounters with the rose. He draws upon Gilles Deleuze and Félix Guattari's model of the rhizome to untangle meanings and forge relationships. Having taken us on a journey that looks at medieval manuscripts, Elizabethan portraiture, sixteenth-century armour, romantic poetry, surreal film, the rose tattoo and bawdy

Artificial roses are invariably integrated with the garments and accessories they adorn, although they can be applied in the form of the corsage. 'Permanent Botanicals: Fashioning Artificial Roses' comprises a comparative study of the artificial flower-making industries in Paris, London and New York, which flourished as vital ancillary trades to the emergent haute couture, elite and mass-production fashion industries. The focus is upon the period *c*.1850–*c*.1914, during which time the industry was at its peak.

18. Hat (detail showing silk roses
that fill the crown), USA, c.1908.
Horsehair, silk, cotton velour
and paper
The Museum at FIT, New York
The Museum at FIT, P83.19.13.
Museum purchase

I explore how faux roses were made, examine their component parts, and consider the differing making processes and working life experiences of the huge numbers of (mostly female) workers involved, who were deemed the aristocrats of the flower-making workforce; they even married 'better'! In Paris, many firms specialised in making just one type of flower, even distinguishing between rose flowers and buds, and makers often worked directly from nature. The ways in which artificial roses are incorporated into fashion design and interface with the body are discussed within the chronological chapters that follow.

Classical civilisation exerted a powerful influence upon nineteenth-century cultures, and many rose 'traditions' and themes that designers continue to draw upon today stem from its later decades. Chapter VI, 'The Nineteenth Century: "I would like my roses to see you"', explores the vogue for floriography; the cultivation, selling and wearing of fresh roses; roses as fashionable motif and applied decoration; rose personification and fancy dress; and roses and rites of passage. A rose-themed evening gown – made for a debutante by the House of Worth using a silk glistening with rose petals, each with a raised and curled edge – is the subject of a focus study. For men, it was the waistcoat (vest) – often embroidered with a flower design – that comprised the single most eye-catching garment of outerwear. This chapter also reveals that rose designs were incorporated into small or concealed textiles surfaces, such as handkerchiefs and braces (suspenders), as well as decorating ceremonial and at-home attire.

Having established, in the context of the nineteenth century, many of the core sociocultural contexts within which roses are still interpreted, 'The Twentieth Century: "A rose is a rose is a rose"' takes heed of the Modernist poet and modern art collector Gertrude Stein, stripping the rose of its symbolism. Here, the work of a number of fashion designers for whom the rose had special meaning, became a hallmark or was incorporated into one significant design, is foregrounded. They include Lucile, Paul Poiret, Boué Soeurs, Madeleine Vionnet, Mainbocher, Christian Dior, Cristóbal Balenciaga, Yves Saint Laurent, Ann Lowe, Claire McCardell, Harry Gordon, Halston, Stephen Jones, John Galliano, Lulu Guinness and Alexander McQueen. The focus study is a Neo-Romantic evening gown, designed by Charles James in 1937, with a décolletage bedecked with silk roses, as worn by an American debutante. During the eighteenth and nineteenth centuries, fashionable depictions of roses were mostly naturalistic; in this period they also took a more stylised guise, expressive of broader movements in art and design such as Art Deco and Pop Art. Roses are also considered in the contexts of the 'Bread and Roses' textiles workers strike of 1912, the First World War, racial segregation and subcultural identities.

In the chapter 'Scent: "The inward fragrance of each other's heart"', Mairi MacKenzie considers the perfume of the rose. Drawing upon the many mythologies inspired by the scent of this exalted flower, she details aspects of its historical use in various cultures, as well as its representations in literature, painting, advertisements and magazines.

Above left
19. Full toilette for a ball,
Journal des dames et des modes, 1802.
Hand-coloured etching
The Metropolitan Museum of Art,
New York
A diadem of pink roses is shown worn
with a white and rose-pink tunic, the
skirt decorated with an asymmetric
swag of matching artificial roses.
Woodman Thompson Collection,
The Irene Lewisohn Costume
Reference Library, The Metropolitan
Museum of Art

Above right
20. Birthday card featuring roses,
1881.
Hand-coloured carte de visite
Private collection
The roses on this rare carte de visite
are painted, one pink and the other
red. With the addition of a printed
greeting, it became a birthday card:
handwritten on the reverse it reads,
'To dear Charlie from Clara,
Nov. 9th/81'.

Below right
21. Birthday card, France,
early 1920s.
Colour-tinted postcard
Private collection

Above left
22. Asahikran, woman wearing a kimono and holding a rose, Tokyo, late nineteenth century.
Studio-portrait cabinet card
Private collection
The gesture of holding a rose is reminiscent of Élisabeth-Louise Vigée Le Brun's portrait of Marie Antoinette (see fig.70).

Above right
23. Woman seated with fresh roses in her lap, USA, early 1920s.
Studio-portrait postcard
Private collection
The sitter here wears a two-piece evening ensemble, adorned by the cluster of fresh roses in her lap.

Below left
24. Two men, each wearing a rose boutonnière, UK, c.1915.
Studio-portrait postcard
Private collection
A touching portrait of two men with matching boutonnières; the standing man touches the rose of his companion.

Below right
25. A couple on their wedding day, mid-1910s.
Studio-portrait postcard
Private collection
The veil and handheld roses render as ceremonial the bride's seemingly everyday dress.

She looks at its ability to act as a carrier of sometimes contradictory social mores, and the more practical horticultural, biochemical, commercial and socio-economic shifts that have impacted upon and facilitated our engagement with – and perception of – rose perfume. In the final section, MacKenzie recounts a visit to the Osmothèque in Paris – a museum dedicated to the preservation of modern and historic scents – where a (small) selection of some of the most important rose-based perfumes in modern perfumery were sampled.

The concluding text examines how and why the exquisite fragility, paradoxical beauty and allure of the rose, with its potential to rupture and draw blood, has been harnessed by an unprecedentedly mobilised and politicised global fashion industry. A focus study is made of the extraordinary *fleurs animées* ensemble featured on this book's cover, designed by Noir Kei Ninomiya for Autumn/Winter 2019, which is interpreted in the contexts of natural modernism and rose personification at its most militant. 'The Twenty-First Century: Roses and Concrete' explores roses and fashion within the critical contexts of racial equality, identity, sexuality, fair trade, the environment and sustainability, alongside the extraordinary innovation, imagination and craft skills of designers who draw upon the rose to flatter, adorn and otherwise provoke. It highlights the vogue for fresh roses on the catwalk and likens the cultivated-rose and fast-fashion industries.

Above right
26. Allan Ramsay,
Flora Macdonald, 1749–50.
Oil on canvas, 74 x 61cm
Ashmolean Museum of Art and
Archaeology, University of Oxford
Macdonald was a farmer's daughter
who assisted in the escape to Skye of
Charles Edward Stuart, the 'pretender'
to the English throne, following his
defeat at the Battle of Culloden in
1746. She wears in her hair, and on the
bodice of her dress, the emblematic
Jacobite white rose, and holds a
garland that alludes to her first name.
IanDagnall Computing/Alamy Stock
Photo

Below right
27. Alexander McQueen,
'Widows of Culloden' collection,
Autumn/Winter 2006.
Mourning and melancholy infused
this McQueen collection, which
highlighted the widows of the
Jacobites murdered at the Battle
of Culloden. Roses, depicted as
tattoos on sheer tops, were teamed
with tailored woollen tartans, here
modelled by Fabiana.
This combination can also be seen in
the Jacobite jacket shown on p.50.
FirstView

CHAPTER I

ON ROSES

⋯

AMY DE LA HAYE IN CONVERSATION WITH NICK KNIGHT

Previous spread
Nick Knight,
Sunday 8th July 2018.
Hand-coated pigment print,
printed 2019, 77.4 x 63.5cm
Edition of 10, with 3 Artist Proofs
Courtesy of Nick Knight

Opposite
28. Nick Knight,
Saturday 10th October, 2015.
Hand-coated pigment print,
printed 2019, 63.5 x 63.5 cm
Edition of 10, with 3 Artist Proofs
Courtesy of Nick Knight

Amy de la Haye: There is a poignant phrase in a T. S. Eliot poem about the roses having the look of flowers that are used to being looked at.[1] When did you first really *look* at roses?

Nick Knight: It was in 1993, when I was invited by the architect David Chipperfield to do a permanent exhibition at the Natural History Museum in London [*Plant Power*, which ran from 1994 to 2009]. It was about humanity's relationship with flowers and plants: looking at cotton in relation to the American economy and slave trade; seaweed and its use in cosmetics; the use of the oak tree for building boats and churches. I split my team into three groups, to search for relevant materials: the perfect Meissen teapot to exhibit with the tea plant, an ancient church roof made of oak, etc. It took us nine months. I contacted my local rose nursery and asked if I could come and cut some blooms, for 50 quid or something. I took them back to my studio and started looking at them through the 8 x 10" camera, really scrutinising them; it's a very considered process, you've only got 20 shots. I liked some of the things the roses evoked in me: they look like strokes from an artist's brush, a couture dress or feathers, and they have a poetic tragedy. They announce, 'Here I am, I'm so beautiful and I'm about to die, enjoy my glory now but I won't last.' Roses are very much to do with death.

Amy: They've also been the cause of death. I'm thinking of Roman excess – the banquets where a huge mass of rose petals would be showered on to guests and some became engulfed and suffocated [see pp.42, 44–5]

Nick: [Smiling] Did that happen a lot?

Amy: I don't think it happened a lot, Nick!

Nick: My mother's middle name was Rose, Beryl Rose; the only tattoo I have is of a rose.

Amy: When did you have it done?

Nick: In 1978.

Amy: So it predates the Natural History Museum?

Nick: Yes, by miles.

Amy: So why the rose, then?

Nick: Fat Jock at the tattoo parlour in the Pentonville Road couldn't draw a cat for some reason, but he said he could do a rose.

Amy: Well, that's what happens when you ask a question and expect a profound answer!

Nick: Because we worked for the Natural History without being paid, they asked if they could do something to thank us. I said I'd like to see the works held in the Herbarium and they offered to pull some specimens. I said I wanted to look at everything. There was a curator there, an amazing woman called Sandra Knapp, and she agreed. The Herbarium houses millions of specimens: lots of grasses that are brown and dried, but other plants have retained their colour or the colour has changed over time. As my wife Charlotte and I looked, it became apparent that some scientists had an artist's eye, from the way they had arranged the specimens on the paper for other scientists to look at. I photographed lots of them – the prints are on my wall.[2]

29. Nick Knight,
Rose VII, 2012.
Hand-applied pigment print and
acrylic paint on polyester,
107.6 x 101.6cm
Unique
This dramatic image captures and
highlights a moment in time, rather like
a vanitas painting or Salvador Dalí's
Surrealist painting of melting clocks
titled *The Persistence of Memory*
(1931). The title *Dog* references the
common name for the wild rose.
Courtesy of Nick Knight

Amy: Did you see any wild roses?

Nick: All we saw were some very old, very tiny, dried roses, which I photographed. But I kept hoping I'd find more.

Amy: You carried on photographing roses after this project ended?

Nick: Photographers photograph flowers and one naturally looks to the people one respects: Irving Penn made albums of roses and [Edward] Steichen photographed roses. About 20 years ago I started photographing roses and sending them out as Christmas cards. Still do. It gave me a reason.

Amy: You photograph roses at home on weekends, working alone.

Nick: Yes. It's very different being solitary and in total control. I enjoy working with other people – with art directors, models and designers: seeing Alexander McQueen through Alexander McQueen's eyes, working with Kanye West... That is a main part of the interest for me. I enjoy the human interaction involved in creating images. When I first moved into the house where I presently live – a house my parents lived in in the 1950s – there were masses of the roses they had planted. The soil was good and somehow through neglect they'd survived; huge tea roses, I recall. I remember picking them and photographing them at night with lights.

Amy: Do you grow the roses you photograph now?

Nick: Yes, but they don't take much... A lot of them came from a job; they stay in pots on my terrace. A lot of people comment to me on Instagram how much they'd love to see my garden;

my garden's quite nice, but it's all ivy and silver birches – the roses stay in pots in a central courtyard. If one dies, it's sad, but it dies.

Amy: There's something about handling the bulk and fragility of a rose in bloom that makes it unlike other flowers, almost corporeal – do you feel that?

Nick: No, it's not an important part of the process for me; it's generally annoying, getting spiked, and picking them up and they fall to pieces in your hands – you can go from visual ecstasy to nothing.

Amy: As a curator I really examine the clothes I exhibit and write about and so I thought I should do the same for roses. In order to understand their component parts and structure, I dissected an open flower and a bud from my mother's garden. It felt a bit like a premeditated act of violence, not at all like chopping a carrot. Have you done that? Could you do that? You studied as a biologist...

Nick: No, I don't think so. But I could. I intended to go to medical school but didn't study for my A levels properly, so I went to university to study human biology; my idea was to do really well the first year and reapply to medical school. I was hopeless because I had no application. I'd rather misbehave, and so I photographed my misbehaviour.

Amy: And now you photograph misbehaving and imperfect, as well as exquisitely perfect, roses.

Nick: When the iPhone came out, Instagram provided me with a platform for instantly creating a picture and getting it out to an audience immediately – no lights, no assistant. It took me back

Opposite
30. Nick Knight,
Friday 8th June, 2018.
Hand-coated pigment print,
printed 2019, 77.2 x 63.5cm
Edition of 10, with 3 Artist Proofs
Courtesy of Nick Knight

1. '... the roses/Had the look of flowers that are looked at.' Eliot 1936.

2. The prints hang in Knight's office, above his studio. They were published in Nick Knight and Sandra Knapp, *Flora* (Munich: Schirmer/Mosel, 2004). On his shelf sits a small, dark red rose set in a Perspex block by Azuma Makoto, whose Tokyo studio he has visited.

3. Nick Knight's *Roses* was on display at Michael Hue-Williams's gallery Albion Barn, near Oxford, from 23 June to 22 September 2019, touring to Russia, France and Hong Kong.

to the totally basic reasons why I got into photography in the first place: seeing something I liked and photographing it. Instagram is a shortcut, it goes straight to the audience and – unlike a magazine or exhibition, where the audience is mute – it allows the audience to talk back to me, and I like that.

To take the rose images from Instagram to the very large scale exhibited at Albion Barn took some consideration.[3] We found an AI that would sharpen the images and put detail where it didn't exist – [adding] about 30 per cent. If you give the AI a very high-resolution file with lots of information it doesn't do so well, but if you give it a low-res image with gaps it makes them sharper, so we res-down our images before we start.

With the 'drip' rose images [p.30], you step from one medium – photography – into painting. The prints are 6 x 4 [feet] so you need someone to do it with you – it's fun and it's physical. I print the image on to a paper that doesn't accept the ink, so [the ink] pools and runs, and we then carry it into a steam room so the paint gets heavier and runs faster. I work with a kettle or a steamer and move round the image to work on particular areas. The biggest challenge is then to get the paint to stop running, without adding granularity or changing its viscosity – maintaining clarity and colour; it is a process that took seven years to develop.

Amy: You exploit the latest technologies in your work. Do you have any feelings about genetically engineered roses? Like the blue rose?

Nick: No, I think human inventiveness is to be encouraged, so I don't have an anti-intelligence stance.

Amy: Can I ask about the black rose photograph you have framed in the studio?

Nick: In real life the rose was bright orange, called tequila sunrise or something awful like that [*Rosa* 'Tequila Sunrise']. Some film is sensitive to certain lights so I processed a colour transparency film and put it through a negative developer, which meant the reds went black. It's the same technique I used to make Kate Moss turn black [for *VERTIGO* magazine in 2016]; her skin looked black because of the printing process.

Amy: You don't photograph red roses.

Nick: No, red's a funny colour to photograph. Instagram and iPhone overcompensate on the reds and they get garish very quickly, they have no depth to them. They don't seem to have as much latitude as other colours, or the same dynamic range. If you have a white rose you can take it from white to black and blue – any colour you want really. But with a red rose... it's almost like it pushes you out, but that makes it very interesting. I was going to do a project where I look at all my prints under red light, which would make you add colour to compensate and combat the red. It would be interesting to see what happens when you turn the white light on.

Amy: In the harsh light of day, could you fall in love with another flower?

Nick: No, I'm loyal and I'm monogamous.

CHAPTER II

RAVISHING

...

THE ROSE IN CONTEXT

JONATHAN FAIERS

...

One day she brought him a bunch of roses, and he was so moved that tears streamed from his eyes. He kissed the flowers, lay them in bed beside him, hugged them to him. But when they faded, that hurt him so that he forbade Albine ever to gather him roses again.

...

Émile Zola, *The Abbé Mouret's Sin*, 1875[1]

Blush, briar, rambling, garden, wild, miniature, floribunda, cabbage, climbing, dog, moss, damask, grandiflora, hybrid, shrub, tea. The abundance of linguistic shading used to describe different forms of rose is matched only by the vibrant richness of the genus *Rosa* itself: a chromatic seduction ranging from virginal white to carnal crimson encompassing startling orange, delicate peach, decadent yellow, faded mauve and fleshy pink, joined by fabled blooms of black, blue and silver.

The beauty of the rose seduces, its heady perfume intoxicates, its cruel thorns punish and its glorious petals all too swiftly fade and fall. More than any other bloom it has fired the imaginations of poets, painters and composers and, for centuries, has been utilised as a political symbol and as a sign of altered states of consciousness, exemplifying both warfare and romance, innocence and immorality, mysticism and transformation.

It is unsurprising, therefore, that the rose has played a key role in the history of appearance and, since ancient times and across the globe, has been used to adorn and perfume our bodies. This chapter explores some of our political, emotional and cultural encounters with the rose, and, as befits such a varied subject, it will adopt an organic, even botanical form – taking root, entangling, proliferating and blossoming in a surprising variety of terrains.

Successful rose cultivation relies on expert horticultural knowledge and so, to guide us through the often dense and

thorny thickets of the rose, this chapter will refer to expert literary gardeners for advice. These include Émile Zola, who has supplied the rose lover with an unparalleled bouquet in his 1875 novel *La Faute de l'Abbé Mouret* ('The Abbé Mouret's Sin'), which conveys magnificently our obsession with the rose as a symbol of desire. Georges Bataille's considerably shorter, but no less pungent account of the rose in his 1929 essay 'The Language of Flowers' offers us an alternative understanding of the rose, as speaking a 'language' at once overtly sexual, fleeting and deathly – a language that is redolent of William Blake's celebrated poem 'The Sick Rose' (1794; fig.31). Bataille's text interrogates the earlier nineteenth-century publication *The Language of Flowers* (first published in English in 1820; see pp.122–3), which has had a lasting influence on our perception of the symbolism of flowers in general, and the rose especially.

Lastly, to help us plan our rose garden, we will follow Gilles Deleuze and Félix Guattari's model of the 'rhizome' in order to understand the rose's complexity. While the rose itself is not strictly rhizomatic in form – like the iris or lily of the valley, for example – and most commonly has deep, vertical, rather than horizontal anchor roots with finer, radiating tap roots, the spread of these roots is surprising, and they often run far and wide. It is their capacity to spread considerable distances and, emblematically, touch and feed into an astonishing variety of philosophical and cultural landscapes that is understood rhizomatically. Like that structure, the rose can connect 'any point to any other point' and is 'composed not of units but

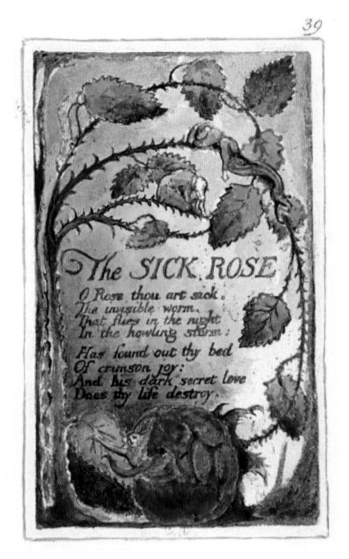

39

of dimensions, or rather directions in motion. It has neither beginning nor end.'[2]

Throughout this wood, natural paths had formed, some narrow, some broad, lovely covered-in rides, where one could walk in fragrant shade. There were cross-roads in this rose world, broad clearings.
One moved cradled among tiny red roses and one walked between walls covered with tiny yellow roses.

Émile Zola, *The Abbé Mouret's Sin*, 1875[3]

In the medieval French poem *Le Roman de la Rose* ('The Romance of the Rose', 1225–30/c.1280), written in sections by two separate authors, the rose is both the object of the narrator's desire and a symbol for female sexuality (fig.32).[4] The poem's first, dream-like part is set in a walled garden – an enclosed floral universe where the lovers and the roses growing there become one, in an ecstatic vision of rosy love. It is a veritable paradise, which is fitting given that the modern derivation of the word 'paradise' comes from the ancient Iranian *pairidaeza*, meaning a walled park or floral enclosure – this sense is recognisable from both *Le Roman de la Rose* and Zola's 'Paradou Park', the setting for his lovers' floral ecstasy.

Above
31. William Blake, 'The Sick Rose', published in *Songs of Experience* (London, 1794).
This memorable illustrated poem, warning its readers against spiritual, moral and social corruption, remains one of the most salutary literary uses of the rose's beauty and its inevitable decay.
The Picture Art Collection/ Alamy Stock Photo

Right
32. Illuminated manuscript of Guillaume de Lorris and Jean de Meun, *Le Roman de la Rose*, published in the fifteenth century.
The medieval lovers of *Le Roman de la Rose* reach fulfillment in a rose-rich, walled paradise, where the bloom is both the object of noble veneration and corporeal desire.
Bibliothèque nationale de France

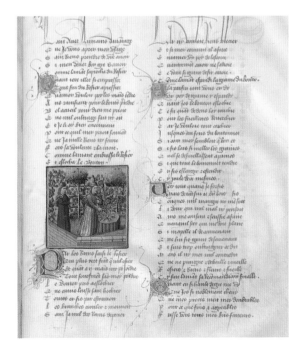

The second, later section of the poem takes a far more worldly view of the rose and includes a satirical treatise on the 'arts of love', which shocked contemporary audiences with the frankness of its language and still unsettles today with its knowing amalgam of carnality, misogyny and double entendres. Replete with puns centred on rosy deflowerings, pricking, scattering seed and seizing young buds, *Le Roman de la Rose* provides one of the earliest and most comprehensive accounts of the sexual rose, at once sensuous and visionary but also carnal and covert.

The remarkable ability of the rose to signify blushing, young love and full-blown desire has ensured its metaphorical ascendancy as the pre-eminent sexual flower. Its seductive petals belie an unparalleled licentiousness – a factor Bataille noted when he highlighted the fact that a rose's petals are the sign, only, of desire: 'It is evident, in fact, that if one expresses love with the aid of a flower, it is the corolla, rather than the useful organs, that becomes the sign of desire.'[5] This he asserts is, in itself, a form of deceit, and goes on: 'Moreover, even the most beautiful flowers are spoiled in their centres by hairy sexual organs. Thus the interior of a rose does not at all correspond to its exterior beauty; if one tears off all of the corolla's petals, all that remains is a rather sordid tuft.'[6]

Below left
33. Music hall entertainer Max Miller in his characteristic floral suit, 1940s. Max Miller's bold floral suits matched his equally outrageous stage show, which consisted of jokes and songs abundant with flowery double entendres.
AF archive/Alamy Stock Photo

Below right
34. Carlos Schwabe, poster for the first Salon de la rose + croix, 1892. Lithograph, 191.4 x 81.4cm Victoria and Albert Museum, London
This design, a masterpiece of Symbolist graphic decadence, depicts a figure, freed from the shackles of materialism, being guided by faith, dressed in white, to enlightenment – on a staircase that mysteriously sprouts roses and lilies. The scene is framed by the repeated motif of a cross surrounded by a rose, the symbol of the Salon de la rose + croix.
© Victoria and Albert Museum, London

The seductive camouflaging of the rose's true sexuality in its delicate petals and floral innocence is fundamental to our cultural understanding of the sexual rose – a form of secrecy, even duplicity, that has allowed it to feature richly in sexual allegory, from medieval poetry to twentieth-century music hall and the figure of the rose-suited comedian Max Miller (son of a flower seller), master of the floral double entendre (fig.33). His popular song 'Down Where the Rambling Roses Grow' was often accompanied by suitably scurrilous flowery limericks from his notorious blue joke book:

When roses are red,
They're ready for plucking,
When a girl is sixteen,
She's ready for... [7]

In contrast to the worldly vulgarity of Miller, the rose has also long been associated with religious mysticism, and the Virgin Mary in particular. Mary, especially for those of the Catholic faith, is often referred to as the 'mystic rose', or the 'rose without thorns', in an allusion to the belief that roses in the Garden of Eden grew without thorns and developed them only after Adam and Eve's expulsion. The immaculate Mary, therefore, is a rose without thorns, whom believers ask to intercede on their behalf while reciting the rosary. Within the context of Catholic mysticism, the scent of roses is a chief note in what has become known as the odour of sanctity: a floral, often rose fragrance, emanating from the body of saints and stigmata. Most notably, the celebrated stigmatic Padre Pio's wounds smelled of roses, as did the body of Saint Thérèse of Lisieux at the time of her death. Lisieux, also known as 'The Little Flower', had a passion for roses, espousing the concept of a 'shower of roses', both literal and metaphorical, as evidence of God's presence.

The association of the rose with Catholicism was also fundamental to the development of Rosicrucianism, a movement that arose in seventeenth-century Europe and was founded upon a heady mixture of ritual and doctrinal components drawn from alchemy, the Kabbalah, Christian mysticism and freemasonry. Followers of the rosy cross held a fundamental belief in transformation and rebirth, symbolised by a cross surmounted by a rose, or, alternatively, a rose with a cross in its centre. Fairly characterised as an esoteric society concerned with esoteric beliefs, one of its most interesting offshoots was the Ordre du temple de la rose + croix, presided over by the flamboyant Joséphin (or Sâr, a title he claimed he had inherited from a Babylonian king) Péladan. This, in turn, led to the celebrated series of Salon de la rose + croix meetings – quasi-religious, occult events promoting spirituality in art, literature and music held in 1890s Paris, which did much to promote the Symbolist art movement of the late nineteenth century (fig.34).

The deployment of the rose as a symbol for secrecy can be traced back to Classical mythology and the story that Cupid used a rose to bribe Harpocrates to remain silent about his mother Venus's various amorous indiscretions (Venus herself the goddess of beauty and love and often associated with the rose). In reference to this story, the ceilings of Roman banqueting rooms were often decorated with roses in order to remind revellers dining beneath that what was spoken of under the sign of the rose should not be mentioned outside. By the Middle Ages, the sign of the rose was being used to encourage discretion on the part of councillors meeting to discuss affairs of state, and Henry VII's recently adopted Tudor rose decorated his private chamber, where political decisions were made; hence the term *sub rosa*, still used today to demand group members' discretion.

Alongside its legalistic uses, the rose has retained its function as a symbol of sexual secrecy and cultural subversion. We can only guess at the identity, and source of anguish, of Nicholas Hilliard's celebrated *Young Man among Roses* (c.1587; fig.36) as he pines in the midst of his rosy bower, while the rose-obsessed Aubrey Beardsley depicted his hermaphrodite navigating a path not only through thorny floral excess, but multiple sexual identities, with evident ease ('Hermaphrodite Among Roses', 1894; fig.37). This arrangement of secrecy, spirituality, decadence and erotic desire has produced some of the most memorable and seductive of bouquets, as our head gardener Zola confirms:

...

The roses had their own way of living. Some would but bring to bud, half opened, facing each other, all timidity, blushing at the heart, while others had corsage ready loosened and were breathing hard, roses fully open, as if of loose muslin, flesh crazed to the point of death.

...

Émile Zola, *The Abbé Mouret's Sin*, 1875 [8]

...

*For some minutes it rained roses in heavy
downpour, blossoms splashing down like
thunder showers of colour, and in the holes
in the flooring the petals made brilliant
puddles.*

...

Émile Zola, *The Abbé Mouret's Sin,* 1875 [9]

The all-consuming state of rosy ecstasy that Zola's lovers experience in their secret walled garden demonstrates the rose's remarkable capacity to create sensory spaces – spaces that engulf and territorialise, submerge and transform the body, in perfumed universes of seductive colour and beauty. From the most discreet of rose tattoos to Dante's limitless white rose of paradise (fig.35) – a floral cosmos made for, and by, the faithful – the rose inscribes and engulfs the lover and the disciple alike. Our groundsmen Gilles Deleuze and Félix Guattari understand not only the spatial potential of root systems, but have explored other means of territorialisation, noting:

How very important it is, when chaos threatens, to draw an inflatable, portable territory. If need be, I'll put my territory on own body, I'll territorialise my body: the house of the tortoise, the hermitage of the crab, but also tattoos that make the body a territory. [10]

The rose grows rampant on the tattooed body, from barely-there ankle bud to lush floral territorialisation, with buttocks, nipples and backs becoming both the canvas for, and the centres of, inky roses (fig.38). The illustrated rose honours lover and mother alike; colonises the bodies of sailors, soldiers and prisoners; and even grows in no man's land – an early-twentieth-century tattoo design featured the head of a Red Cross nurse emerging from or surrounded by roses. The design originates from the First World War description, in popular song, of the nurses who risked their lives attending to soldiers in the trenches and who were dubbed 'The Roses of No Man's Land'.

Ba-ra-kei, translated as 'Ordeal by Roses', is the name given to a remarkable series of photographs, the result of a collaboration between two of post-war Japan's most startling thinkers: the novelist Yukio Mishima and photographer Eikoh Hosoe. Commissioned by Mishima, Hosoe produced a set of dazzling auto-erotic tableaux, the most celebrated of which feature Mishima enacting the themes of love and death while clutching, inhaling and being engulfed by roses, their petals and thorns simultaneously representing beauty and pain.

More recently, the rose, or at least its petals, have featured in another series of memorable erotic scenarios. In the 1999 film *American Beauty*, directed by Sam Mendes, Lester Burnham – an advertising executive undergoing a mid-life crisis – becomes infatuated with a friend of his daughter, the nubile Angela Hayes. As Burnham's obsession grows, he starts to receive visions of Angela amid a sea of rose petals and, in an especially visionary sequence, Burnham, suffering from mounting, unrequited sexual desire, imagines himself beneath a shower of falling rose petals in a carnal, cinematic reworking of Saint Thérèse's beatific shower of roses (fig.40).

Chap. riv.

It is to the Classical world, however, that we are indebted for possibly the first and most notorious instance of rosy immersion:

that practised by the juvenile and hedonistic Roman emperor Heliogabalus and unforgettably imagined by the Victorian painter Lawrence Alma-Tadema (fig.41). The work itself – titled *The Roses of Heliogabalus* – is a product of unseasonal rosy extravagance, given that Alma-Tadema painted it in the winter months of 1888 and, in order to recreate the scene in his studio, had roses delivered from the French Riviera every week until the work was completed. The incident depicted is derived from a, probably apocryphal, account featured in the collection of imperial Roman biographies known as the *Augustan History*, which relates the delight Heliogabalus took in suddenly releasing a torrent of flower petals on his unsuspecting guests from the retractable roof of his banqueting hall. Many of the drunken revellers were unable to crawl out from beneath this sudden deluge and died in floral suffocation. Whether historically factual or not, this fragrant slaughter has fired the imagination of successive writers and artists ever since – a perfumed reminder of the dangers of rosy excess.

Whether Heliogabalus's murderous roses were part of his larger political machinations, or merely evidence of his ingeniously sadistic pleasures, remains unknown; the rose, however, has featured as the emblem for an astonishing range of political and ideological projects throughout history and continues to be utilised in this way today. Any account of the political rose must address what, it could be argued, is the appropriation of the flower in its most partisan guise, as the symbol of the opposing forces in the fifteenth-century English Wars of the Roses. At the Battle of Bosworth Field in 1485 – the conflict's climax – Henry Tudor, leading the Lancastrian forces under the emblem of the red rose, defeated Richard III's Yorkist forces marching under the white rose. This famous, floriated confrontation might equally be remembered for the opposing armies' heraldic tinctures – Henry's red dragon and Richard's white boar – but, as in so much of the rose's cultural formation, the contrast of military might with the delicate rose proved irresistible.

Above
38. Rose tattoo
The rose is an enduringly popular tattoo design which, like fashionable dress, evolves stylistically over time.
Getty Images

Right
39. Alvin Lustig, cover design for Tennessee Williams, *The Rose Tattoo* (New York: New Directions, 1951). Book and typeface designer Alvin Lustig produced more than 70 cover designs for New Directions publishing house. The daring simplicity of this 'negative' image of a red rose, combined with a floating typeface, is typical of Lustig's approach.

Irresistible also to William Shakespeare, who, recounting the
events leading up to the Wars in *Henry VI, Part 1* (1591), has a
group of noblemen pick either red or white roses in the Temple
Gardens to declare their allegiances (see fig.42). Shakespeare
embellishes this scene with the suggestion of possible defection
made real as illustrated by the threat from the rose's thorns, and
has the Lancastrian Somerset deliver the famous warning to the
supporters of Richard Plantagenet:

...

Prick not your finger as you pluck it off,
Lest, bleeding, you do paint the white rose red,
And fall on my side so against your will.

...

William Shakespeare, *Henry VI, Part I*, 1591 [11]

It is tempting to see this poetic warning against floral turncoating
reflected in that other famous scene of a royal house making
nature conform to political ideology: the Red Queen instructs
her knaves to paint white roses red, her favoured colour, in Lewis
Carroll's 1865 *Alice's Adventures in Wonderland* (see fig.44).

40. *American Beauty*,
dir. Sam Mendes, 1999.
Film still
Lester Burnham, the leading
protagonist in *American Beauty*,
receives visions throughout the
film akin to the rosy imaginings of
medieval religious mystics, in which
both he and the object of his desire,
cheerleader Angela Hayes, are
showered by rose petals.
PictureLux/The Hollywood Archive/
Alamy Stock Photo

Previous spread
41. Lawrence Alma-Tadema,
The Roses of Heliogabalus, 1888
Oil on canvas, 132.7 x 214.4cm
Private collection
This evocative painting captures
perhaps the most celebrated instance
of 'death by roses': the moment
when the decadent Roman emperor
Heliogabalus released a torrent of
roses on his unsuspecting guests.
incamerastock/Alamy Stock Photo

Above right
42. Henry Arthur Payne, *Plucking
the Red and White Roses in The Old
Temple Gardens* (design for the mural
in the east corridor of the Palace of
Westminster, London), 1908–10.
Pen, watercolour, gold leaf and oil
Palace of Westminster
Henry Arthur Payne's mural design
captures in Edwardian splendour the
scene from William Shakespeare's
Henry VI, Part 1 (1591) in which the rose
serves as an expression of allegiance
in the ensuing Wars of the Roses.
Art Collection 3/Alamy Stock Photo

Below right
43. Attributed to Nicholas Hilliard,
Queen Elizabeth I (the 'Pelican'
portrait), *c*.1573–75.
Oil on panel, 78.7 x 61cm
Walker Art Gallery, Liverpool
For Elizabethan viewers, this portrait
of Elizabeth I, the 'Virgin Queen', with
its abundance of rosy decoration,
would have been read as an image of
their ruler as an English 'rose without
thorns': incorruptible and pure.
Image courtesy of National Museums
Liverpool, Walker Art Gallery

Opposite
44. Sir John Tenniel,
'Painting the Roses Red',
illustration for Lewis Carroll's *Alice's
Adventures in Wonderland* (London:
Macmillan, 1865).
Lewis Caroll's unforgettable image
of living playing cards scrambling to
paint white roses red to avoid the
wrath of the Red Queen is brought
to surreal life in Tenniel's illustration.
The half-painted roses convey at once
the futility of the task, the destruction
of natural beauty and the threat of
impending violence.

...

For flowers do not age honestly like leaves, which lose nothing of their beauty, even after they have died; flowers wither like old and overly made-up dowagers, and die ridiculously on stems that seemed to carry them to the clouds.

...

Georges Bataille, 'The Language of Flowers', 1929[12]

45. Armour garniture of George Clifford, 3rd Earl of Cumberland, 1586.
Steel, gold, leather and textile
The Metropolitan Museum of Art, New York
The magnificent garniture, or set, of armour was made under the direction of the master armourer Jacob Halder at the Royal Workshops in Greenwich, London. The armour represents a dazzling amalgam of defence and decoration, with the Tudor rose an essential part of the design.
The Metropolitan Museum of Art, New York. Munsey Fund, 1932

Following his victory at Bosworth Field, Henry VII amalgamated the white and red roses to form his personal dynastic emblem, the Tudor rose – a remarkably early and highly successful public relations exercise that proved so effective it came to represent not only the Tudor dynasty, but England itself, in an instance of the rose as nation branding. The rose in England from this point onwards becomes increasingly politicised, in an iconography easily deciphered by emblematically literate Tudor viewers, who encountered it in architecture, applied arts and portraiture. The so-called 'Pelican' portrait of Elizabeth I, attributed to Nicholas Hilliard (fig.43), depicts the Virgin Queen, the 'rose without thorns', practically overgrown with roses. A prominent Tudor rose hovers against the dark ground on the queen's right side, delicate blackwork roses adorn her undershirt, jewelled rose embellishments are placed symbolically at her abdomen, and even the large fan that appears at the bottom of the image takes the form of a rose composed of feathers. Contemporary with this portrait, the magnificent 'Cumberland' armour of 1586 (fig.45), made for the queen's champion and favourite George Clifford, is emblazoned with Tudor roses and the cipher of Elizabeth – consisting of two Es back to back; it is an expression in gilded steel of allegiance, patriotism and prowess.

The rose continued to be cultivated in the British political landscape and, in the eighteenth century, the white rose was adopted as a political symbol by allies of the Jacobite cause. Seeking the restoration of the Catholic House of Stuart to the thrones of Scotland, England and Ireland, prominent Jacobite supporters, to show their allegiance to the cause, would be painted holding or wearing white roses. An extremely rare example of Jacobite fashion is a magnificent late-eighteenth-century tartan coat linked to the Ancient Caledonian Society (fig.46), which bears in each of its dazzling red squares a woven silk rose and two buds, symbolising James III of England and Ireland and VIII of Scotland (the 'Old Pretender') and his two sons Charles ('Bonnie Prince Charlie') and Henry Stuart. The jacket is an exceptional example of the rose incorporated into a sartorial expression of political ideology – a tacit, silken sign of dissent.

Today the rose has survived not only as the floral symbol of England – memorably joining the Scottish thistle, the Welsh leek and Irish shamrock, along with other flora of the Commonwealth, as part of the horticultural heraldry adorning Norman Hartnell's coronation robes for the present queen – but, since the 1980s, as the emblem of the British Labour Party (fig.49), joining a spray of international socialist red roses. So symbolically potent is the rose that the causes it espouses are as varied as the forms the species itself takes: from the intellectual Nazi resistance group called the White Rose, formed in Munich in 1942 (see fig.50), to the modern-day deployment of a torn and bleeding rose in the fight against female genital mutilation (fig.47).

But roses wilt, their petals drop and perfume fades, and their moment of perfection is short-lived. Such is the shock of vanished beauty, of abundant growth withered and dying, that the rose is often understood as a symbol of the passing of time, of transformation and decay. As Shakespeare observed in his Sonnet 35, 'And loathsome canker lives in the sweetest bud', so Blake declared 'O Rose thou art sick', and Orson Welles, as Citizen Kane in the 1941 film of the same name, gasped the word 'Rosebud' with his dying breath (fig.48).[13] This latter rosy death rattle ushers in a temporal revolution, as we are catapulted back through the dead tycoon's life in search of the enigmatic rosebud, his personal symbol of lost love and happiness. Equally disruptive is another cinematic rose – a perfect specimen that, in the hands of 'Conductor 71' in Michael Powell and Emeric Pressburger's 1946 masterpiece *A Matter of Life and Death*, can both halt time and turn the world from black-and-white to colour (fig.52). The Conductor, a foppish aristocrat who has been guillotined in the French Revolution, travels through time and space connecting his black-and-white 'other world' to Technicolor wartime Britain in order to save crashed fighter pilot David Niven's life. He demonstrates his ability to freeze time with the aid of his pale pink rose, declaring 'After all, what is time? A mere tyranny.'[14]

These time-defying roses are perhaps a response to the real rose's all-too-fleeting existence; occasionally, however, even dead roses can live again. One of Vaslav Nijinsky's most celebrated early roles was in *Le Spectre de la Rose*: the spirit of a fading rose –

Opposite
46. Tartan dress coat for the Ancient Caledonian Society (and detail), Scotland, c.1786.
The Scottish Tartans Authority
The Ancient Caledonian Society, founded in 1786, was a forerunner of subsequent Caledonian Societies, including that founded in London in 1839. It was comprised of a group of like-minded professional Scots, sympathetic to the Jacobite cause and whose aim was the advancement and maintenance of Scottish cultural and philanthropic interests. The coat is a unique example of floral political dress, using the Jacobite white rose as a sartorial expression of ideology.

Above left
47. Anti-FGM (Female Genital Mutilation) campaign image
This startling image of a decimated, bloody rose makes a powerful statement for the campaign against FGM, drawing on established concepts of beauty defiled, and the rose's proximity to violence.
Maren Winter/Shutterstock

Below left
48. *Citizen Kane*, dir. Orson Welles, 1941.
Film still
A child's sledge decorated with a rosebud becomes the central, enigmatic motif in Welles's masterpiece. Representing lost youth, innocence and love, 'rosebud' is the last word uttered by the dying plutocrat Kane and introduces a series of narratives in which we see both his wealth and power grow, along with his increasing isolation and unhappiness. The rosebud's significance is lost, however, on those who tend the dying Kane and the sledge with its painted rose is consumed by flames at the end of the film.
Photofest

Right
49. Steve Speller,
Peter Mandelson, 1988.
Cibachrome print, 9.2 x 29.1cm
National Portrait Gallery, London
British politician Peter Mandelson is reincarnated as a latter-day lovesick Elizabethan courtier with his symbolic red rose. As the Labour Party's director of communications, Mandelson re-envisioned the traditional Socialist symbol of the red rose as part of the rebranding of a new, centrist party.

Far right
50. Inge Scholl, *The White Rose*, (Connecticut: Wesleyan Press, 1983).
Book cover
The White Rose Group were an intellectual, non-violent, anti-Nazi resistance group organised by students attending the university of Munich. The short-lived group conducted an anonymous campaign of leafleting and graffiti against the Nazi regime from 1942 to 1943.
Cover image by David Wolber, Performance Network Theatre, Ann Arbor 2001, Wesleyan University Press

THE WHITE ROSE
Munich 1942–1943

INGE SCHOLL
Introduction by Dorothee Sölle   Translated by Arthur R. Schultz

a memento from a ball that a young girl lets slip from her fingers as she falls asleep (fig.54).[15] As she slumbers, the ghost of the dead rose appears and dances with the still-sleeping girl. The ballet ends with the spectre exiting with a dazzling leap through her window as she awakes and kisses the fallen bloom. Nijinsky's spectacular final leap ensured the ballet's immediate success and increased the dancer's fame. His costume, designed by Léon Bakst, was covered with individual silk rose petals; Nijinsky had to be stitched in for each performance, and such was his fame that the petals he shed as he danced were collected by his servant and sold as souvenirs to adoring fans.

Transformation is also central to the rose, whether, as in the previous examples, the transformation of time and space ushered in by magical roses, whose floral power alters our perceptions, or the more fundamental transformation from beauty to decay, from life to death. At the heart of all fairy stories are transformative processes, and the rose features in one of the most blissful of all: *La Belle et la Bête*, originally written by Gabrielle-Suzanne Barbot de Villeneuve and published in 1740, and later brought to the screen in Jean Cocteau's ravishing 1946 film version of the tale (fig.53). The rose, plucked unlawfully from the beast's garden, acts as a catalyst for a series of subsequent transformations that structure the rest of the narrative. Ugliness turns to beauty, anger turns to forgiveness, and revulsion turns to affection. A simple rose is all that Beauty asks of her father, and it is this modest gift, unlawfully obtained, that leads eventually to the lifting of the curse laid on the beast and the reversal of Beauty's fortunes.

...

All round them the rose-bushes flowered, with crazy profusion, lover's profusion, all scarlet laughter, pink laughter, white laughter. The living blooms revealed their petals as when corsages reveal the naked riches of the bosom. There were yellow roses brushing the skins of barbarian maidens, straw roses, lemon roses, sunshine roses, every shade possible of blooms bronzed by blazing skies.

...

Émile Zola, *The Abbé Mouret's Sin*, 1875 [16]

Equally fantastic are the many fabled roses whose existence resides only in horticultural fantasies; blue roses, for example, abound in folklore and fairy tale. An instance in *One Thousand and One Nights* inspired, in turn, a memorable scene in Nikolai Rimsky-Korsakov's fairytale opera *Sadko*, premiered in 1898, in which the power of true love is so great that a white rose is perceived as blue.

Blue roses are often associated with deception due to their fabrication (they are usually dyed white roses), as in the Chinese legend that tells the tale of an emperor's daughter who demands a blue rose in exchange for her hand in marriage. Each of her prospective suitors attempts to deceive her by presenting her with 'blue' roses: one made from sapphire, a dyed specimen obtained from a florist, and even an illusion conjured up by a wizard that disappears once the empress tries to touch it. A reworking of this legend can be found in Rudyard Kipling's poem 'Blue Roses', first published in 1887, in which a lover's gifts of red and white roses are rejected, leading him to go on a fruitless search for a blue rose, only to return empty-handed to find his lover dead.[17]

The impossible shades of the blue rose, whether dyed, or made from silk or other materials, have, until very recently, only been achieved artificially, and it is artifice, ironically, that resides at the heart of much of our cultural understanding of roses of all hues.[18] Bataille, typically, takes this 'deception' enacted by the rose to its extreme conclusion:

In fact, after a very short period of glory the marvellous corolla rots indecently in the manure pile – even though it seemed for a moment to have escaped it in a flight of angelic and lyrical purity – the flower seems to relapse abruptly into its original squalor: the most ideal is rapidly reduced to a wisp of aerial manure.[19]

In Richard Strauss's 1911 opera *Der Rosenkavalier* (The Rose Cavalier), an artificial silver – or in some productions, blue – rose is the central motif in a work that is at its heart a story about artifice, ageing, transformation and infidelity (fig.51). The legend of the silver rose laced with oil of roses presented to an intended fiancée was a ritual made up by Hugo von Hofmannsthal, on whose libretto the opera is based. The plot revolves around four main characters: the ageing Marschallin; her young lover, Octavian (sung by a mezzo-soprano in male dress); her oafish, licentious cousin Baron Ochs; and the object of his amorous attentions, the nouveau riche Sophie. Octavian is persuaded by the Marschallin to act as the Baron's 'Rosenkavalier' and offer Sophie the silver rose on his behalf. Inevitably the young couple fall for one another and the Marschallin gives in to the power of young love and relinquishes her hold on Octavian.

The intentionally artificial plot, set in the eighteenth century – the age of artificiality and the same artifice-loving era from which *A Matter of Life and Death* hails and during which *La Belle et la Bête* was first penned – collapses time, overlaying its inauthentic Rococo setting with themes of sexual and psychological instability reflecting the concerns of the period in which the opera was written.

Top
51. Production of Richard Strauss's
Der Rosenkavalier, Glyndebourne,
dir. Richard Jones, 2018.
Richard Jones's controversial
production of this opera featured a
blue rose in place of the customary
silver bloom presented as a token
of love, emphasising the themes of
artificiality and disguise that permeate
Strauss's interrogation of fidelity and
fading youth.
Photograph by Robert Workman

Middle
52. *A Matter of Life and Death*,
dir. Michael Powell and
Emeric Pressburger, 1946.
Film still
The perfect pink rose held as a
nosegay by the time-travelling
eighteenth-century French aristocrat
symbolises his mastery over time itself
and marks the film's transition from
black-and-white to colour.
Photofest

Bottom
53. *La Belle et la Bête*,
dir. Jean Cocteau, 1946.
'...my dear sir, you steal my roses.
You steal my roses, the things I love
most in all the world.' So says La Bête
to Belle's hapless father in Cocteau's
film version of the classic fairytale.
Photofest

An artificial rose is placed at the centre of a fictional operatic bouquet, consisting of women masquerading as men, aristocrats pretending to be servants, the twentieth century pretending to be the eighteenth, anachronistic waltz tunes of the nineteenth century not quite disguising modern atonality, and characters adopting different dialects according to their status and true feelings, all masked by ritual and formality.

The rose, especially the fashionable varieties, is capable of endless reinvention – manifestations in cloth, precious stones or fragrance, which in turn transform their wearers. The Alexander McQueen Autumn/Winter 2019 collection (fig.55) is a masterly example of this rosy transformation – a vestimentary bouquet made up from precisely cut, draped and tailored blooms, where roses bloom from shoulders as botanical leg-of-mutton sleeves, recalling Louis Aragon's marvellous Surrealist poem in which he offers: 'I'll reinvent for you my rose as many roses/As there are diamonds in the waters of the seas.'[20]

But it is not just in fairy tales, on stage, film or high fashion's runways that roses have the power to transform; throughout history, the simple addition of a rose worn in a buttonhole, added to a corsage, or placed in a vase has transformed the wearers into princes and princesses, their homes to palaces. Roses elevate and sanctify, they signify simplicity and excess, beauty and decay, love, cruelty and perfection. They beautify our most sacred spaces and our most important rituals; our unions, our conflicts and our departures:

...

There Albine lay, panting, exhausted by love,
her hands clutched closer and closer to her heart,
breathing her last. She parted her lips, seeking
the kiss which should obliterate her, and then the
hyacinths and tuberoses exhaled their incense,
wrapping her in a final sigh, so profound that it
drowned the chorus of roses, and in the culminating
gasp of blossom, Albine was dead.

...

Émile Zola, *The Abbé Mouret's Sin*, 1875[21]

Opposite
54. Vaslav Nijinsky in the Ballets
Russes production *Le Spectre de la
Rose*, Théâtre de Monte-Carlo,
Paris, 1911.
Nijinsky's seductive personification of
the spirit of a rose, with its mixture of
dazzling athleticism and delicate floral
beauty, enraptured audiences and
remains one of the seminal moments
in the history of the Ballets Russes.
Historic Collection/Alamy Stock Photo

Right
55. Alexander McQueen, designed
by Sarah Burton, rose-sleeved suit,
Autumn/Winter 2019.
Some of fashion's hardiest blooms
decorated McQueen's womenswear
collection for 2019. Androgynous,
bovver-booted neo-punks sprouted
masterfully draped, printed and
gathered blooms, forming memorable
bouquets of toughened sartorial
fragility.
Firstview

CHAPTER III

EIGHTEENTH-CENTURY FASHION

...

PERENNIAL REIGN

COLLEEN HILL

...

Within the garden's peaceful scene
Appear'd two lovely foes,
Aspiring to the rank of queen,
The lily and the rose.

The rose soon redden'd into rage,
And swelling with disdain,
Appeal'd to many a poet's page
To prove her right to reign.

...

William Cowper, 'The Lily and the Rose', 1782[1]

The 1799 publication of *The Laboratory; or, School of Arts*, then in its sixth edition, included this metaphor: 'The spring opens her bountiful treasure each year, and clothes and enamels the earth with endless charms of beauty; she invites us to imitate her as near as possible in all her splendour.'[2] Although elegantly written, *The Laboratory* was in fact a practical handbook for artisans, which boasted a range of trade secrets, experiments and techniques for the manufacture of artistic goods. This passage, taken from a section devoted to the design of botanical patterns for silks, embroidery and printing, offers a clear reference to the rich connections between nature and textile design that developed during the eighteenth century in Western Europe.

The discovery and collection of rare plants and flowers flourished in Renaissance Europe and continued into the Enlightenment. Foreign specimens from both near and far – the Netherlands, Eastern Europe and Asia – were especially prevalent. During the sixteenth and seventeenth centuries, scholars and scientists often maintained plants in research gardens associated with universities and medical schools.[3] Decorative, privately owned flower gardens also began to thrive during this time. These gardens were initially made for people of wealth and status. The renowned naturalist, gardener and curiosities collector John Tradescant the Elder, for example, travelled the world to collect plants, including roses, for the gardens of English noblemen. By the eighteenth century, the middle classes had begun planting seeds in their own decorative gardens.[4] Rose bushes appeared even in New England, adding beauty to gardens otherwise devoted to hardy vegetables and medicinal herbs.[5]

Designers of textiles in eighteenth-century western Europe incorporated imagery of new and exotic flora into their work, but the elegant rose remained a perpetual motif. This popularity was perhaps bolstered by the momentous arrival of the China rose (*Rosa chinensus*), introduced to Europe around mid-century. This flower quickly made a radical impact on rose breeding in Europe, and many modern breeds of roses are the result of its cultivation and hybridisation. 'By the end of the eighteenth century,' observes François Joyaux, a scholar and collector of old garden roses,[6] 'the rose was not only in minds and in gardens: it was everywhere, in home decor, the ornamentation of furniture, [and] the adornment of women.'[7] Joyaux's statement must also be expanded to include men's dress.

Representations of roses in eighteenth-century dress are seen regularly in silk – the fabric which, as an indicator of both status and taste during this era, will be the focus of this chapter.[8] Roses were woven, embroidered, painted and shaped from fabric, and their appearances varied according to larger trends in textile design. During the late seventeenth and early eighteenth centuries, textile designers rendered silks in 'extreme and unnatural patterns' that gave no hint of the interest in naturalism to come (fig.56).[9] Yet a progression into more botanically correct flowers in textile design was indeed approaching: by the end of the 1720s, floral motifs had become larger and more lifelike. The tendency toward naturalism persisted well into the 1740s and was integral to the century's renown for intricate and luxurious textile designs.

56. Sample of 'Bizarre' silk,
France, 1685–90.
Silk and gilt-metal yarn brocaded on
silk damask ground, 121.6 x 51.8cm
Los Angeles County Museum of Art
Textile motifs from the late seventeenth
and early eighteenth centuries favoured
the fantastic over the realistic. The bold,
asymmetrical designs from this era are
commonly referred to as 'Bizarre' silks
and they were influenced by goods
imported from Asia.
Costume Council Fund, M.2000.204.8

PURVEYORS OF NATURALISM

The trend toward naturalism in fashion was related to larger developments in Western science and culture. Scholarly studies of botany – and, with them, more accurate renderings of plant life – were presented during the Renaissance and the field made greater strides in the seventeenth century. Importantly, such studies were not undertaken exclusively by men. Highly accomplished drawings by the German naturalist Maria Sibylla Merian were intended not only for scientific study but also as designs for embroidery. Her 1675 watercolour study of a rose, in the collection of the Staatsbibliothek Bamberg (fig.57), is drawn with long, curling, shaded lines that resemble needlework. This watercolour was made in the same year that she published her first work, *Florum Fasciculus Primus* ('Nosegay of Flowers').

The Swedish botanist Carl Linnaeus, known as the 'father of taxonomy', developed a system of classifying living organisms with genus and species names. While Linnaeus's interest in and ability as regards drawing is debated, his groundbreaking taxonomical work *Systema Naturae*, first published in 1735, provided the impetus for botanical illustration to thrive.[10] Like Merian's work of the previous century, pictorial scientific publications in the 1700s could have multiple functions. In 1730, the Flemish painter Pieter Casteels III worked with two Englishmen, the engraver Henry Fletcher

and the horticulturalist Robert Furber, to publish *Twelve Months of Flowers*. Conceptualised as a seed catalogue, this book doubled as a suitable reference for needlework, tapestry weaving, woodcarving and flower painting.[11] Casteels, Fletcher and Furber represented more than 400 species among the 12 plates, including numerous roses. The plate for June – the month in which many roses reach their peak bloom – features seven varieties of the flower (fig.58).

The artist Mary Delany provides an example of how books of botanical illustrations might have been translated into designs for fabric. Delany is renowned today for her intricate and realistic representations of flowers in cut paper, which she began making at the age of 72. Working in this medium until her death at age 88, Delany produced 985 cut-paper flowers, including numerous roses (fig.59).[12] While Delany's paper flowers are undoubtedly compelling, of particular note for our purposes is a design for an embroidered petticoat, completed many years before, in 1740 (fig.60). Delany was skilled in needlework – a bed cover embroidered by her is in the collection of the Ulster Museum in Northern Ireland – but the petticoat seems to have been designed by Delany and executed by professional embroiderers. The surviving panel of this garment has lost none of its lustre. Black silk satin provides a dramatic background for densely embroidered flowers, rendered primarily in shades of ivory, red and pink. The design includes a pale pink rose, complete with delicate rosebuds and tiny thorns.

Opposite
57. Maria Sibylla Merian,
Study of a rose, 1675.
Watercolour, 8.6 x 13.7cm
Staatsbibliothek Bamberg
Maria Sibylla Merian was a German
naturalist and scientific illustrator.
Most naturalists during the
seventeenth century were men,
but Merian's drawings could also
be used as designs for embroidery –
a suitably feminine pursuit.
Courtesy Staatsbibliothek Bamberg,
I R 90. Photograph by Gerald Raab

Right
58. Pieter Casteels III (artist),
Henry Fletcher (engraver), Robert
Furber (horticulturalist), 'June',
from *Twelve Months of Flowers*, 1730.
Engraving, 42.7 x 32.2cm
Private collection
This series of twelve engravings
featured detailed depictions of more
than 400 species of plants, including
many roses. The images originated
as illustrations for a seed catalogue,
but they also proved valuable to the
textile arts.

The intricate naturalism of these embroidered flowers, as well Delany's decision to have them embroidered on a black background, strongly prefigures the aesthetic of the cut-paper designs that she would not begin for another three decades.

A 1776 painting of Philippe de Lasalle, likely a self-portrait (fig.61), depicts the esteemed Lyonnaise textile and embroidery designer sitting at a simple wooden desk adorned with flowers, including pale pink roses. He holds a small flower in one hand as he gazes at the viewer. A sculpture of Flora, the Roman goddess of flowers and spring, stands on a plinth at the right edge of the painting, while sheets of paper and a drawing tool resting on the desk indicate that the designer is ready to begin his work. Lasalle was evidently – and justly – proud of his talent for drawing flowers. Lesley Ellis Miller explained the importance of the skill possessed by creators like Lasalle:

The involvement of artists, designers or draughtsmen in the conception and execution of [luxury] textiles made them stand apart from some of the cheaper ranges of furnishing and dress textiles, which were devoid of designs or whose designs were simpler. Ambitious to imitate nature closely, these artists created cartoons or designs that were for exact reproduction either through weaving or printing.[13]

Lasalle's self-portrait not only underscores the importance of his ability to draw, a talent for which Lyonnaise designers were particularly renowned, but it also deliberately highlights his ability to render flowers. The painting provides evidence of how important the study of nature was to eighteenth-century textile design. It also lays the foundation for the role of the rose motif in fashion during this era.

Opposite above
59. Mary Delany,
'Moss Province Rose', 1775.
Collage of coloured papers with
bodycolour and watercolour,
26.9 x 18.9cm
British Museum, London
While she is credited with perfecting
the art of paper collage, Mary
Delany's depictions of flowers also
possess scientific value. Delany
recorded details of where and when
each collage was created and each
example is labelled with the plant's
Linnaean and common names.
© Trustees of the British Museum

Opposite below
60. Mary Pendarves (designed by
Mrs Mary Delany), front petticoat
panel (detail, left half), England,
1740-41.
Silk embroidery on satin
Private collection
Delany designed the floral pattern for
this petticoat, which she may have
worn to a ball hosted by the Prince of
Wales in 1741. It was likely paired with
a gown made from ivory silk, opened
at the front skirt to reveal the elaborate
undergarment.
Photograph by John Hammond

Right
61. Philippe de Lasalle,
Self-portrait, 1776.
Pastel, 36 x 29.1cm
Musée des Tissus, Lyon
This painting, widely considered a
self-portrait, highlights Lasalle's skill
for drawing and the importance
of flowers to his designs. By 1775,
Lasalle's patrons included such
important figures as Catherine the
Great and Voltaire.
MAD 2274. Don Pin, 1969 © Lyon,
Musée des Tissus, Pierre Verrier

LYON AND SPITALFIELDS:
PLANTING THE SEEDS
OF NATURALISM

Although Lyon was not the only region in France where silk was made, it was undoubtedly the leader: roughly one third of its population worked in the silk industry during the eighteenth century.[14] Beauty and quality had established Lyon's dominance, as did innovations pertaining to naturalistic design. By the 1730s, the process of *points rentrés* (colour shading) – a relatively simple but highly effective technique for producing complex designs on silk cloth – had been achieved by interlocking threads in a different way on existing looms.[15] Designers were able to produce florals that appeared more three-dimensional and thus more lifelike, as is exemplified by a silk brocade *robe à la française* from c.1735, on which pink roses mingle with other colourful flowers and topiaries (fig.62). Notably, the flowers are much larger in scale than the shrubbery. Although some threads have worn away, the shading of the flowers and leaves is unmistakable.

While this silk may not have been made in Lyon, its style bears a strong resemblance to a contemporaneous fabric that is certainly attributed to the silk-weaving centre (fig.63). The fabric is in the style of Jean Revel, frequently referred to as a silk designer but determined by Miller to be a businessman who worked in the silk industry.[16] The style associated with Revel was one of bold naturalism and exemplary of the work executed in Lyon.

While Lyonnaise silks were highly prized in the eighteenth century, they were rivalled by those of another silk-weaving centre: that of Spitalfields, England, now part of the City of London. Spitalfields boasted several well-known male designers, including Christopher Badouin, Joseph Dandridge and James Leman. Yet the creator of Spitalfields' most enchanting floral designs was a woman: Anna Maria Garthwaite. Little is known about this prolific and important artisan, who appears to have begun her work in around 1726. As a designer, Garthwaite drew compositions – largely florals – in watercolor and pencil on grid paper, and weavers would translate these into patterns.

Opposite
62. *Robe à la française* (and back detail), France, c.1735.
Multicoloured silk brocade
The Museum at FIT, New York
Patterned silks and cottons gained importance in France during the reign of Louis XIV. As textile designs rapidly evolved, weaving centres such as Lyon became integral to the elite fashion industry. People of more modest means tended to wear clothing made from fabrics in solid colours.
The Museum at FIT, 2006.56.2.
Museum purchase

Right
63. Silk design in the style of Jean Revel, Lyon, France, c.1735.
Plain-weave silk with supplementary warp and wefts, 74.8 x 54.2cm
The Chicago Art Institute
The shift toward naturalistic silk designs began during the 1730s, when new techniques for colour shading on silk looms resulted in more figurative and dimensional patterns. Over the decade, motifs shifted from being oversized and dramatic to subtle.
Restricted gift of Mr and Mrs John V. Farwell III, 1988.469

Success as a designer required an understanding of the machinations of fabric looms, for which Garthwaite appears to have had a keen eye. Her drawings frequently include technical notations, and there is often little discrepancy between the drawings and the finished silks.[17] While the details surrounding the import and export of silks between France and England are too complex to mention here, the general perception was that French silks were superior in quality and design.[18] Early in her career, Garthwaite was clearly interested in learning from her peers across the Channel. She was in possession of a number of French designs from the 1730s, which appear to have affected Garthwaite's own work from that time.[19] The beauty and precision of her work can be seen in a number of drawings held in the collection of the Victoria and Albert Museum, London. A drawing from 1739 (fig.64) is a rare example of a Garthwaite design that does not feature an assortment of blooms. Its plain ivory background is scattered only with roses – in shades of pale pink and lavender, and complete with buds and tiny thorns.

1739

Left
64. Anna Maria Garthwaite,
Design for a woven silk,
Spitalfields, England, 1739.
Watercolour on paper, 61.3 x 50.5cm
Victoria and Albert Museum,
London
Nearly 900 of Anna Maria
Garthwaite's drawings for textiles
survive and are preserved at the
Victoria and Albert Museum. The grid
that Garthwaite used for accuracy is
still visible in this example. Her interest
in naturalism is evidenced by the tiny
thorns on the roses' stems.
© Victoria and Albert Museum, London

Opposite
65. Dress (and detail),
England, c.1840.
Spitalfields multicoloured silk
brocade dating from c.1760
The Museum at FIT, New York
Eighteenth-century silks – especially
brocades – were costly, and gowns
were frequently remodelled to keep
up with changes in silhouette. While
brocaded silk was not suited to
the lightweight dresses of the early
nineteenth century, it had resumed
its place and value by the 1830s.
The Museum at FIT, P87.20.7.
Museum purchase

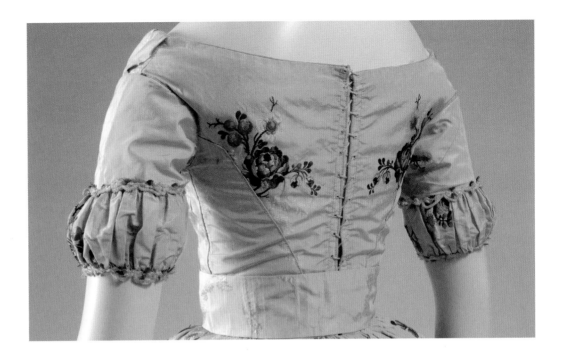

Although Garthwaite realistically rendered the roses here, the naturalism in her silk designs would not reach its peak until the early 1740s. Due to her skill and that of her peers at Spitalfields, some historians argue that English silks surpassed those of France in naturalism during the 1740s and into the following decade.[20] Silks from Spitalfields often retained value well beyond their initial consumption. The Museum at FIT, New York, owns a dress made from silk attributed to Garthwaite, the fabric of which dates to c.1760 (fig.65). The silhouette of the dress, however, identifies it as being made c.1840. While the reuse of valuable silks was common, the number of extant gowns that were remade using Spitalfields silks is noteworthy.[21] This silk design is more stylised than those of the 1740s, and features the intermingling of flowers and berries that is typical of Garthwaite's style, yet its mauve roses stand out as the largest and best-articulated motif.

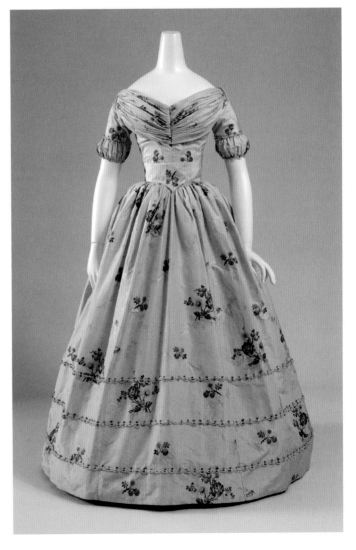

. . . .
FOCUS STUDY
. . . .

PAINTED SILK

. . . .

By the seventeenth century, imports from China, India and Turkey were prevalent in Western Europe. The development of an 'exotic' style appropriated from such goods came to be known as Orientalism. Adam Geczy has noted that patterns of trade 'introduced cottons and silks in ever-rising quantity ... These fabrics were more desirable than jute, flax, wool and linen because they were lighter, suppler and – because of that least measurable of economic variables, perception – they were different.'[1] Painted silks, originating in China for import to Europe, were a significant component of eighteenth-century trade. In an intriguing development, the chinoiserie patterns that became fashionable in Europe were sent to China to be copied, and the painted silks were then shipped back to England or France.[2]

A length of fabric from the Museum at FIT's collection dating to the late eighteenth century shows none of the earlier fashion for chinoiserie, but it is nonetheless a noteworthy example of painted silk (fig.66). The swathe is painted with a fashionable late-eighteenth-century European design, mixing bold stripes with small sprigs of flowers and bouquets linked by curling strands of ribbon. Pink roses predominate in the bouquets, but the rose motif seems to be utilised again, in a highly stylised form, on the blue stripes. This charming, meandering design emphasises the freedom afforded by painting as opposed to weaving. By the late 1700s, painted silks could be either imported to or fully produced in Europe, and it is difficult to determine the origin of this example.

Although numerous extant gowns are made from painted silk, the demand for this material was less substantial than for silk brocade. Entire dresses could be made from painted silks, but gowns with borders of painted fabric were also *à la mode*. Researching painted fabrics is challenging, as this material is not always acknowledged as such in fashion plates and can be difficult to discern from a printed textile. Fortunately, *Galerie des modes et costumes français* published descriptive captions that occasionally mention painted fabric. An example from 1778 (fig.67) describes hand-painted 'country' borders that include pink roses. Real or artificial roses also spring from the bosom in a jaunty nosegay and are used to decorate the figure's bonnet.

Notes
[1.] Geczy 2013.
[2.] Mahieu 1995, p.71.

Below left
66. Painted silk, China or France, late eighteenth century.
Silk, 162.5 x 39.4cm
The Museum at FIT, New York
Painted silks from China were an important part of trade to Europe during the eighteenth century. This design, in which bold stripes mingle with roses and ribbons, may be an example of a fashionable European style that was produced in China. The Museum at FIT, 84.90.1. Gift of Anne S. Kraatz

Below right
67. Thomas LeClerc, fashion plate showing *robe à la polonaise* with painted borders, *Galerie des modes et costumes français*, 1778.
Fashion magazines began to appear regularly during the 1770s. This enhanced means of disseminating information on dress also accelerated the pace of fashion. The detailed plates and descriptions of *Galerie des modes et costumes français* (published 1778–87) offer invaluable insight into French fashion from the period.

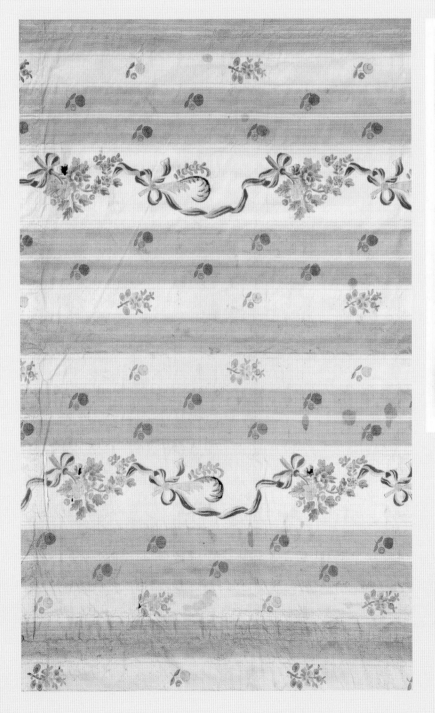

Dessiné par LeClerc   Gravé par Le Roy
Polonaise de toile bleue et blanche vermicelée garnie à plat de bandes de toile peinte de toutes couleurs sur fond blanc

THE COURTLY ROSE:
MADAME DE POMPADOUR AND MARIE ANTOINETTE

Madame de Pompadour, born Jeanne-Antoinette Poisson in Paris, was Louis XV's official mistress from 1745 to 1751. She retained influence in the French court during that time and thereafter served as an important friend and advisor to the king until her death. Pompadour was not of the nobility, but she was from a well-connected bourgeois family. As Thomas E. Kaiser has written, 'From the beginning, Jeanne-Antoinette's career was associated with her artistic interests, talents, and connections.'[22] She received instruction in dance and music from the renowned teacher Guibaudet, and learned about literature from Montesquieu. Beautiful, charming and cunning, she became the king's mistress by means unknown to modern scholarship, but it is evident that she was able to quickly and adroitly establish herself as a leader of fashion at the court of Versailles.

Madame de Pompadour's appreciation for beauty – in the forms of fashion, decorative arts and gardens – is well documented. Several portraits indicate her predilection for roses, typically in the form of large nosegays woven into the fabric of fashionable gowns or worn as hair ornaments. François Boucher's striking 1756 portrait (fig.68) is a superior example, showing Madame de Pompadour wearing roses. Her green silk taffeta gown is adorned with dozens of pink silk roses, forming a garland that traces the edges of the bodice and skirt; she also wears a small spray of flowers (either real or artificial) in her hair and a substantial nosegay made with fresh roses. Nosegays were, in part, a practical element of eighteenth-century life. The painter Élisabeth-Louise Vigée Le Brun wrote about the necessity for women of carrying bouquets of flowers, recalling that when the posies were 'combined with the strongly scented powder with which each one perfumed her hair, [they] made the air we breathe seem almost embalmed'.[23] Men, too, wore nosegays or corsages.

Boucher's painting was shown at the Salon of 1757 – begun in 1667, this was the official art exhibition of the Académie des beaux-arts in Paris – where the art critic Friedrich Melchior, Baron von Grimm, asserted that the dress was 'overloaded with ornaments' – a complaint that was partly prompted, in all likelihood, by the fact that the gown overwhelms the lower half of the painting.[24] Yet Madame de Pompadour was unmistakably a fashion leader. Her large wardrobe was impressive even by the standards of the court, and it can be used as a measure of fashionableness.[25] 'With her rosy cheeks, curly tendrils and bows at the bosom, Madame de Pompadour was one of the earliest and most successful self-image makers', Suzy Menkes wrote in a review of an exhibition dedicated to the king's mistress at the National Gallery, London, in 2002.

Opposite
68. François Boucher
Madame de Pompadour, 1756.
Oil on canvas, 212 x 164cm
Alte Pinakothek, Munich
Madame de Pompadour was famed for her elaborate wardrobe. As Aileen Ribeiro has written: 'Louis XV liked fashionable women around him. Of all his mistresses, Madame de Pompadour was the most influential in the dissemination of French taste and fashions; she was almost the personification of the playful, three-dimensional elegance of the rococo style in dress.' (Ribeiro 1984, p.18.)

Above
69. Fragment of a court dress petticoat believed to have been worn by Marie Antoinette, France, 1780. Embroidered and embellished ivory silk, 107 x 59cm
Museum of London
Like Madame de Pompadour, Marie Antoinette was often portrayed wearing or carrying roses. Very little of her wardrobe survives, but this fragment of one of the queen's petticoats depicts a spray of deep pink roses.
© Museum of London

Right
70. After Élisabeth-Louise Vigée Le
Brun, *Marie-Antoinette*, after 1783.
Oil on canvas, 92.7 x 73.1cm
National Gallery of Art,
Washington, D.C.
This is a copy of one of two paintings
of Marie Antoinette by Élisabeth-
Louise Vigée Le Brun that depicted
the queen in the same pose, holding
a pink cabbage rose in her left hand.
National Gallery of Art, Washington,
D.C., Timken Collection

Opposite
71. Thomas LeClerc, fashion plate
showing *grand robe à corps ouvert* and
*pouf, Galerie des modes et costumes
français*, 1778.
The *pouf* hairstyle sometimes blended
pure artifice with elements of nature.
The roses and ribbons on this example
mirror the ornamentation on the
fashionable lady's dress. Both fresh
and artificial flowers were used to
adorn hair.

'The pretty woman who was Louis XV's mistress became not just a household name in history, but a lasting icon of rococo frivolity.'[26]

While Madame de Pompadour clearly enjoyed considerable influence on fashion, Marie Antoinette – who entered the court of Versailles in 1770, six years after Pompadour's death, and became queen in 1774, when her husband Louis XVI ascended to the French throne – has become the pre-eminent fashion icon of the eighteenth century. A number of scholars, including Caroline Weber and Kimberly Chrisman-Campbell, have undertaken extensive research on Marie Antoinette's wardrobe. The focus on roses in the queen's wardrobe here will offer an interesting perspective to add to their findings.

Marie Antoinette is often associated with the rose as evident in its presence in portraits or the roses seen embroidered on a fragment of a 1780 petticoat worn with court dress, now part of the collection at the Museum of London (fig.69). Other connections made between Marie Antoinette and roses are difficult to verify but intriguing nonetheless. A 1913 publication on artificial flowers relayed that a man named Joseph Wenzel fashioned white artificial roses for Marie Antoinette at the request of her friend, the comte d'Artois, which resulted in Wenzel's appointment as merchant to the queen, as well as a considerable enthusiasm for artificial blooms in French fashion.[27] A more fantastical reference to Marie Antoinette can be found in an 1803 publication by the travel writer John Carr, who alleged

that the queen 'like the Idalian goddess ... used to sleep in a suspended basket of roses' in her bedroom at the Petit Trianon.[28] Idalia is an epithet for Aphrodite, the goddess of love, beauty and pleasure.

Élisabeth-Louise Vigée Le Brun painted more than 30 portraits of Marie Antoinette, but none is perhaps more famous than the picture showing the queen in a white muslin *chemise* gown – a style named for its resemblance to a commonly worn undergarment (fig.70). Even Marie Antoinette's 'simple' *chemise* gown ensemble is opulent. A swathe of sheer ochre fabric is tied in a voluminous bow at her back waist, and her wide straw hat is trimmed with a shiny blue ribbon and several large blue plumes. Despite all this, the rose stands out. It is a *Rosa x centifolia*, or 'rose of one hundred petals', also commonly known as the Provence or the cabbage rose. Although the exact origin of the centifolia is unknown, this impressive variety was likely developed in the Netherlands in the late sixteenth century and may be a hybrid of numerous ancient rose types, including the Gallica (*Rosa gallica*), the Damask (*Rosa x damascena*) and the Alba (*Rosa x alba*).[29] The flower quickly became a favourite among painters.[30]

Although the queen favoured this informal style in her personal life, its representation in a portrait, especially when shown in a public setting – the Salon of 1783 – proved to be highly contentious. It was removed from the Salon and replaced by another Vigée Le Brun painting from that same year, this time featuring Marie Antoinette in a status-appropriate blue silk gown embellished with delicate lace and ribbon. While the queen's dress was changed, her pose remained the same. In both paintings, she gazes out at the viewer, holding a nosegay with a prominent pale pink rose in her left hand and grasping a ribbon that encircles its stems with her right hand.

It was not only Marie Antoinette's dressed appearance that was consistently scrutinised by aristocrats and commoners alike, but also her physical characteristics – particularly her fine complexion. In her memoirs, Vigée Le Brun wrote that the queen's skin 'was so transparent that it bore no umber in the painting ... I had no colours to paint such freshness, such delicate tints, which were hers alone, and which I had never seen in any other woman.'[31] When any tint of her skin was mentioned, it was often compared to a rose. Weber has noted that an Alsatian noblewoman named Henriette-Louise de Waldner described Marie Antoinette's skin as 'literally blending lilies and roses' and explained that this particular comment held political weight.[32] The rose was a well-known symbol of Marie Antoinette's family, the Habsburgs, while lilies represented Louis XVI's family, the Bourbons. The queen's physical appearance, therefore, was interpreted as an alliance of the two.

Marie Antoinette was only 14 when she married. It appears that she was conscious of ageing in the public eye and what effect that might have on her wardrobe. Thirty was considered middle aged during the eighteenth century, according to Aileen Ribeiro, and was the stage in life at which many women ceased to wear the 'frivolities' of fashion that included pastel colours, feathers and flowers.[33] This sentiment may have originated with Marie Antoinette herself. A 1785 passage from *Mémoires secrets*, written by the French nobleman Louis Petit de Bachaumont, stated that the queen began to eschew feathers and flowers just before turning 30.[34] Yet she may have begun to doubt the wearing of flowers at an even earlier age. According to the memoirs of Henriette Campan, first lady-in-waiting to Marie Antoinette:

…

Before the Queen was five and twenty she began to apprehend that she might be induced to make too frequent use of flowers and of ornaments, which at that time were exclusively reserved for youth. [Milliner] Madame Bertin having brought a wreath for the head and neck, composed of roses, the Queen feared that the brightness of the flowers might be disadvantageous to her complexion.

…

Mme Campan, *Memoirs of the Court of Marie Antoinette*, pub. 1900[35]

In any case, these two recollections underscore Marie Antoinette's love for and connection to flowers, particularly roses, even if her wearing of them was short-lived.

Dessiné par Le Clerc   Gravé par Voysard

Petite Maîtresse en Robe Lilas tendre garnie de gaze
a la promenade au Palais Royal.

HEADWEAR AND HORTICULTURE

Marie Antoinette's influence extended to one of most notorious fashions of the eighteenth century: the *pouf*. A thick padding used to craft and support a towering hairstyle, the term *pouf* became synonymous with the style itself. Linda Festa explains its construction:

To create these immense confections, natural and artificial hair was combed up over wire scaffolding or over large pads made of wool, felt, and gauze, coated with a gum-like paste called pomatum, composed of the fat of bears or calves, and covered with colored powder.[36]

Taking shape during the mid-1770s, the *pouf* was viewed by hairdressers as another surface to be ornamented. Some of the most conspicuous styles were those decorated to represent an important social or political moment. The 1778 victory of the French frigate *Belle-Poule* over a British vessel, for example, resulted in a hairstyle featuring a small replica of a warship 'sailing' atop a sea of curls. Although relatively restrained in its original iteration, the style soon became the subject of caricatures, which remain oft-referenced 'representations' of eighteenth-century extravagance.

Both fresh and artificial flowers were used to adorn *poufs*. Hairdressers used small vases of water that could be nestled within mounds of hair, similar to those that were used to prevent nosegays from wilting, for fresh flowers.[37] British politican Horace Walpole described one of these vessels in a letter from 1754: 'I know nothing more but a new fashion which my Lady Hervey has brought back from Paris. It is a tin funnel covered with green ribband, and holds water, which the ladies wear to keep their bouquets fresh.'[38] Fresh-cut flowers, whether displayed in the home or forming part of a fashionable appearance, were a luxury. They necessitated attention from and replacement by servants, and also indicated an indifference to extravagance and waste.[39]

Little about the *pouf* could be described as natural, though flowers, feathers and fruits were its more common forms of adornment. Even these 'simple' embellishments were applied to creative excess, however (fig.71). A 1775 issue of the *Correspondance Secrète* described some themes popularised by Marie Antoinette: 'These head-dresses represent high mountains, flowery meadows, silvery streams, forests, or an English garden. An immense crest of feathers supports the edifice at the back.'[40] *Poufs* adorned with 'natural' elements were not immune to caricature: a 1776 plate by the prominent London-based printmakers Mary and Matthew Darly, entitled 'The Extravaganza, or the Mountain Headdress' (fig.72), shows a slender woman smiling beneath an enormous structure of pale hair.

The style is adorned with colourful feathers and garlands of flowers, including swags of roses in yellow, red and blue that fall off to one side. The impossibility of the blue rose in nature simply adds to the satirical commentary on fashion artifice. *Poufs* were in decline by the early 1780s, replaced by straw hats and bonnets ornamented with feathers, ribbons and flowers. Many fashion plates from this decade indicate that such hats were only marginally less extravagant than the *pouf*. A fashion plate from *Galerie des modes et costumes français* of 1780 (fig.73) shows a woman wearing a gown of pink, blue and ivory silk that is remarkably free of embellishment, but it is paired with an enormous hat with a straw brim and a tall crown of gathered fabric. Pink roses form a hatband and extend energetically from the crown. Like those used to adorn *poufs*, these flowers could have been natural or artificial. Understandably, such hats were large, cumbersome and heavy, and they were not suited to every occasion. As Chrisman-Campbell discovered, a heatwave in Paris in the summer of 1787 resulted in many women abandoning such hats in favour of bandeaus and turbans. Some even sported simple, elegant garlands of roses.[41]

THE EXTRAVAGANZA.
OR THE MOUNTAIN HEAD DRESS OF *1776*.

Robe à la Turque, la même expliqué au vingt septieme Cahier N.º 159. elle eſt ici developé de
Profil ou Trois quart

Dessiné par Le Clerc   Gravé par Dupin

ROSES IN MENSWEAR

Aristocratic men's fashion during the eighteenth century was extraordinary in its luxury and detail. Wearing elaborate fabrics was considered a sign not of femininity, but of status. As Sharon Sadako Takeda has written of this period, 'the splendid man's attire was frequently festooned with flowers. Designs on textiles and dress mirrored the elaborate architecture and floriculture of the landed gentry's domestic gardens.'[42] Embroidery in particular was inspired by flowers, though men also wore brocade fabrics patterned with florals. An example of the latter is seen used to fashion a waistcoat of c.1780, held in the collection of the Museum at FIT (fig.74). Roses in shades of red–orange are interspersed with smaller, stylised posies rendered in metallic thread. Gold embroidery – now appearing mostly silver, indicating that the threads were made of gilded silver wrapped around a silk core – outlines the buttonholes, pockets, centre opening and bottom edges of the waistcoat.[43] The use of metallic thread indicates that this garment may have been worn at court, while the difficulty of embroidering with metallic threads reveals that the work was completed by a professional, rather than one of the many amateur embroiderers of the day.[44]

Waistcoats, worn as part of a matching ensemble or paired with a coordinating jacket and breeches, were an important component of men's wardrobes in the late eighteenth century. The fashion for waistcoats changed rapidly and was subject to mandates of season and occasion, requiring the well-dressed man to own a significant selection. As in women's fashion, pale colours predominated and served to highlight colourful embroidery. In a waistcoat dating to the 1790s (fig.75), the pink rose is the largest flower among a delicate tangle of pansies, bluebells, sunflowers and several other small, indistinct floral designs. The rose is, once again, the most intricately rendered flower, though every bloom is highly stylised. Worn with a yellow silk coat from c.1790 (fig.76), this garment and its mate resemble those seen in a 1785 fashion plate from Galeries des modes et costumes français (fig.77), in which a 'friendly seducer' presents a box of jewels to a fashionably dressed woman. He wears a yellow silk suit and a cream waistcoat embroidered with garlands of pink flowers that appear to be roses. In his 1770 book Art of the Embroiderer, Charles Germain de Saint-Aubin, designer to Louis VX, advised on the art of shaded embroidery:

Not only must stitches curve following veins of leaves to express movement, but one must also place colors appropriately and must avoid heaviness ... One must avoid, especially for flowers, too many shades of color. Poor Workers believe they can never have enough. They dare not consider skipping one or two shades to heighten an effect.[45]

Opposite
72. M. Darly, 'The Extravaganza, or the Mountain Headdress', 1776. Engraving
Caricatures of fashionable dress were common during the eighteenth and nineteenth centuries. The pouf was a particular target for mockery, as its extreme proportions were easily exaggerated.

Above
73. Thomas LeClerc, fashion plate showing robe à la turque, Galerie des modes et costumes français, 1780.
As the pouf fell out of fashion, large hats took its place. The embellished hats were heavy and cumbersome, making them scarcely more practical than towering hairstyles.

A French court suit from *c.*1785 (fig.78) demonstrates the use of
embroidery on a matching set of coat, waistcoat and breeches.
Made from dark green velvet striped with beige, the ensemble's
very colour indicates its value, as green was a colour difficult to
achieve using contemporary dyes and thus expensive.[46] Intricate
embroidery further underscores the ensemble's opulence, and its
designer appears to have incorporated Saint-Aubin's advice.
Each rose is crafted from contrasting shades of pink, ivory, yellow
and pale blue. While the flowers may not be naturalistic, their
depth and definition underscore the skill of the embroiderer.

Below left
74. Waistcoat (detail), France,
*c.*1780.
Ivory silk brocade with gold metal
embroidery
The Museum at FIT, New York
The lavish menswear styles of the
eighteenth century indicated the
wearers' status and good taste.
Flowers, including many roses, were
popular design motifs. The use of gold
thread indicates that this waistcoat
was worn at the French court.
The Museum at FIT, 93.132.4.
Gift of Thomas Oechsler

Below right
75. Waistcoat,
USA or Europe, 1790s.
Cream silk faille with multicoloured
silk embroidery
The Museum at FIT, New York
Waistcoats were an integral
element of men's attire during the
late eighteenth century. Examples
embroidered with flowers were
especially common. Waistcoat
styles changed regularly, and their
embroidery precluded them from
being altered to adapt to new
silhouettes.
The Museum at FIT, 87.120.1.
Gift of Dr & Mrs Roger Gerry

Above left
76. Cutaway coat,
USA, c.1790.
Silk
The Museum at FIT, New York
An embellished waistcoat might
be part of a matching three-piece
suit, but could also be worn with a
coordinating jacket and breeches
made from plain fabric. Even when
paired with bright yellow silk, the
intricate embroidery of this waistcoat
is eye-catching.
The Museum at FIT, P80.5.8.
Museum purchase

Above right
77. François-Louis-Joseph Watteau,
fashion plate, *Galerie des modes et
costumes français*, 1785.
*Galerie des modes et costumes
français* was an important source for
men's clothing as well as the most
fashionable women's dress. This plate
shows a man wearing a yellow silk suit
complemented by a white, floral-
embroidered waistcoat, similar to that
shown in fig.76.

THE FABLES OF FLORA

John Langhorne's *The Fables of Flora*, first published in 1771, consists of stories of moral prose. While fables often anthropomorphise animals, Langhorne's stories are told by flowers, foreshadowing the larger trend towards flower personification in nineteenth-century literature.[47] Fable IV, 'The Garden-Rose and the Wild-Rose', is especially charming. In short, the wild rose feels overshadowed by her more cultivated rival, the garden rose. The story's narrator, a poet, is surprised by her woes and responds:

…

Though this courtly rose …

Is gay, and beauteous to behold

Yet, lovely flower, I find in thee

Wild sweetness which no words express,

And charms in thy simplicity,

That dwell not in the pride of dress.

…

John Langhorne, *The Fables of Flora*, 1771[48]

Later editions of the book, dating to the late eighteenth and early nineteenth centuries, feature detailed engravings by Alexander Anderson (fig.79). These illustrations are not only of the flowers, but of their personifications. The title page for 'The Garden-Rose and the Wild-Rose' portrays a group of four young women – presumably the wild roses – elegantly posed and encircled by thorny stems. Their simple, white muslin gowns underscore their humble nature and align with the fashion of the day. Lavish, floral brocaded silks had little place in French fashion during the waning years of the eighteenth century but, as demonstrated throughout in this book, rose motifs were never out of style for long.

FABLE IV.

THE GARDEN-ROSE AND THE WILD-ROSE.

AS DEE, whose current free from ftain,
Glides fair o'er MERIONETH's plain,
By mountains forced his way to fteer
Along the lake of PIMBLE MERE,

Opposite
78. Court suit, France, c.1785.
Silk velvet with multicoloured silk embroidery
The Museum at FIT, New York
The court suit comprised a matching jacket, waistcoat and breeches. Roses predominate in the embroidered pattern of this example; although not naturalistic, they are carefully shaded and detailed to provide the illusion of depth.
The Museum at FIT, P83.19.10.
Museum purchase

Right
79. Alexander Anderson, 'The Garden-Rose and the Wild-Rose' (1794), from John Langhorne, *The Fables of Flora* (London: B. Crosby, 1804).
Alexander Anderson's personification of wild roses portrays the flowers as a group of elegant young women, nestled among leaves and thorns.
The Morgan Library & Museum, New York

CHAPTER IV

THE ROSE

...

THE UNFADING FLOWER
OF JEWELLERY

GEOFFREY MUNN

...
No jewels,
Save my eyes,
Do I own,

But I have a rose
Which is even softer
Than my rose lips
...

Vladimir Nabokov, *Pnin*, 1957[1]

In 1653, the physician and astrologer Nicholas Culpeper wrote in his *Complete Herbal*, 'What a pother have authors made with roses! What a racket they have made!'

The same racket has echoed across the centuries, from Classical antiquity to the present day, when the rose maintains [its] very special place in the human imagination. There is no synonym for the rose and this is further evidence of its supremacy; as the lion is absolute in the animal kingdom, so the rose has always been paramount in floriculture. This is probably because its unique beauty affects all five senses with equal intensity. Consequently, it was readily assimilated into myths and legends. In the ancient world, the goddess Aphrodite and her Roman incarnation Venus were identified by a variety of attributes, including shells, pearls, doves, myrtle flowers and, above all, the rose.[2] Its message is always amorous but a harsh warning is implicit; hidden among the sensuous beauty of the leaves and petals lurk thorns and the danger of hurt. Thus, in almost every age and every culture, the rose is emblem of both the pleasure and the pain of love. This provides a colourful palette of imagery to artists far and wide, who have been quick to exploit it when rendering every permutation of human emotion. In 1545, it was brought to a very shrill pitch, when Florentine artist Bronzino painted *An Allegory with Venus and Cupid* – a highly erotic composition in which a confetti of rose petals is a central ingredient of an already tortuous allegory. Just over 40 years later, in London in around 1587, Nicholas Hilliard used the eglantine (*Rosa rubiginosa*, or 'sweet briar'), in his miniature entitled *Young Man among Roses*

(see fig.36) to imply the agonising yearnings of first love. Beautiful from bud to bloom, the rose, in common with every flower, is by its very nature impermanent and, just as the scent grows faint and the petals drop, so even ideal love is inevitably superseded by grief. In 1633 Venetia Stanley, Lady Digby, died suddenly in her sleep and her grief-stricken husband asked Sir Anthony van Dyck to paint her fast-fading beauty on her deathbed. In this arresting image it seems that Venetia is simply sleeping. The only obvious clue to her mortality is the rose on the hem of her sheet.It is not only full-blown but some of the petals have fallen. Thus, we see the symbolic meaning of the rose expanded to encompass even love beyond the grave. It is in this gloomy capacity that it is used to great effect in *memento mori* paintings, funerary sculptures and, tellingly, in jewellery design (fig.80).

As it was in art, so too in literature; there again the rose reigned supreme, its amorous symbolism giving writers vivid inspiration for a variety of narratives. As early as 615 BCE the Greek poet Sappho is believed to have written the 'Song of the Rose' and, 1,000 years later, we find that there are more than 90 mentions of the flower in the complete works of William Shakespeare.

As the native beauty of the genus *Rosa* was enriched by hybridisation, the references to it intensified, and never more exquisitely than in William Blake's famous lyric 'The Sick Rose' (fig.31). Blake was one of dozens, probably hundreds, of writers to be inspired not just by the beauty of the rose, but by its time-honoured association with both pleasure and pain. John Keats, in his 'Ode on Melancholy' of 1819 (published in 1820), urged his reader to 'glut thy sorrow on a morning rose' and Algernon Swinburne's 'The Year of the Rose' (1874) is, as the title suggests, an allegory of love. Oscar Wilde's short story 'The Nightingale and the Rose' (1888), is a tragic account of devotion that is not only devalued but cruelly spurned. Imbued with such symbolic intensity, it is not surprising that the rose is widely found not just in painting and literature, but in every aspect of decorative art, including dress and jewellery. Here, in equal measure, we see roses decorating the surface of a variety of stuffs, including woven and painted silks, damasks and even cloth of gold where, on the Imperial Mantle worn by the British sovereign, it appears as an emblem of England.

In jewellery design specifically, we see that roses are not simply decorative but carry dozens of covert messages, the majority of which are amatory and most of which derive from the language of flowers. The charming but completely artificial system laid out here has its origins in antiquity but was greatly expanded in the eighteenth and nineteenth centuries. It was then that dozens of small books were published, listing every possible meaning for each and almost every flower. In these little floral lexicons, we read once again that the rose is peerless and, in honour of its special importance, it carries no less than 40 meanings. One of the more lugubrious is that of the dried white rose, which stands for 'death rather than loss of innocence'.

It is said that jewellery is the highest form of dress, and it is true that its function is almost always far beyond the merely decorative. More often it is an emblem of love, magic or power, and occasionally all three. This was never more apparent than in the ancient world, where, among the many and varied forms of jewellery, head ornaments were literally the crowning glory of the goldsmith's art. These remarkable objects, almost sculptural in their complexity, were wrought from 'native' gold (found and mined in its pure, unalloyed form) and the malleability of the precious metal allowed it to be worked into delicate leaves and flowers.

80. Locket, England, c.1810.
Enamelled gold set with plaited hair
Victoria and Albert Museum,
London
A gold mourning jewel of unusual complexity, made to frame a lock of plaited human hair. This is a highly emotive piece of jewellery, which seems to imply a sense of guilt regarding the loss of the deceased in the phrase, 'I snapped it, it fell to the ground'.
© Victoria and Albert Museum, London

Favourites for both men and women were wreaths of laurel, oak and olive, and preternatural garlands of roses were observed in their every detail and delicacy. In this way it seemed as if, by a wave of the alchemist's wand, the fleeting beauty of the rose, being transmuted into gold, was finally rendered undying and perpetual. It is even possible that these fragile, paper-thin jewels were seen as representing the triumph of love over the grave itself, because they were worn by both the living and the dead.

One of the most lyrical examples of such a wreath was found in the funerary treasure of Philip II of Macedon (fig.81). It is a delicate combination of roses and – another attribute of Venus and an emblem of marriage – myrtle leaves and flowers in full bloom. Among this elaborate foliage sits evidence that the Greek jewellers had something of a sense of humour, as, occasionally, they include butterflies and bees within their already complicated composition: insects perpetually pollinating the unfading flowers of pure gold.

Although the Romans admired much about the culture of the Greeks, and sometimes slavishly copied their art and architecture, there is next to no evidence that their interest extended into jewellery design. In the hands of the Roman goldsmith, precious ornaments of all sorts lost most of the delicacy of their Hellenistic predecessors. Gone were the delicate observations of nature, and in their wake came diadems, necklaces, bracelets and earrings of an almost monumental stature. More often than not, these jewels were designed to frame precious stones, largely unavailable to the Greeks, that included amethysts, emeralds and pearls.

We know that the Romans were inordinately fond of roses and used them on all manner of festal occasions, including banquets both official and private; in homage to the pain of separation, they were often used in rites for the dead.[3] Surprisingly, they are not often found in Roman jewellery design. Instead there was a distinct preference for snakes, knots of Hercules, cameos, even the baleful head of Medusa; if there were roses, they were conventionalised into simple rosettes.

The cultivation of the rose probably began in China 5,000 years ago but it was in the modern (post-Classical) world that it became widespread throughout the northern hemisphere. It is a flower associated with warmer climes, however, and it was not until the thirteenth century that it became popular in Europe. Even then, its representation in art and jewellery design was frowned upon in early Christian asceticism, owing to its close association with the pagan world. Nonetheless, little by little, these prejudices faded away and the rose earned a new identity in the Christian world. The floor of the Chapter House at Westminster Abbey, London – laid down for Edward III in the mid-fourteenth century – is decorated with a Latin text that translates:

'As the rose is the flower of flowers so this is the house of houses.' The rose became a favourite plant in the medieval garden, even an emblem of the Virgin Mary herself (see p.39).[4] As it was in cultivation, so it was at the jeweller's bench, where the rose was as much an ornament as an heraldic device. In 1498, Anne, Lady Scrope, left her stepson a 'White roose with a baleys' (red spinel).[5] It must have borne a striking resemblance to the brooch in the form of a white rose that figures in the miniature painting of a Burgundian pendant now in the Historisches Museum in Basel (fig.82). The endless threat to the survival of intrinsically valuable jewellery is fashion, and constant remodelling and resetting of precious stones has resulted in the loss of the vast majority of jewellery that has had any intrinsic value at all. Consequently, the historian relies heavily on external evidence, including painting, sculpture and wills. A rare surviving example is a fifteenth-century jewel of similar design to the Burgundian pendant, now preserved at All Souls College, Oxford (fig.83).

In the early Renaissance, jewellers who had previously focused their attention on Christian subjects were given a wider remit. Inspired as much by the ancient world as their own freedom of expression, the goldsmiths of the sixteenth and seventeenth centuries embraced every aspect of floral design and, inevitably, this included the rose and its time-honoured lore.

At this time, the typical artist/craftsman was trained in all manner of skills, including painting, sculpture, goldsmithing and, indeed, jewellery making. This was the rebirth of learning, which relied heavily on the antique and its pagan gods. Always naked, but clothed in a new academic respectability, Venus returned to centre stage, identified by her many attributes. Sandro Botticelli's *Birth of Venus* (1482–5), for example, shows her born from the sea in a shell, propelled by a zephyr of pink roses.[6]

A number of the greatest masters of the time had some expertise at the jeweller's bench and these included Antonio Pollaiuolo, Albrecht Dürer, Hans Holbein the younger and even Leonardo da Vinci himself. Needless to say, all of these artists and their contemporaries were conversant with the rich heritage of plants and flowers, and Leonardo, already fascinated by botany, made at least one detailed study of a single rose. Although there is no surviving evidence that these famous artists used the rose in their goldsmithing work, there is no reason to doubt it. Nonetheless, representations in Renaissance jewellery are tantalisingly rare. One, most touching in its modesty, is found on the reverse of the newly discovered, gold-enamelled Fettercairn Jewel (fig.84), probably made in Scotland in the mid-sixteenth century. Probably the most emphatic of all, however, is the Phoenix Jewel (fig.85), in which the image of Elizabeth I is framed by red and white roses of Lancaster and York entwined with her own emblem – none other than the eglantine (*Rosa rubiginosa*).[7] In another pendant ornament, known as the Heneage Jewel (fig.86), the image of the queen appears not once but twice: as a medal and in a painted miniature. The locket is backed by a gold panel on which a full-blown rose is framed by a wreath of its own leaves. Around it runs a Latin motto alluding to fast-fading beauty, which translates as, 'Alas, would that virtue endured with such beauty might, inviolate, enjoy perpetual light.'

In the seventeenth century, exploration and colonisation brought precious stones to Europe in unprecedented variety and volume. Consequently, the delicate mannerist ornamentation that had characterised the previous century made way for the scintillation of emeralds, topazes, chrysoberyls and diamonds, cut to a dazzling new level of sophistication and brilliance.[8] Nevertheless, the close yet contradictory relationship between the everlasting beauty of precious stones and the transient charm of leaves and flowers was never completely forgotten.

Indeed, in some medieval wills the word 'flower' is a synonym for a jewel. In goldsmiths' work, there could be no real competition between these brilliantly coloured gemstones and detailed subtle representation of the plant world and so, relegated to the back of jewellery, flowers were rendered in delicate painted enamels on the reverse of stomachers, necklaces, slides and all manner of jewellery. There, quite hidden from public view, bouquets and posies were reserved for the private delectation of the owner, though they were occasionally shown as cabinet pieces in their own right.[9] In the Low Countries in the first half of the seventeenth century, it was not the rose that was at centre stage but the tulip, introduced from Turkey to the West by the sultan Suleiman I (known as 'the Magnificent') in the sixteenth century. However, this fresh challenge to the ancient heritage of the rose, known as 'Tulipmania', was particular to the Low Countries, and even there it was comparatively short-lived.[10]

Opposite
84. The Fettercairn Jewel (back), probably Scotland, c.1560–80.
Gold, enamel and almandine garnet
National Museums Scotland
The front of this gold locket is set with a large red almandine garnet and the back is decorated with champlevé enamelling. A small yellow rose is one of the emblematic flowers gathered in the blue vase to the left of the composition.
Image © National Museums Scotland

Overleaf left
85. The Phoenix Jewel, England, 1570–80.
Gold and enamel
The British Museum, London
The gold here takes the form of a bust of Elizabeth I, Queen of England, cut out in silhouette. On the back of the pendant is a device of a phoenix in flames under the royal monogram, crown and heavenly rays. The central image is enclosed by a wreath of enamelled red and white Tudor roses.
© The Trustees of the British Museum

Overleaf right
86. Nicholas Hilliard (painter), The Heneage Jewel (back and front views), England, c.1595.
Enamelled gold, table-cut diamonds, Burmese rubies, rock crystal and a miniature
Victoria and Albert Museum, London
A gold locket made to frame a miniature of Elizabeth I by Nicholas Hilliard. The front of the jewel displays a gold relief portrait of the queen, secured under a panel of rock crystal. On the back is a ship in full sail, emblematic of the Church of England, navigated safely through troubled waters by the queen. The inside of the locket, opposite the miniature, shows a Tudor rose framed by a wreath of its own leaves.
© Victoria and Albert Museum, London

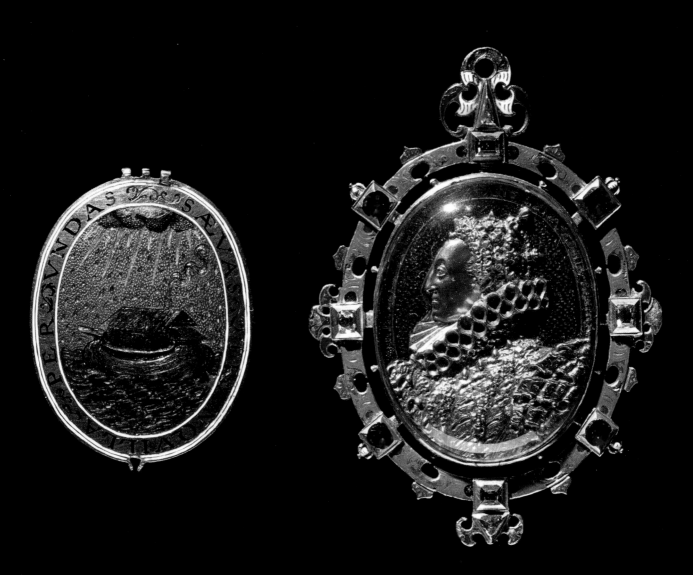

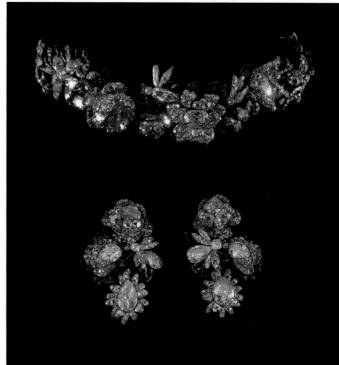

The eighteenth century has been described by the antiquary and jewellery historian Joan Evans as the age of light and lightness, both in the decorative arts and in the mind. This was particularly true of both dress and jewellery. Daring décolleté dresses allowed for an extravagant display of necklaces, and fiercely boned corsages were the perfect platform for all manner of stomachers set with coloured stones and diamonds. The variety of available gemstones was even greater than in the seventeenth century and the invention of the brilliant-cut diamond was everything its name suggests – brilliant. The finest jewellery was worn in the evening and the diamond's natural affinity with candlelight meant that both men and women blazed in refracted light, from their jewelled buckles right up to their complicated wigs, even to their gem-set combs and tiaras. Immense bouquets were the order of the day and the rose was central to all sorts of completely improbable floral sprays. Often, gem-set flowers and buds were set on watch springs, and there they trembled and oscillated with the slightest movement of the wearer, accentuating a return of light quite beyond all previous imaginings. The fashion was so successful that it continued well into the nineteenth century (fig.87).

In diamond jewellery of this sort, the rose may have lost its colour but not entirely its meaning. In the lore of the lapidary, the diamond stands for constancy, and in conjunction with the rose it means eternal love. In one extremely rare example, the jeweller had access to the best of all worlds in both colour and form. Supported by the seemingly limitless budget of the Russian

imperial court under Empress Anna, he was free to create one of the greatest masterpieces of the jeweller's art (fig.88). An array of coloured diamonds was brought together to make a garland of roses and matching earrings.[11]

In the nineteenth century, it seems that decorative artists – in contrast with those operating amid the vital splendour of the Baroque and Rococo – had lost confidence, if not in their technical prowess then in their own artistic integrity. Consequently, the majority believed that the best way forward was to look back. This attitude, already apparent in the 'Empire' style of the 1820s, and nurtured by the teachings of a number of art critics including John Ruskin, dominated the aesthetics of the century. Jewellers and jewellery designers were quick and willing to follow suit.

Standing for Christian virtue and authority, the Gothic style was one of the first to be emulated in nineteenth-century Europe. It seemed that the plant world as a source of inspiration had been subsumed into medieval convention and so the rose in that particular revival is not easy to find; the decorative schemes that followed the Gothic Revival were equally conventionalised. However in parallel with the revival of Greek, Roman, Assyrian and Renaissance styles, there emerged a renewed enthusiasm for nature and the natural sciences. Once again, it was in gem-set jewellery that the rose bloomed anew.

Opposite left
87. Bodice ornament,
probably England, c.1850.
Diamonds set in silver,
backed with gold
Victoria and Albert Museum,
London
This large ornament features roses,
carnations and other flowers entirely
set with diamonds. The heads of some
of the flowers, including the roses, are
set on watch springs called 'tremblers',
to increase the return of light.
© Victoria and Albert Museum, London

Opposite right
88. Suite consisting of a wreath and
matching earrings, Russia, 1730–40.
Coloured diamonds and enamel
The Diamond Fund, Moscow
The jeweller of this matching set was
likely inspired by the gold wreaths of
antiquity and, in homage to his ancient
predecessors, has even placed bees
among the diamond-set flowers and
naturalistically enamelled leaves.
Part of the celebrated Russian crown
jewels, the parure is composed of
some of the rarest and most valuable
stones ever sourced for jewellery.
Reproduced from *Joyaux du Trésor
de Russie* (Bibliothèque des Arts:
Paris, 1901). Photograph by Nicholai
Rachmanov

Below
89. Brooch,
England, c.1840.
Gold and red-stained ivory
British Museum, London
© The Trustees of the British Museum

Below left
90. Cartier, rose clip brooch,
London, 1938.
Platinum and diamonds
The Cartier Collection
Princess Margaret wore this brooch
to the coronation of her sister,
Queen Elizabeth II on 2 June 1953
at Westminster Abbey, London.
Vincent Wulveryck, Collection Cartier
© Cartier

Bottom left
91. Cartier, 'Chinese Vase' brooch,
Paris, 1928.
Gold, platinum, diamonds,
emeralds coral, lapis lazuli and
enamel
The Cartier Collection
Vincent Wulveryck, Collection Cartier
© Cartier

In Paris, at the benches of the jeweller Theodore Fester and his contemporaries Frédéric Boucheron and Octave Loeuillard, several of the finest flower pieces were made. It was Fester who made the magnificent corsage brooch in the form of a rose in bud and bloom owned by Princess Mathilde, the daughter of Jérôme Bonaparte; it became the centrepiece of her world-famous collection of jewellery. In around 1900, a similarly ambitious brooch was made by Fabergé in Russia, in homage to the Danish origins of the Empress Maria Feodorovna, whose family emblem was the yellow rose. It featured a delicate budding flower, set with coloured diamonds to witty and dazzling effect.

There is only one word for jewellery in the English language but, conveniently, the French have two: *joaillerie* for the kind of gem-set ornaments described in the previous paragraph, and *bijouterie* for those jewels that rely heavily on the value of technique and superlative craftsmanship. These *bijoux* are generally of a more intimate and sentimental nature, and this is where the imagery of the rose took firm root again. During the nineteenth century, the flower was used to convey its familiar message in all manner of gold pendants, lockets, brooches worked in coloured golds – sometimes incorporating stained ivory to naturalistic effect (see fig.89) – and, occasionally, fobs set with seals. After the hot red sealing wax had cooled on the tip of an envelope, the imprint of a rose, applied with a seal, was the first hint of a private love message within. However, to describe certain jewels as *bijouterie* simply because of their relatively small intrinsic value is inappropriate and diminishing. This was never more obvious than in the case of René Lalique. He was at the vanguard of a movement of designers and craftsmen looking for a unique and modern method of expression with only one definable source of inspiration – nature itself. Its vortex was in Paris and it grew under the name of Art Nouveau, 'the new art', though the movement spread elsewhere in Europe as Jugendstil.

America, too, was ready for this artistic revolution, and there it was Louis Comfort Tiffany who was the most important protagonist. It thrived internationally in various degrees of popularity, but in every aspect of Art Nouveau design there is a faint atmosphere of disquiet. Lalique's restless, occasionally macabre imagination embraced not only the transient beauty of nature but also its eventual decay and corruption. Leaves and petals are shown not in a state of complete perfection, but occasionally overblown, perished, gnawed by teeming insect life. The animals that roamed Lalique's psyche have a strange unnatural beauty – beauty from the beastly. On one occasion he designed an enamelled gold pendant in the form of vultures gorging on carrion.

Nevertheless, the rose worked its special magic on Lalique and we see it through his eyes and in an entirely new vision (fig.93). As always, art and effect were paramount and it mattered very little how they were achieved. Yes, Lalique used precious stones, but,

if the composition required it, then ivory, humble glass and even worthless cows' horn would do as well. Lalique died in 1945, by which time his work had fallen out of fashion and was only appreciated by a small contemporary elite that included his most important patron, the millionaire financier Calouste Gulbenkian.[12]

It is hard to identify a single characteristic of the Art Nouveau movement, but an organic curvilinear line defines most of the work. However, as a result of a fierce reaction to this decadent aesthetic, it was superseded in the early 1920s by the angular geometric style known as Art Deco. One might reasonably wonder how the organic form of the rose could survive an aesthetic shock of this magnitude and it hardly did. This time, Cartier, Boucheron, and Van Cleef & Arpels took up the mantle, supported by a cast of adventurous materials that included rock crystal, lapis lazuli and every imaginable hardstone – even ancient Egyptian faience and Chinese lacquer; despite all this richness, the rose was scarcely to be found (figs 90, 91). It seemed that for the moment it had been banished from jewellery to more decorative pieces, including card and vanity cases, where it was often represented using carved emeralds and rubies. One of the most bizarre examples was commissioned as a group of Christmas presents by James de Rothschild of Waddesdon Manor, England, in 1926. This was a series of roses, designed to predict the weather with a hidden hygrometer, each of which was mounted in a laquer vase by Cartier.

Following the First and Second World Wars, society as it once was changed forever. The vast fortunes made in Europe and America in the late nineteenth and early twentieth centuries were diminished and, as a result, the lavish entertainments and the wearing of elaborate jewellery was greatly reduced. Previously, patrons of the decorative arts, including dress and jewellery, were willing to spend money literally for the sake of spending it, and they did so lavishly, with little or no regard for the future. Occasionally, an enormously expensive dress was made just for one night and, in the same way, a costly jewel was purchased not for investment but simply for pleasure. When those heady days were over, so too was the cultivated patronage that demanded the finest and the best of the jeweller's art. Regrettably, customers at the great jewellery houses of Europe and America began to buy as an investment rather than to spend on innovative design and superlative craftsmanship; this change was to mark the beginning of a steep decline in jewellery as an art form. Where, once, precious stones were selected for the concept of a fine necklace or tiara, now all manner of jewels were made simply to flaunt costly gems in artless jewels.

Nonetheless, the rose survived as an emblem of love and a small number of jewellers managed to incorporate it into this new aesthetic and the most successful example is the brooch made by Cartier to accommodate the rare and valuable pink diamond given to Princess Elizabeth as a wedding present in 1947 (fig.92). It also continued to be represented in all manner of relatively semi-precious materials, giving colour and depth to the more abbreviated forms of the 1940s. These included coral, ivory and sometimes simply polished coloured gold, heightened with diamond sparks.

And yet, the future of the rose in contemporary jewellery houses seems uncertain. One notable exception to the general rule is the firm JAR, founded in the late 1970s by Joel Rosenthal and operating in the Place Vendôme in Paris. Here, in a flurry of exotic flowers, petals and butterflies wrought from coloured stones and diamonds, Rosenthal has taken a fresh look at the rose as a source of inspiration. Through the use of rare and exotic gemstones he has identified its very essence, evoking the rose's velvety softness with some of the hardest precious materials known to man. Pavé-set in delicate grades of colour, in heady combinations of red, pink and purple, JAR's jewels are not slavish copies of nature but adventurous interpretations (fig.94), truly redolent of the scented rose.

Today it seems JAR stands almost alone in fascination with the rose. It is hard to find it blooming in any form in the over-lit window displays of New York, London and Paris, but, considering the famous beauty and charm, the very quintessence of the rose, perhaps this temporary die-back mirrors the endless cycle of nature. During the winter the rose is quite unseen, dormant in the icy darkness, waiting for the first warm rays of the sun before it burgeons again in all its unrivalled splendour. As it is in nature, so surely must it be in art. We will not have to wait too long before the rose reclaims its rightful supremacy at the goldsmith's bench, rising triumphant once again in the endlessly beguiling history of jewellery design.

94. JAR, Brooch, Paris, 2013.
Rubies, sapphires, spinels and diamonds
JAR Paris

CHAPTER V

PERMANENT BOTANICALS

···

FASHIONING ARTIFICIAL ROSES

AMY DE LA HAYE

...

You must always have the rose before
you or know it by heart.

...

Petal Dyer, Paris, 1910[1]

'Permanent Botanicals' is the name given to the first artificial
flowers based on natural blooms such as the rose (something
'artificial' is here defined as being made or produced by humans,
rather than occurring naturally, and usually a copy of something
natural; 'natural' refers to objects existing in or derived from
nature, not made or caused by humans). This chapter explores
the history, design, making and materiality of such artificial roses
and examines the diverse kinds of training and the working lives
of the people, mostly women and young girls, who made them.
Following a brief historical context, artificial flower making in
Paris, New York and London – the leading fashion cities when
this trade flourished – is explored. The chapter touches upon
the making of black flowers in Manchester, England, and the
German artificial flower-making industry.

By the mid-nineteenth century, with the mass production of
metal tools, textiles and dyestuffs, artificial flower making had
become an ancillary trade to the elite fashion industries, serving
haute couture houses, dress and hat makers, and the mass-
production clothing industries. Most historical evidence about
the industry dates from the mid-nineteenth to early twentieth
centuries, when artificial flower making was at its peak.
Apart from slumps during both world wars, the business of
artificial flower making generally thrived until the 1960s, when
fashion became more informal, less substantial and more
modernistic, and hat wearing declined.

Published research on artificial flower making is scant within
fashion studies and these products have not – with the exception
of the *Artisans d'élégances* touring exhibition, initiated by Musée
national des arts et traditions populaires, Paris (1993–4) – been
foregrounded within exhibitions.[2] However, there does exist a
wealth of primary sources upon which to draw, within which
the rose, as a most popular flower, and the rose maker – an elite
member of the flower-making workforce – are often prominent.

Opposite
95. Attributed to the German
Strasbourg workshop, 'Two
Riddles of the Queen of Sheba',
c.1490–1500.
Wool, linen and metal,
80 x 101.6cm
The Metropolitan Museum of
Modern Art, New York
The Metropolitan Museum of Art,
New York. The Cloisters Collection,
1971

Right
96. Christian Dior skull cap (detail),
Paris, c.1950.
Silk velvet, with silk roses
The Museum at FIT, New York
One of two clusters of cream-
coloured silk roses, buds and green
cotton leaves on stems, each cluster
itself resembling a large rose bloom.
The stamen-less roses – six in the
right-hand cluster, and five in the left
– are made in four different sizes. The
roses and buds have long, stiffened
cotton sepals dyed dark green on
the face and a lighter green on the
reverse.
The Museum at FIT, 72.81.38.
Gift of Doris Duke

Surviving artificial roses permit material culture analysis of flowers, buds, stems and leaves; thorns, which could snag material or skin, are omitted. Applied to garments and hats, they reveal how flowers interface with apparel and the fashionable body. Like lace and buttons (fig.97), flowers are sometimes removed from one item of apparel to accessorise another, or might be preserved in the form of a memento. However, unlike buttons and lace, which attract masses of collectors and can command high prices, artificial flowers are generally less revered; they can also be more fragile and awkward to store.

The making of permanent botanicals, originally crafted in times when the earth no longer yielded natural flowers, dates back to ancient Egypt, where flowers were made from shavings of stained horn; to China, where silk, porcelain, gold, paper and the marrow from bamboo were used; and to ancient Greece, where they were finely tooled from gold and silver metals. Traders took the craft to Rome, where silk cocoon and, later, wax, were employed. China and Rome were to achieve a fine degree of botanical accuracy, but it was in Paris, where the industry evolved

slowly between the fourteenth and the mid-nineteenth centuries, that artificial flower making was to find its most refined and creative expression in fashion. From the mid-eighteenth century, French Protestants fleeing religious persecution took flower-making skills to London, and by the early nineteenth century, those emigrating to New York had done likewise.

Even though artificial flowers can be made year-round, they are worn primarily when those they imitate are in bloom. Until the late twentieth century, when the shape of the fashion industry's year came to be more fluid and less powerfully oriented around bi-annual seasonal presentations; this seasonality exerted a profound impact upon the structure and organisation of the industries and their workers. Some firms combined flower making with feather work, as feathers generally trim winter apparel, in order to ensure employment throughout the seasons. While the working environments required were similar, the two industries involved different supply chains (the most brilliantly coloured feathers were imported from Latin America) and skills. As feathers do not replicate roses they are not considered here.

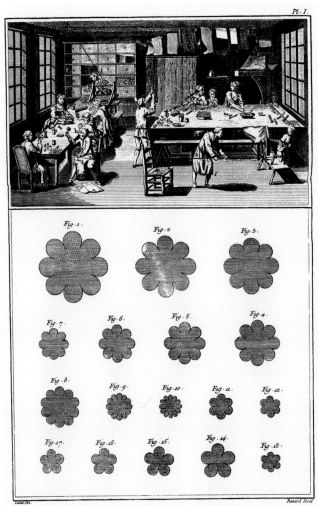

Fleuriste Artificiel, Plans d'emporte-pieces de Feuilles de Fleurs.

MAKING ROSES
IN PARIS

By the early eighteenth century, the artificial flower-making trade had become concentrated in rue Saint-Denis and the surrounding streets, supplying flowers for the fine art market as well as fashion. An early Parisian firm, established in rue des Petit-Champs in 1727, was the predecessor of Maison Legeron, which continues to supply the elite fashion market today. One of the first visual records of the trade was published in *Encyclopédie, ou dictionnaire raisonné des sciences, des arts et des métiers* (1751–72) by Denis Diderot, French philosopher and art critic. It comprises eight prints, made from engravings by Bernard Fecit, the first of which depicts a spacious, light-filled workshop with 12 people – six women, two children and four men – working at wooden tables (fig.98). Subsequent plates depict tools for flower making and patterns for various petals and leaves, including roses.

In 1776 the Corporations des marchands de modes, plumassiers et fleuristes was formed to support this emergent trade. Artificial flower makers (*bouquetières-décorateurs*) and fresh flower workers (*chapelèirs en fleurs*), whose work included making rose garlands and chaplets (circlets for the head), were regulated and protected by the same guild. When the national Trade Assembly abolished the guild system in 1791, anyone was able to enter the trade, but it nonetheless grew slowly: in 1820 there were just 100 artificial flower-making firms in Paris.[3] Associated trades included toolmakers and silk, cotton, muslin, paper and *papier serpent* (crinkled paper), liquid and powder dye, cardboard, wire muslin, India rubber, wax and scent suppliers. In 1859, real and artificial flower workers were brought together again by the newly formed Chambre syndicale des fleurs, plumes et modes. Henceforth, flower makers became vital suppliers to the emergent haute couture industry and to luxury hat designers. The most exclusive flower makers were situated in the rue Vivienne area.

By 1865, there were some 10,000 artificial flower makers working in Paris, 80–85 per cent of whom were women and girls; they accounted for about 10 per cent of Paris's female workforce.[4] By 1896, the number had more than doubled to 24,000 workers.[5] Artificial flower making in Paris was a respected and relatively well-paid occupation. Extensive training was provided: the trade was learned from family members engaged in the trade or by serving a parentally funded, three-year apprenticeship. An organisation called Assistance Partinelle was formed in 1866 to tutor children on Sunday mornings, from October to July, in the study of natural history and design as applied to making flower and feather decorations. In 1869, the Chambre syndicale des fleurs, plumes et modes established the Société pour l'assistance partenelle des fleurs et des plumes to provide apprenticeships, schooling and accommodation for artificial flower-making trainees.

Opposite
97. Button, probably Limoges, France, mid- to late nineteenth century.
Hand-painted porcelain,
4cm diameter
Private collection

Above
98. Artificial flower-making workshop and flower shapes, from Denis Diderot, *Encyclopédie, ou dictionnaire raisonné des sciences, des arts et des métiers*, 1751–75.
Print from engraving by Bernard Fecit
Image courtesy of Fashion Institute of Technology | SUNY, FIT Library Unit of Special Collections and College Archives

While some Paris firms produced a variety of flowers, fruits, leaves and grasses, many specialised in making just one flower type, sometimes distinguishing between rose flowers and buds. In 1876, the newly established American trade paper *Millinery Trade Review* reported that even when flower sales were down, roses always sold well.[6] Furthermore, rose makers were the elite of the flower-making workforce. In her research on the industry in the late nineteenth century, Marilyn J. Boxer reports that, in 1896, makers of *petite fleurs* – including lily of the valley and forget-me-nots – earned about 90 centimes for a nine-hour working day, whereas a rose maker could earn 4 or 5 francs. It appears that rose makers even married 'better': just 9 per cent of rose makers married unskilled workers, compared to 32 per cent of *petite fleurs* makers.[7] Boxer concludes:

A flowermaker who could design a model and produce a lifelike blossom, especially a large rose of a specific variety, had a true vocation, a métier, which could support her well, even into old age, as long as her fingers remained strong (despite splaying, a common deformity) her eyes sharp (despite long hours of close work), and her head clear (despite gas fumes and lead-based red dyes).[8]

Toxic red dyes were used extensively for rose making. While some workshops offered good working environments, many were overcrowded and poorly ventilated; smoke led to asphyxiation and carbon monoxide caused lung disease. The combination of poor lighting and intricate work also had a detrimental effect on eyesight. In her intriguing book *Fashion Victims* (2015), Alison Matthews David reveals that in the 1850s and early 1860s a number of flower workers, and some wearers, were also poisoned by arsenic-based green dye; the pigment was used in dust form on foliage (also to colour taxidermied birds for millinery and on fashion plates). So toxic was this dyestuff that, in 1862, the *London Times* reported that the quantity of dust applied to a single leaf was sufficient to kill a child (see fig.109).[9] Thereafter it was rarely used.

In New York in 1910, the Women's Work section of the Russell Sage Foundation investigated working conditions in the flower-making industry: in order to obtain historical context and make a comparative analysis, a Miss Elizabeth S. Sergeant was dispatched to Paris. She was advised by the Chambre syndicale des fleurs et des plumes that there were some 30,000 flower workers in Paris and surrounding districts – twice as many as in New York. Sergeant reported that top-quality flowers were usually made by small family firms that employed 'few' well-trained workers and provided year-round, often lifelong, employment. She observed, 'They love their work, which is for them a craft in the best sense of the word.'[10] Many firms had retail premises below the workrooms.

Sergeant made a site visit to a firm believed to make 'the most beautiful roses in the world'.[11] It was owned by 'Madame A.'

and her married sister: 'refined, gracious, and well-dressed women, sitting each at a daintily arranged little table on opposite sides of the reception salesroom, working, one at a moss rose, and one at a yellow tea rose. The real flowers stood in water beside them.'[12] It was widely accepted that the finest flowers were copied directly from nature. Madame A., who learned her craft from her mother and often spent four or five hours making a single rose emphasised that, 'You must love flowers and love your trade to succeed: apprenticeship lasts all your life.'[13]

They proceeded to tour the workrooms. Two men and a boy apprentice were undertaking the preliminary processes that involved preparing the cloth, and cutting and dyeing the petals. The oldest man, aged between 45 and 50 years, had dyed petals since the age of seven; he advised that to make a truly beautiful product, 'You must always have the rose before you or know it by heart.'[14] In the larger workshop, five females, including an apprentice, were completing an order of blue roses for a milliner. If petals required shading – painting the centre darker than the edges, for example – the women undertook this work. This gendered division of work was typical, although it was – at this time – unusual for women to occupy more skilful workplace roles. Apart from foliage, all parts of the flower, including the stamens, were made in-house. Once married, women generally left the workplace, although many continued to work at home by necessity. Madame A. employed 12 or so married homeworkers, including her own daughter, all of whom had served an apprenticeship with her.

Exquisitely crafted and often naturalistic, artificial flowers were objects of French national pride and were displayed within international exhibitions from 1878, when Madame Roux Montagnac, who had hand-painted the petals of the flowers she made, rather than tinting them with dyes, exhibited in the painting salon. Thereafter they were shown in the contexts of horticulture (1844), clothing (1855), and fans and toys (1878). In 1925, at the Paris Exposition, they were shown in *classe 22*, a category dedicated to millinery, flowers and feathers.

Opposite
99. Samuel Melton Fisher,
Flower Makers, 1896.
Oil on canvas, 56.4 x 43.7cm
Walker Art Gallery, Liverpool
An idealised portrait of a flower-making workshop, in which the rose maker is foregrounded.
Courtesy National Museums
Liverpool, Walker Art Gallery

MAKING ROSES
IN LONDON

In London, and also New York, speed of assembly and competitive pricing generally took precedence over craft and creativity. Artificial flower making was subdivided, permitting workers to learn quickly 'on the job'; the trade was seasonal and involved extensive use of exploited homeworkers. The first census of England, Wales and Scotland, which recorded the names of people, their type and place of occupation, was published in 1801. Surprisingly, this and those submitted across the ensuing four decades do not include artificial flower workers. However, records of the Royal & Sun Alliance Insurance Group (stumbled upon by this author when researching early flower-making firms) list their artificial flower-making clients as early as 1791. That year, the sole entry was for Louis Flarent Catherine, of 24 Broad Street, Carnaby Market: 'artificial flower maker and dessert ornament maker'.[15] Up to five firms are listed in sporadic entries up until 1816 – mostly firms with women's names located in London's West End (close to the elite dressmaking industry), who also worked with feathers. Mrs Peachey, who supplied flowers for Queen Victoria, was based at Rathbone Place. By 1851, the census identified 885 workers in London and 32 in Lancashire (see p.110). However, the existence of homeworkers, mostly women and children, was 'hidden'.

Two primary sources provide core evidence on the British industry: the *Report on Artificial Flower and Ostrich Feather Makers* (1865) written by W. H. Lord for the Children's Employment Commission, and the work of social reformer Charles Booth, whose investigations on *Poverty* (1889) and *Industry* (1891), comprised part of his seminal 17-volume series, *The Life and Labour of the People of London*. Both make extensive use of oral testimony and foreground the human experience, rather than products made. The sole reference to roses is made by Booth, who wrote, 'The trade is a season trade, and is also extremely irregular in season, owing to changes in fashion. Very skilled hands, mounters, can earn 18s a week, and a rose maker at home can earn over 20s; good workers in the factory can earn from 10s to 1s, but the majority earn from 8s to 10s, and do not have constant work.'[16] It would thus appear that in London, as in Paris, rose makers were the elite of the flower-making workforce.

The British trade was divided into makers of coloured and black flowers, the latter a national speciality feeding into the lucrative market for etiquette-correct mourning dress (p.141). A few London firms made both, but in Manchester, Lancashire – until around 1863, when there was some diversification – the focus was on mourning flowers, which were less subject to fashion changes and seasonal demand. Lord's research, undertaken between 1862 and 1863, revealed that flower-making apprenticeships were not available in London, but that some Manchester firms offered two-year bound schemes.[17]

Girls usually entered the trade aged ten, although some started as young as six – the latter (unpaid) brought in to assist female relatives. Delicacy of touch was important and children's tiny fingers proved useful for intricate processes such as separating the cuts or layers of petals using pincers or pliers, which would often blister their thumbs and forefingers. Boys were not employed until they were aged 13 years. The standard working day was 12 hours, often extended significantly during busy times.

By the 1860s, the industry had congregated in north-east and East London, where rents were lower. Mr Vernon, owner of a factory on City Road, told Lord that fashions were so variable they never made stock.[18] He and other employers advised that the long hours and seasonality of artificial flower making had led many employees to migrate to more regular work: making caps or machine sewing.

MAKING
A ROSE

. . . .

...

*The rose seems even to outdo the natural in their
close resemblance and to flatter the roses of nature
in their beauty. They appear in many varieties,
interesting montures showing combinations of infant
and half-blown buds, full-blown blossoms, and wind-
torn blossoms bereft of petals and with only the
stamens and pistols crowning the petiole.*

...

Millinery Trade Review, 1889[1]

Here follows an account of how an artificial rose was made from
the mid-nineteenth century to the early twentieth: processes
that have changed little over time, although today the gendered
division of labour is less rigidly defined. The making of an
artificial rose can be divided into four core stages:

1. Design In Paris, flower makers often worked directly from
nature, copying natural roses or buds. Botanical engravings
were also used as source materials. The cheaper end of the trade
copied flowers made by the exclusive firms.

2. Cutting and dyeing The fabric used to make the corolla (the
petals of a flower) was stretched and starched prior to being cut,
using heavy hammers (sometimes bound by hide), or a stamping
machine. Lightweight fabrics, like silk and muslin, were cut 16
layers at a time, while more dense fabrics like cotton or silk velvet
(often used in winter) were cut in layers of four. The petal shapes
were then tinted using dyes and spread out on porous paper to
oven dry.

3. Forming the flower Each petal was goffered (curved into a
cupped form) using a tool with a metal shaft ending in a ball
form, heated by flame or gas jet. Elizabeth Sergeant observed,
'The rosemakers, when the petals are ready, attach the inner ones
to a wire stem, stick its end into their potato standard, and add
petals, crimp the edges, and form the flower as it hangs head
downwards before them.'[2] The petal edges were then crimped
(curled) by hand or using tweezers. A dusting of potato flour was
used to create the effect of 'bloom'. Buds were made of wadding,
finely covered with silk, over which individual petals and
sometimes sepals were added.

4. Composition This, the final and most highly skilled stage, was
known as 'branching'. The stalk, formed from wire, was crowned
with the seed vessel and stamens; glue was added to the base of
these and the corolla threaded onto the stalk and pressed onto
the seed vessel. The calyx or culot was fixed in the same manner.
Any leaves were then wired to the stalk, before it was covered with
silk thread, fabric and/or paper, a process requiring a finely tuned
rotary movement of the thumb and forefinger of the left hand.

Left
100. Artificial roses (detail of hat), USA, 1908.
Horsehair (hat), with silk roses, cotton velour and paper leaves
The Museum at FIT, New York
Rows of finely crafted dark red silk roses decorate the crown of a (now very fragile) American hat. There are six silk roses and three rosebuds on stems, with autumnal coloured leaves. Each rose (and bud) has a fabric sepal, is composed of a profusion of tightly clustered silk petals and measures about 7cm in diameter. On the hat brim, tucked beneath a large black silk bow with silk velvet edging, is a single stem with three rosebuds.
The Museum at FIT, P83.19.13.
Museum purchase

Above left
101. Lewis Wickes Hine, 'Colouring the petals', published 1913.
Photograph
New York Public Library
©NYPL

Below left
103. Lewis Wickes Hine, 'Cutting flower petals by hand', published 1913.
Photograph
New York Public Library
©NYPL

Above right
102. Lewis Wickes Hine, 'Artificial flower maker goffering (curling) rose petals', published 1913.
Photograph
New York Public Library
©NYPL

This movement, practiced extensively and perfected during apprenticeship, was also employed when making rosebuds. Sometimes flowers were fragranced. Among the specialist suppliers were Stafford Allen & Sons of London, 'essential oil distillers and manufacturing chemists', who made scents, including rose, for artificial flowers.

Leaves These were made using starched paper or fabric, cut and dyed in a manner similar to that used for petals and then veined using a two-part iron tool, the die of which represented, in relief, one of the faces of the leaf, and the counterpart, the matrix, securing the iron in place. In 1871, *Harper's Bazaar* reported that a French chemist had developed an effective way of colouring artificial leaves that involved mixing water-soluble dyes with a mucilaginous gum; this gum was poured onto glass tablets that were hardened in an oven and was then ground to form a powder that achieved a fine degree of colour and transparency. He recommended using synthetic aniline dyes; tincture of curcuma (or turmeric tincture), combined with a solution of soda, provided a beautiful chestnut; a solution of alcohol and curcuma with fuchsia, a striking scarlet red; and the same combined with aniline blue, a handsome greenish-yellow.[3]

To achieve a glossy surface, leaves were given a wash of gum. The dull, velvety, texture of the leaf reverse was created by sprinkling dyed cloth powder on to the fine gum coating. Leaves were not always made to appear perfect. In September 1876, *Harper's Bazaar* reported the latest Paris trend for naturalistic, thickly set branches and thickets of artificial flowers featured autumnal-coloured leaves, 'spotted as if by decay'.[4]

Stamens Unbleached silk was fixed onto brass thread and steeped in glue to create greater rigidity. Once dried, each end was garnished with paste and plunged into a bath of yellow dye.

Notes

[1] *Millinery Trade Review*, February 1889, p.19.

[2] Kleeck 1913, p.158.

[3] 'Coloring Artificial Flowers' 1871.

[4] *Harper's Bazaar*, September 1876, p.563.

Opposite above
104. Artifical rose dress ornament, Paris, c.1935.
Organza, paper and chenille
The Museum at FIT, New York
This magnificent ornament comprises the sole flower decoration on an unlabelled (possibly Molyneux) silk crêpe evening dress, printed with a graphic design of Classical urns and rose garlands. It is unusually sited, 46cm from the hem and at the tip of a pleated yellow silk godet; at 15cm in length and unsupported by the body, it is a robust decoration for a fine silk dress.
The Museum at FIT, 90.33.6.
Gift of Arne Ekstrom

Opposite below
105. Straw hat, New York, c.1924.
Silk rosebuds, chenille and silk velvet ribbon
The Museum at FIT, New York
Above and, most profusely, below, the wide, pale blue silk-lined brim of this black straw hat are pink silk rosebuds with green chenille-like thread, very similar to those illustrated on the business card of the New York-based 'Parisian Flower Company' (see fig.116).
The Museum at FIT, P83.18.6.
Museum purchase

Above
106. De Pinna, Heart-shaped hairline cap, New York, mid-1950s.
Fabric, paper, plastic and wire
The Museum at FIT, New York
The leaves that surround the prominent red silk rose at the centre back of this cap are each made from two layers of stiffened fabric, with crimped edgings. The face fabric is dyed green, with a white-painted central vein and powdered bloom; the underside is white. The leaves are attached to paper, and then to plastic-wrapped, padded and wired stems.
The Museum at FIT, 82.3.66.
Gift of Frederick Supper

Left
107. Lewis Wickes Hines, 'Margaret Ciampa, 29 January 1917'.
Photograph
Aged 14 years at the time this photograph was taken, Margaret Ciampa is shown finishing real roses dipped in wax for the Boston Floral Supply Co., 347–57 Cambridge St. The firm also made artificial flowers. The original caption to this photograph states that this was the only flower maker in Massachusetts.

108. Census of flower makers. The figures from 1851–1901 are taken from the England, Wales and Scotland census. The figures from 1911 are from the England and Wales census (Scotland was not included that year).

YEAR	LONDON FLOWER MAKERS	LANCASHIRE FLOWER MAKERS
1801–41	No artificial flower makers listed	
1851	885	32
1861	1,123	134
1871	Statistics not available at time of research	
1881	781	114
1891	1,008	120
1901	928	93
1911	1,652	61

The largest London factory Lord visited was Messrs Lockyer of Shaftesbury Street, New North Road, which, during the busy season, engaged 250 employees, 150 of whom worked on the premises. Lord noted:

Much of the work is still given out to be done in a small place, where a family works with two or three others to help them. This is particularly the case with mourning flowers, violets, and other simple and common goods. In such cases the workplaces are mere dwelling rooms, sometimes back kitchen or basement. These are often dirty and foetid.[19]

Mr R. Johnson of 120 Packington Street, Islington, told Lord, 'It is a very dirty trade, though you would scarcely think so. It takes three persons here every Saturday from 5 or 6 till nearly 12pm to wash and clean the four rooms thoroughly.'[20] Mr W. H. Boulton, of Quadrant Road, Islington, who employed ten females, told Lord, 'I am bound to admit that the French workpeople in this trade excel ours: they take so much more interest in their work and have a pride in it; ours use their hands – make up what you put before them – but do not use their heads.' Booth reported similarly and also noted that fear of German imports was 'only dreaded in the commoner class of work', which he described as the making of 'unnatural flowers', i.e. *fleurs de fantasie*, not roses.[21] The German industry, based in Sebnitz, focused on low-quality, high-volume production until the First World War, when imported cheap materials were hard to obtain and higher quality materials were bought from Switzerland.

A training scheme was offered to differently abled women living in London. It was established by John Alfred Groom, a silver engraver in Clerkenwell, East London, who became so concerned about the plight of local flower and watercress sellers who were blind or amputees (often as a result of factory accidents) that in 1866 he founded the 'Watercress and Flower Girls' Christian Mission' to provide food and washing facilities (fig.112). Ten years later, with private financial backing, he provided accommodation and schooling for 350 girls and training for young women to work with fresh, and make artificial, flowers.

By 1894, the Mission had moved to larger premises, and subsequently opened another branch in nearby Clacton-on-Sea, Essex. When Queen Alexandra launched Alexandra Rose Day in June 1912 she commissioned Groom's organisation to make thousands of pink artificial rose badges, and continued to place orders for what became an annual event (fig.111). In 1932, high rents and a reduction in demand for artificial flowers saw the factory diversify into other areas.

In 1891, Charles Booth reported that there were 4,587 artificial flower makers in London, 576 of whom were male.[22] He references 'learners', who worked for two or three years and earned between two and eight shillings a week, which suggests apprenticeships were then available. By comparison, male petal cutters earned 9–12 shillings and mounters (women) 12–18 shillings.[23]

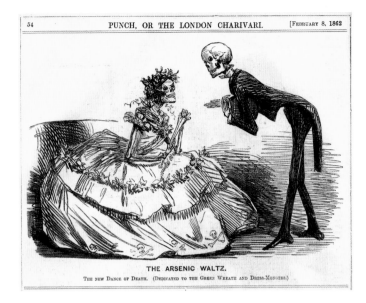

THE ARSENIC WALTZ.
THE NEW DANCE OF DEATH. (DEDICATED TO THE GREEN WREATH AND DRESS-MONGERS.)

Booth reported that some lower-middle-class makers chose to work at home in preference to working 'with a class of labourers whom they considered beneath them'.[24] Booth's work was seminal, but he was also highly judgemental about flower workers who undertook sex work, writing 'The substance is thrown away for the shadow. These girls do not sell themselves for bread; that they could easily earn. They sin for the externals which they have learnt to regard as essentials.' He was referring to fashion.[25] Similar criticisms were made of Parisian workers. In a fictionalised account of the trade in Émile Zola's *L'Assommoir* (1877), the protagonist's daughter Nana is about to start work in a flower factory and a discussion between family and friends ensues about the morality of the workers, to which the forewoman Madame Lerat retorts, 'But they have a sense of decorum, and when they go off the rails they exercise a certain taste in their choice ... Yes that comes from the flowers ... Now in my case what kept me pure...'[26]

In 1903, Grace M. Oakeshott, Inspector of Women's Technical Classes for London County Council, wrote an article called 'Artificial Flower-Making: An Account of the Trade and a Plea for Municipal Training' for the March issue of the *Economic Journal*. Arguing the case expressed in her title, she, too, stressed the superiority of the Parisian industry and bitterly criticised what she perceived to be lack of work ethic, commitment and creativity amongst London's flower makers: 'The majority of the girls do their work mechanically and unintelligently. They are without ambition, even without interest, in their trade.'[27] She stressed that as women were expected to stop working once married, their working life was too short for them to care what form it took.[28] A manufacturer she interviewed told her, 'The Frenchwoman's rose ... was La France in perfection, with its beautiful curves – the Englishwoman's something she would call a rose, though its shape might resemble a shuttlecock.'[29] She conceded that, 'Whilst an English flower-maker is expected to make any flower, a French woman makes rose petals only, or rosebuds, and nothing else. With clearer water and clearer skies, it is said that their eyes are more delicate and clear than ours. A Frenchwoman, moreover, has a higher ideal of perfection than an Englishwoman.' Presaging the Russell Sage report, she noted that 'Much of the good quality work is copied from the French models and can be done by anyone who has deft fingers, a good training and will be a faithful copyist.'[30]

Oakeshott highlighted the fact that, while many firms could not keep pace with fashion changes, poppies and black roses were made continuously, 'as England leads in the matter of black flowers, and there is a steady demand for a small quantity of mourning flowers always.'[31] In summary, Oakeshott stressed that employers were aware how effective a two- or three-year apprenticeship was, but that the women would 'not be bound'.[32] She argued that the best place to train young women was in a school or college, which is precisely what happened with the foundation of the fashion trade schools in the early years of the twentieth century.

Top
109. 'The Arsenic Waltz. The New Dance of Death. (Dedicated to the Green Wreath and Dress Mongers)', *Punch* cartoon, 8 February 1862.

Above
110. Artificial flower makers working for C. & H. Chaplin & Horne, posing in an exhibition or demonstration setting, *c*.1860. Stereoscopic photograph (one side) Private collection

MAKING
BLACK ROSES

Although there are no truly black flowers in nature (the pigment that flowers employ to colour their petals does not produce black), makers of mourning flowers were known as 'black workers', the flowers being crafted from silk and the same matte-black crape fabric that was used for women's mourning dress (see fig.157). Mourning flowers were less subject to changes in fashion and, while more complex flowers, such as roses, were made, surviving objects and evidence suggests that many were simpler, easy-to-assemble 'abstract' forms. (Platt Hall, part of Manchester Art Gallery, has two mourning bonnets: a ruched silk one from the 1850s and the other, made from straw, dating from the 1880s, both decorated with abstract crape flowers.)[33] Structured black flowers were made by threading black glass or jet beads onto wired threads to form aigrettes for bonnets. When W. H. Lord visited a Mrs Stowe of Penn Street, Hoxton, who employed six persons including her own daughter, who was 13, she rued:

It is a poor trade; any one can start as a crape flower maker who can buy a pair of scissors and some wire and some odds and ends of crape that would commonly be thrown away as rubbish; a guinea [£1, 1s] is a large capital to begin with. That's how it is that all the trade is in the hands of small people; scarce any employ more than we do, and most have less.[34]

She advised that black was easier to work with than red or white materials, which 'dazzled' the eyes. 'I have known girls with their eyes nearly out of their sockets with making white flowers by gaslight in winter.'[35] Manchester-based Mrs Doherty, who had made mourning flowers for 12 years, told Lord they were made by girls aged 10 to 16 years, who started work by twisting crape round wire stems to form stalks and progressed to making buds and flowers. She employed between 12 and 20 workers. Black flowers were the one product that could be made during quiet times. The situation was similar in New York, where, in 1910, a factory owner stated, 'If you only could find out what the style is going to be, you'd get rich, but you cannot make stock on anything but black flowers.'[36]

MAKING ROSES
IN NEW YORK

In flower making, it is not machinery but the organization of the market which has turned an art into a trade.

Mary Van Kleeck for the Russell Sage Foundation, *Artificial Flower Makers*, 1913[37]

The artificial flower-making industry did not emerge in New York until the early nineteenth century. In 1910, research for the Russell Sage investigation, discussed above, was initiated, as it was felt that flower making exemplified the core industrial problems of seasonal work – that is, child labour, and unskilled and homeworking. At this time, New York accounted for 75 per cent of all artificial flower production in North America and was the major importer of high-grade flowers from Paris.
The findings of the investigation, published in 1913, were written up by Mary Van Kleeck, whose research involved 980 site visits, 590 of which were to workers in their homes and 390 to factories located in an area of Manhattan she described as a 'congestion' of flower shops – 'a small and flowerless district south of Fourteenth St and west of Broadway'.[38] It was in the midst of this dismal environment that author Edith Wharton located her novel *Bunner Sisters* (written 1891, published 1916), a tragic tale of sisters Eliza and Evalina, who barely eke out a living making artificial flowers for New York's hat trade and for private clients, working from their tiny basement home that also serves as manufactory and shop.[39]

Van Kleeck stated that in 1840 there were just ten manufacturers who made artificial flower and feather decorations, of whom T. Chagot, based at 24 Maiden Lane, who also imported flowers, was the largest. By 1847, the number had more than doubled to 24 and by 1880 had increased to 174 firms. The industry reached a peak in 1890, when there were 251 firms employing 4,343 employees and the vogue for artificial flowers was at its peak. By 1905, the industry had declined to 213 firms due to reduced demand, but five years later it had not only revived but expanded considerably, employing some 6,000 workers.[40] Most New York firms made multiple flower types. Echoing London voices, Van Kleeck wrote, 'the artificial flower manufacturer in New York accepts as an immutable fact the superiority of the Parisian flower maker.'[41]

Huge quantities were imported. Even in 1905, a poor year for the trade, the value of imported flowers and feathers in the US was $2,369,015; domestic production was $5,246,822. In 1908, the value of imported flowers and feathers had risen to $3,747,021. As in fashion clothing and millinery, artificial flower companies aligned themselves with the international fashion capital, some even taking its name (see fig.116).

The importance of fashion meant that – as in the UK – many companies could not create stock, unless of black flowers and roses.[42] One employer, however, advised he was compelled to cut the price of a dozen roses from 35 cents to 30 cents in the slack period, and a rose maker who earned $9 a week in the busy season was only employed for three days a week at half the daily rate.[43]

The American trade was organised not by industry bodies, as in Paris, but by unions. In 1910, the Flower Makers Union (est. 1907) was replaced by the Educational League of Flower Makers (named thus because many young women were reluctant to join a union), but such organisations were powerless to support unregulated homeworkers. Kate Richards O'Hare, unionist and pacifist (a mother with four children, she was imprisoned for her political beliefs in 1917) exploited melodrama and the symbolism of roses to raise awareness about working conditions in her 1904 fictive account of a fellow artificial flower worker, 17-year old Italian Roselie Randazzo. In one scene from 'He Counteth the Sparrow's Fall', Randazzo lets out a shrill scream while making red satin roses:

As I lifted her up the hot blood spurted from her lips, staining my hands and spattering the flowers as it fell ... The blood-soaked roses were gathered up, the forelady grumbling because many were ruined, and soon the hum of industry went on as before. But I noticed that one of the great red roses had a splotch of red in its golden heart, a tiny drop of Roselie's heart's blood and the picture of the rose was burned in my brain.[44]

The narrative of blood turning flowers, usually white ones, red – here, red on red – draws upon Greek mythology and biblical references, as well as the fictions highlighted in Chapter II. It was widely accepted that those engaged in workshops experienced better job security, work conditions and rates of pay than homeworkers. Of 114 factory owners interviewed by Van Kleeck, only 24 stated that all of their manufacturing was done in the workroom.[45] By reporting in detail on individual circumstances, Van Kleeck rendered the human cost explicit. A family of five – mother, father and three children – paid $10 in monthly rent to live in two rooms on Sullivan Street. The father earned $3–4 a week working as a bootblack; pre-marriage, the mother had worked in a veil shop and subsequently made artificial flowers from home. When the investigators visited, she was making yellow muslin roses for 25 cents a gross (144 roses). The work involved working with five petals of different shapes. With the help of her nine-year-old son, after school, she could make two gross a day, earning $3 a week. For four or five months during the spring and summer she had no work.[46] The *Artificial Flower Makers* report found that regulation of child labour could not be upheld in domestic spaces; it was found that child flower workers had higher non-attendance at school, poor eyesight, respiratory and contagious disease and increased mortality rates.

Documentary photographer Lewis Wickes Hine was commissioned to make a visual record for the Russell Sage report. In order to gain access to factories, he misrepresented himself as an insurance agent, fire inspector or salesman; once inside – and putting himself at considerable risk, both of personal injury and criminal action – he would quickly set up his 7 x 5" glass plate camera, take photos and obtain personal details (included in the captions to his photographs) from the people he portrayed. Hine's work is stark, poignant and empathetic (figs 101–3).

Much of the evidence about artificial flower making, as stated above, relates to the late nineteenth and early twentieth centuries, when demand for flowers was at its peak. However, faux roses continued to decorate fashion in the period 1900–39 and again during the 1950s. By the 1960s, the elite flower-making industries in Paris, London and New York had fallen into steep decline. Daily hat wearing fell out of fashion; the clientele for haute couture shrank, as wealthy young women came to favour more directional, and instantly available, designer ready-to-wear fashions. Furthermore, as evening gowns became 'skimpier', there was less space and 'substance' upon which to place roses. Hippy and pastoral trends favoured meadow flowers and by the 1980s minimalism, and in the 1990s deconstruction, generally negated the use of flowers. When used by directional designers – and notably Rei Kawakubo of Comme des Garçons and John Galliano – roses, when they appeared, were manipulated, self-fabric, suggestions of roses. The fashioning of artificial roses in the twentieth and twenty-first centuries is further discussed within those chapters.

CHAPTER VI

THE NINETEENTH CENTURY

...

'I WOULD LIKE MY ROSES TO SEE YOU'

AMY DE LA HAYE

...

Won't you come into my garden?
I would like my roses to see you.

...

Attributed to Richard Brinsley Sheridan[1]

During the nineteenth century, affluent women were assumed to be fond of flowers: to wear flower-bedecked fashions; to grow and arrange flowers; read about flowers; dry, sketch and paint flowers (in watercolour); model them in wax, paper and shells; knit or embroider them. In addition, some were likened to idealised flowers, usually roses. Roses were incorporated into masculine fashionable dress in fresh flower form, or as patterning on the small or concealed textile surfaces worn in public spaces. More profuse was the rose ornamentation donned by a fashionable groom or worn for leisure at home. In a century when flowers came to be gendered feminine, male interest in the bloom was generally interpreted as scientific enquiry – partly to allay anxieties about non-heteronormative sexuality or gender non-conforming identities. Amid this century's turbulent sociocultural, political, urban and industrial shifts, and with the onset of modernity, nature provided a refuge, the rose garden a haven – variously earthly, romantic, celestial or sublime. Throughout, fashion's depiction of the rose remained fairly constant – mostly naturalistic, only occasionally abstracted. This chapter explores the nineteenth-century vogue for floriography and the cultivation, selling and wearing of fresh roses. It looks at the rose as fashionable motif and applied decoration; rose personification and fancy dress; and the role of the rose in rites of passage.

NEOCLASSICAL ROSES

Until around 1820, the Neoclassical, empire-line cotton chemise remained fashionable for day and evening dress. As it was cheaper than silk, cotton was widely portrayed as egalitarian, although it was a product of colonial domination and slavery. By the 1810s, the mostly plain surfaces of 1800s fashions had given way to a flowering of ornamentation and, as in the Greco-Roman civilisations that were so influential in this century, the rose was pre-eminent. To attend a ball, a woman's hair was dressed with fresh or artificial roses (fig.119); swags of faux roses decorated evening toilette, and individual or clusters of roses punctuated daytime dresses. The millinery trades flourished and hats became a dominant site for artificial roses.

Following the coronation of Napoléon Bonaparte in 1804, Empress Joséphine – working with Louis Hippolyte LeRoy, her feted *marchand de mode* (influential stylist, precursor of the haute couturier) – became a stylish fashion leader in France and beyond. Born in Martinique to a rich French Creole family, she was not – as she is often portrayed – a great rose collector. However, she did plant magnificent gardens at Château de Malmaison, near Paris, and in 1798 commissioned the Belgian artist Pierre-Joseph Redouté to paint portraits of her flowers. Joséphine endorsed the vogue for hand-woven, cashmere shawls as fashion objects of intense desire (see fig.120); some of her own included rose patterning.

Engraved for the Ladies Magazine, Oct.ʳ 1804.

PARIS DRESS.

Above left
118. 'Paris Dress', fashion plate for
Ladies Magazine, October 1804.
Hand-coloured engraving
The figure on the left wears a black
straw bonnet (a hat that ties under the
chin) trimmed with artificial roses and
leaves; the figure on the right wears
a long shawl embroidered with a
floral design.
Gift of Woodman Thompson, Irene
Lewisohn Costume Reference Library,
The Costume Institute, Metropolitan
Museum of Art, New York

Above right
119. Fashion plate showing an
evening toilette, c.1812.
Hand-coloured etching
Archive FIT
The pink roses hair ornament matches
the clusters of artificial pink roses that
accent the self-fabric *rouleaux* on
this white, empire-line dress, which is
teamed with long white gloves, white
slippers and a double-strand pearl
necklace with central ornament.
Image courtesy of Fashion Institute of
Technology | SUNY, FIT Library Unit
of Special Collections and College
Archives

Above
120. François-Pascal-Simon Gérard
*Portrait of Joséphine, the wife of
Napoleon*, 1801.
Oil on canvas, 178 x 174cm
The State Hermitage Museum,
St Petersburg
Joséphine is portrayed seated,
wearing Neoclassical dress with a
dark-coloured shawl, with a posy of
flowers and garden backdrop.
© The State Hermitage Museum.
Photograph by Alexander Koksharov

Opposite above
121. Routzahn & Gilkey tailors,
smoking cap, USA, 1870s.
Silk velvet with hand embroidery
Los Angeles County Museum of Art
This cap, in the style of a Turkish cap
with prominent tassel and design of
pale-pink roses with gold-coloured
leaves and stems, would have been
donned by a stylish and affluent man
in the private spaces of his home.
It was sold by a tailoring firm and
was possibly imported.
Digital Image © 2020 Museum
Associates/LACMA. Licensed by
Art Resource, NY

Opposite below
122. Evening dress (detail),
possibly France, 1810–15.
Embroidered silk twill
The detail of embroidered silk roses
with stems, leaves and thorns is from
the broad panel that encircles the
lower skirt of the dress.
The Museum at FIT, 2020.2.1.
Museum purchase

Shawls were beautiful, divinely soft and provided warmth and coverage over sheer dresses; they also symbolised wealth (they were vastly expensive) and colonial power and fed into prevailing perceptions of an exotic East. Redouté went on to become the foremost rose artist and dedicated the album of prints *Les Roses* (1817–21), his most acclaimed work, to Joséphine's memory (see fig.205). Myth became reality when rose gardens were planted posthumously at Malmaison and a variety of *Rosa gallica* – a loose, large, pink double rose – was named after her.

Throughout the century, the most eye-catching item of men's outerwear was the waistcoat or vest; coats were worn open to display silk, sometimes shiny satin-weave, surfaces decorated with woven or embroidered designs, some of which featured roses. At home, stylish men often wore banyan, which were succeeded by smoking jackets; both were made using fabrics that incorporated rose patterning, as were embroidered smoking caps (fig.121) and beaded tobacco pouches.

THE LANGUAGE
OF FLOWERS

In reaction to Classical diction, the Romantic movement, which blossomed in the early years of the century, gave primacy to the individual, his or her innermost emotions and relationship with nature. It is within this context that the trend, in art, literature and popular culture, for the conflation of (mostly) girls and women with flowers, as well as that for twinning flowers with emotions, flourished. Carl Linnaeus's sexually explicit likening of plant reproduction to human sexuality, which had caused a scandal in the early eighteenth century, also fuelled these literary tropes. From 1819, the publication of one book – *Le Langage des Fleurs* (translated into English by Frederic Shoberl in 1820) – did much to determine the choice of bud, bloom, colour and combination of flowers as they were worn, gifted, depicted and displayed. Moralistic and sentimental in tone, it was aimed predominantly at white, heteronormative, well-off women, many of whom became well-versed in its essentially positive messages. The rose, accorded more attention than any other flower, was personified as female and recognised for its democratic reach:

It might be said that the Queen of the Flowers sports with the air that fans her, adorns herself with the dew-drops that burthen her head, and smilingly meets the sun rays that expand her bosom; it might well be said of this beautiful flower that nature has exhausted herself in striving to lavish on it the freshness of beauty, of form, perfume, brilliancy, and grace. The rose embellishes the whole surface of the earth. It is thus the commonest of all flowers. On the days that its beauty is fully mature it perishes; but nothing restores it to the first graces of its former youth. The emblem of all ages, the interpreter of all sentiment, the rose constitutes an element of all our festivals! [O]f all our joys and griefs. Most justly is it consecrated to Venus, and, rivalling beauty itself the rose, like that, possesses a grace more exquisite even than beauty.[2]

Not surprisingly, it is in this period that the name Rose, in multiple languages, became a favourite. The author of *Le Langage des Fleurs* also attributed meanings to the ways in which a flower was held or worn:

When a flower is presented in its natural position, the sentiment is to be understood affirmatively; when reversed, negatively. For instance, a rose bud with its leaves and thorns indicates fear with hope, but, if reversed it must be construed as saying, 'you may neither fear nor hope'. Again, divest the same rose bud of its thorns, and it permits the most sanguine hope; deprive it of its petals, and retain the thorns, and the worst fears are to be apprehended. The expression of every flower may be thus varied by varying its state or position.[3]

1829.   *Costumes Parisiens.*   (2685)

Coeffure exécutée par M. Alexandre, Rue Neuve des Petits Champs, N.º 101. Robe de tulle garnie de rouleaux de satin et de fleurs.

Costumes Parisiens.

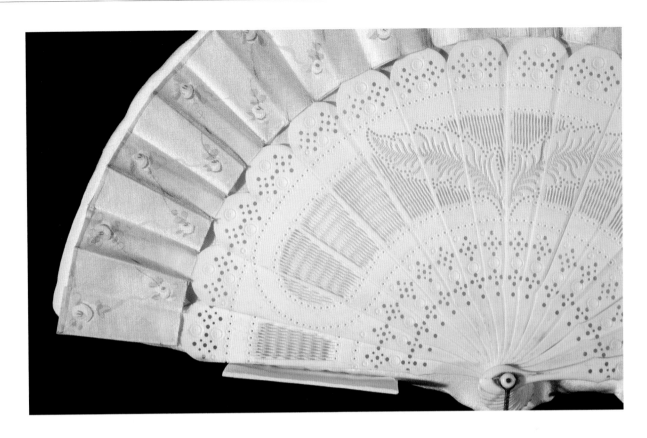

Opposite above
123. Rose-decorated hairstyles and evening gowns, fashion plate for *Journal des dames et des modes*, 1829. Hand-coloured etching
Artificial or fresh pink roses are woven into looped and curled hairstyles and artificial roses accent the tips of the self-fabric, lattice *rouleaux* decoration on these similar dresses, shown in two colourways. The jewellery comprises earrings, a triple strand of pearls and a jewelled brooch that harmonises with the dress fabric.
Image courtesy of Fashion Institute of Technology | SUNY, FIT Library Unit of Special Collections and College Archives

Opposite below
124. Elaborate 'rose basket' hairstyles, fashion plate for *Journal des dames et des modes* (detail), 1830. Hand-coloured etching
Hairstyles were at their most fashionably elaborate in the 1830s. A leading hair stylist, such as the Parisian Monsieur Alexandre, would attend to a woman's hair in her home prior to her attending a ball. This complex rose-basket design might have been composed either with fresh or artificial roses.
Image courtesy of Fashion Institute of Technology | SUNY, FIT Library Unit of Special Collections and College Archives

Above
125. Fan with hand-painted rosebuds, possibly France, *c.*1880s. Hand-painted silk satin and ivory
The Museum at FIT, New York
Fan leaves were usually painted by women, who, like the most exclusive artificial flower makers, often worked directly from nature. Some fans had leaves made from lace with rose motifs, and sticks and guards were variously incised, carved or painted with rose designs.
The Museum at FIT, 69.160.45.
Gift of the Estate of Elizabeth Arden

Le Langage des Fleurs was reprinted multiple times and scores of similar texts followed in its wake. In a period of imperialism and widespread racist attitudes, Asian, African and many European immigrant women were excluded from the metaphors. So, generally, were men.[4]

Another non-linguistic 'language' has been attributed to the fashionable fan as a performative tool (fig.125); twirling one in the right hand, for example, announced 'I Love Another.'[5] As Ariel Beaujot points out in *Victorian Fashion Accessories* (2012), this might be interpreted as empowering for the women doing the communicating, but fans, which originated in China or Japan, simultaneously fed into fetishised notions of Asian women as demure and submissive.[6] In June 1882, *Harper's Bazaar* reported a vogue for perfumery in the handles of fans: a rose-decorated fan might thus have also released rose fragrance.[7]

By 1830, the fashionable female silhouette had fully transitioned from columnar to having a dropped shoulder line with immense gigot sleeves (fig.126); the waist resumed its 'natural' position and skirts became conical in shape. The increased sophistication of print technologies – notably engraved-roller printing techniques – permitted textile designers to create meandering, naturalistic designs such as those featuring trailing roses. Handheld bags became an important fashion accessory, and beaded and embroidered reticules, purses and travel bags featured rose designs. A romantic portrait of the Russian count Vasily Alekseevich Perovsky, by Alexander Brullov (fig.128), depicts the imperial

Russian general and statesman wearing detachable flower-
(including rose-) embroidered suspenders, or braces (see fig.127).
Until 1820 – when the London-based Albert Thurston introduced
ready-made, detachable suspenders – breeches, pantaloons and
trousers were tightened by gusset ties on the rear waistband or
held in place with integral suspenders. The fabric components
of a set of detachable suspenders would be embroidered either
professionally or in domestic spaces, by females, as personal gifts.
In a man's daily urban life, a rose-printed handkerchief (fig.131)
or cravat could provide a fillip to a dark-coloured tailored outfit,
as indeed could a fresh rose boutonnière.

Below
126. Day dress (detail),
USA, 1830–33.
Printed cotton
The Museum at FIT, New York
This lightweight voluminous dress,
with its immense gigot sleeves,
is made from a sheer cotton with a
printed design of rose clusters and a
shadow trailing design of bindweed
(*Convolvulus arvensis*).
The Museum at FIT, 94.92.1.
Gift of Marcia Wallace

Opposite left
127. Brace, probably UK, *c.*1860s.
Embroidered silk satin and
cutwork leather
Private collection
This single surviving brace
(suspender), made from a panel of
dark-red silk satin, has been hand-
embroidered with a trailing design of
pink roses; the reverse is pale-pink
satin. It was probably embroidered
by a woman as a gift; the fastenings
would have been made and attached
by a professional leather worker.

Opposite right
128. Alexander Brullov,
portrait of Vasily Perovsky, 1824.
Watercolour and lacquer on paper,
29.7 x 19.4cm
The State Russian Museum,
St Petersburg
The Russian military general,
described by the artist as 'a wonderful
man who loves a quiet life and the
arts' chose to be portrayed in a
romantic light, strolling through an
idyllic, sun-lit landscape.
© State Russian Museum,
St Petersburg

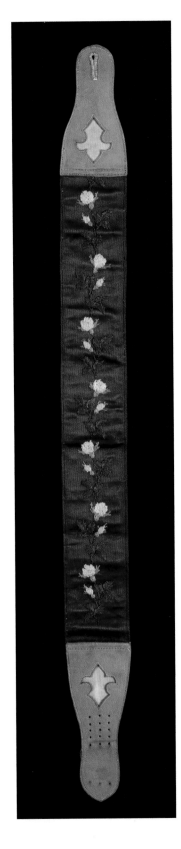

Far left
129. Two men in a garden, fashion plate for *Journal des dames et des modes*, 15 September 1836. Hand-coloured engraving
The man on the right wears a flower-printed handkerchief in his pocket. Image courtesy of Fashion Institute of Technology | SUNY, FIT Library Unit of Special Collections and College Archives

Left
130. Two fashionably dressed men, fashion plate for *La mode: revue du monde élégant*, 21 November 1835. Hand-coloured engraving
The man on the right wears a fashionable shawl-collared, flower-patterned (possibly rose) vest from the atelier of Mr Hummann. Image courtesy of Fashion Institute of Technology | SUNY, FIT Library Unit of Special Collections and College Archives

Right
131. Steinbach Koech, handkerchief swatch, London, registered 27 July 1879. Printed cotton
The National Archives, London
This textile design, registered with the Public Record Office in London (now part of The National Archives), incorporates a foreign or 'unnatural rose', made up of multiple pink roses with fantastical flowers and leaves. Steinbach Koech was a leading textiles firm based in Alsace, France. The National Archives, London

CULTIVATING, SELLING AND WEARING FRESH ROSES

By the mid-nineteenth century, the French led not only international fashion, they had also created the vogue for breeding roses; both industries whetted desires with an ever-tempting array of new colours, textures and forms. Plant breeders crossed remontant (repeat-flowering) roses, brought from southern China and central Asia, with fragrant European roses. The first rose described as modern was introduced in 1867. It was a cross between a tea rose (tea roses are the forerunners of the modern 'hybrid teas', originating from a cross between a China rose and various Bourbons and Noisettes; they have a tea-like fragrance) and a hybrid perpetual (origins not known; these are hardy, vigorous roses with large, fragrant blooms). Named – and claimed with utmost national pride – 'La France', it was hardy, fragrant and, characterised by a single bloom per stem, was immediately adored by florists, gardeners and cut-flower consumers. Henceforth, roses were divided into 'heirloom' (including the gallicas, damasks, albas, centifolias and moss roses, known for their heady fragrance and large blooms; see fig.133) and 'modern' roses (including hybrid tea, grandiflora, floribunda, shrub, climbing and rambling roses) or 'old' and 'new' classes, in an echo of social classifications. By the 1870s, Britain had taken the lead in rose growing. In a reversal of fashion practices, when the French rose 'Madame Ferdinand Jamin' was imported into the US, it was renamed 'American Beauty' and stole the nation's heart. However, hybridisation was not universally popular.

Fashion dissent was unusual in the nineteenth century. In 1800, in Paris, it became illegal for a woman to cross dress, and the ruling extended to fancy dress in 1853. Yet, in France, writer and champion of women's rights George Sand (born Amantine Lucile Aurore Dupin), defied the rigidly defined sartorial gender distinctions and braved the law to don masculine tailored suits, with not a rose in sight. In 'What the Flowers Say' (1876, from *Tales from a Grandmother*) a short story written to inspire her grandchildren to imagine alternative worlds, Sand personifies the garden roses who don't smell like roses and are not 'true' as spiteful and vain, while the 'natural' wild rose is shown to possess grace, gentleness and beauty.

Inspired by the ideas of John Ruskin – anti-capitalist polymath and a visionary conservationist, who painted wild roses (fig.134); an apricot-pink shrub rose is even named after him – the Pre-Raphaelites looked back to the medieval period for inspiration on ways to live and for aesthetic models. Ruskin and William Morris – the Arts and Crafts pioneer and social revolutionary, whose designs for wallpaper and textiles featured wild roses – were vehement critics of engineered flowers.

47.

Paris. Bouquetière du Boulevart Italien.

Lanté delt.   Gatine sculpt.

Above
132. 'Bouquetière du boulevard Italien', from George-Jacques Gatine and Louis-Marie Lanté, *Costume d'ouvrières Parisiennes* (Paris, 1824), p.51.
Hand-coloured etching
Bibliothèque nationale de France
Flower girls contributed to family and national economies and appeared within occupational typographies, but they occupied an ambiguous role within nineteenth-century culture.
Bibliothèque nationale de France

Not dissimilarly, Pre-Raphaelite women including Christina Rossetti, Jane Morris and Fanny Cornforth (fig.135) rejected the synthetic aniline dyes invented by William Henry Perkins in 1856, which generated a vogue for unprecedently vibrant fashion textiles. Instead, they tended to wear anti-fashion, unstructured dresses made from fabrics dyed using natural (plant-, insect- and mineral-derived) sources, and were sometimes portrayed with wild roses in their hair.

By the 1850s, the international cut-flower trade was thriving and cultivated roses had become widely available. Whereas the sale of shrub roses was a male-dominated trade, the buying, arranging and selling of cut flowers was undertaken by women and girls described occupationally as flower girls, irrespective of their age. The most exclusive florists worked from elegant retail premises, but flowers were mostly sold on busy urban thoroughfares. As highly visible workers, selling nature's most beautiful produce to a mostly affluent male clientele, flower sellers occupied an ambiguous role in nineteenth-century culture. Often perceived to have loose sexual morals, their existence fuelled fears of class slippage, yet they were romanticised, and the very poorest captured the attention of social reformers. In London, the eldest of two orphaned sisters told social investigator Henry Mayhew, 'The best sale of all is, I think, moss-roses, young moss-roses. We do best of all on them.'[8] Mayhew's statistical analysis of cut flowers and rooted shrub sales provides substantive evidence that the rose was the most popular flower, selling more than twice as many as its closest rival, the wallflower.[9]

Fresh roses or buds were worn singly or clustered, usually applied to the left side of a dress bodice, close to the heart and best positioned to be in the sight-line of a male walking companion (who, customarily, would take the right side). Corsages (the term an abbreviation of the original French *bouquet de corsage*) were made by specialist florists. In the late 1870s, there was a vogue for pinning flowers at the waist. On the subject of wearing fresh flowers as hair ornaments, Mary Haweis, author of *The Art of Beauty* (1878), was emphatic that only through 'ignorance' or 'absolute tastelessness' would a woman opt for an artificial flower, which lacked the wondrous 'refraction of lights on myriads of little cells and breathing pores, giving sometimes the appearance of sparkling'.[10] She abhorred the commonplace practice of mis-matching flowers and leaves in unnatural pairings such as that of roses paired with ferns (see fig.141). Fresh roses were also handheld, sometimes to dramatic effect. In 1884, *Harpers Bazaar* reported, 'It has been no unusual thing at the dinners and at the large balls this season to see a young lady carrying a bouquet considerably larger than her head. These bunches of roses often contain four dozen of large hybrids. Twenty four roses are frequently attached to a fan of straw.'[11]

Masculine floral adornment usually comprised a single rose or bud, as a boutonnière, also known as a favour or buttonhole,

worn in the uppermost buttonhole. Simply formed, these were often sold alongside bunched flowers by street sellers. In their study of marriage attire, dress historians Phillis Cunnington and Catherine Lucas reported that, 'By 1865 the "flower-hole" had gained the day and it sometimes had "a piece of broad ribbon put under the turn to hold a glass flower bottle" (*West End Gazette*, 1865).'[12] The wearing of 'exotic' flowers such as orchids, or 'unnaturally' coloured flowers, such as the green carnation associated with Oscar Wilde, became indications of non-heteronormative masculinity. *The Green Carnation* was an 1894 novel by Robert Hichens, whose lead characters were based on Oscar Wilde and his lover Lord Alfred Douglas; homosexuality being illegal in the UK, the book caused a scandal. Here the definition of the term 'natural' embraces culturally constructed, and often oppressive, perceptions.

In the 1880s, fashionable rose-themed garden parties were held at the break of day or in moonlight, when the flowers were at their most fulsome and fragrant. In winter 1884, the Vanderbilt family – whose vast fortune was based on shipping and railways – ordered 50,000 cut roses (at $1 a stem) for their New York house-warming party for 1,000 guests. That same year, one fashion writer had observed sagely, 'If only you have a great many flowers of a very expensive kind, you cannot go amiss in the distribution of them. Other times have loved flowers for their beauty: we value them for their muchness and their cost.'[13] As the most ephemeral of fashion items, fresh flower ornaments might be interpreted as the ultimate in luxury, yet the addition of a rose

to an otherwise unremarkable outfit or tucked into the hair could be transformative. The sort of occasion on which a rose was worn could be recorded for posterity by a visit to a portrait photographer's studio (figs 138–42).

Photography revolutionised visual culture and mass communication. The first relatively cheap form of photographic portraiture was the carte de visite, introduced in 1854. Today, masses of orphan (single, without provenance) portraits survive, many of which reveal how roses interfaced with the body and comprised part of fashionable and everyday dressed appearances. They also show how, across continents, the flower was utilised as a handheld emblem, in poses often derived from painted portraiture (fig.22). Occasionally, a photographer hand painted, in brilliant pink or red ink, a single rose or a bunch on to an otherwise 'rose-less' portrait (figs 20, 21), or added rose blush to a woman's cheeks. In the 1870s, larger scale, more costly cabinet cards became available, and these were succeeded by the picture postcard in around 1900.

Opposite
133. Henri Fantin-Latour,
Roses, 1886.
Oil on canvas
The French painter and lithographer Henri Fantin-Latour was acclaimed for his sensitive and sensuous portrayal of roses. Fellow artist Jacques-Émile Blanche wrote, 'The rose – so complicated in its design, contours and colour, in its rolls and curls, now fluted like the decoration of a fashionable hat, round and smooth, now like a button or a woman's breast – no one understood them better than Fantin' ('Fantin-Latour', *Revue de Paris*, 15 May 1906, pp.311–12). A full-petalled, blush-pink, centifolia old rose was named 'Fantin-Latour' in c.1900.
Art Heritage/Alamy Stock

Above
134. John Ruskin,
Study of Wild Rose, 1871.
Watercolour and bodycolour over graphite on paper, 42.2 x 26.8cm
Ashmolean Museum, University of Oxford
Rosa canina, or the dog rose, may have come upon its name because it was used to treat dogs with rabies in the eighteenth century; the name may also simply be pejorative.
© Ashmolean Museum, University of Oxford

Opposite
135. Dante Gabriel Rossetti,
Fair Rosamund, 1861.
Oil on canvas, 51.9 x 41.7cm
National Museum of Wales
The woman portrayed is Fanny
Cornworth, the artist's lover and muse.
She wears an 'anti-fashion', loose,
flowing dress decorated with a flower
design that echoes the flower placed
in her hair.
© National Museum of Wales

Above left
136. Francis Grant,
Sir Daniel Gooch, 1st Bt, 1872.
Oil on canvas, 142.2 x 111.8cm
National Portrait Gallery, London
Gooch was a member of parliament
and chairman of the Great Western
Railway. The pink of his dog's
slathering mouth is echoed by the
single delicate component of this
otherwise robustly masculine portrait:
a rose boutonnière, possibly worn as
the national flower of England.
National Portrait Gallery, London

Below left
137. Henri Manuel, comte Robert de
Montesquiou-Fézensac, Paris, late
nineteenth century.
The count dressed to suit his moods;
his ensembles also included a
pistachio suit teamed with a white
waistcoat and a mauve shirt, worn
with a cluster of pale violets at the
throat in place of a necktie.
Hirarchivum Press/Alamy Stock Photo

Below left
138. Jabez Hughes & Mullins,
Oscar Wilde, Isle of Wight, 1884.
Studio-portrait cabinet card
Collection of Mary Viscountess Eccles
Later, Wilde was satirised, often
cruelly, for being openly homosexual at
a time when it was illegal in England.
In the media, Wilde was twinned with
oversized or impossibly coloured 'unnatural' flowers. Here, he chose to be
photographed wearing a rose.
© British Library Board. All rights
reserved/Bridgeman Images

Below right
139. John Ferguz,
standing woman with rose,
Scotland, mid-1880s.
Studio-portrait cabinet card
Private collection
This elegant lady wears a fashionable
bustled dress and clasps a rose as an
emblem in her upright left hand.

Below
140. Seated man in studio setting,
late nineteenth century.
Studio-portrait cabinet card
Private collection
The sitter, probably a groom, wears
a rose boutonnière and poses with a
vase of flowers, baskets of flowers,
books and a rolled document,
possibly a certificate.

Above right
141. A. K. P. Trask,
portrait of woman with corsage,
Philadelphia, USA, 1885.
Studio-portrait cabinet card
Private collection
The sitter wears a large corsage of
rose buds. The reverse is annotated
'Aline B. E. Roussel, December 1885'.

Below right
142. A. B. Cornstock, woman with
flower bouquets, New York,
late nineteenth century.
Studio-portrait cabinet card
Private collection
The subject, probably a bride, wears a
prominent rose corsage on the bodice
of her lace-decorated dress and poses
with multiple baskets of flowers (many
of them roses) with greeting cards.

Above left
143. Franz Xaver Winterhalter,
*Queen Alexandra when Princess of
Wales*, 1864.
Oil on canvas, 162.6 x 114.1cm
Royal Collection Trust
The princess wears roses in her hair, a
beribboned white ballgown, gold and
pearl jewellery and the badge of the
Order of Victoria and Albert, which
she was given upon her marriage
to Prince Albert Edward in 1863. As
queen (from 1901) she launched the
charitable Alexandra Rose Day (fig.111).
Royal Collection Trust/© Her Majesty
Queen Elizabeth II 2020

Above right
144. Day dress, USA, *c.*1855.
Silk taffeta
The Museum at FIT, New York
This dress is of silk taffeta printed
with a design of polychrome roses
and a blue flower, possibly borage.
Dresses in this period were composed
of two pieces: skirt and bodice. This
one was made with both a short-
sleeved evening and long-sleeved
daywear bodice.
The Museum at FIT, 76.208.10.
Gift of Mrs Van Nostrand

Opposite
145. Winter day dress (detail),
USA, *c.*1865.
Printed wool challis
The Museum at FIT, New York
The Museum at FIT, P85.88.2.
Museum purchase

ROSES IN HAUTE COUTURE AND FASHION DISSEMINATION

International womenswear trends were led by the Paris haute couture houses: notably Félix, Jacques Doucet, Worth, Pingat, Redfern, Lanvin and Callot Soeurs. London's court dressmakers and tailoring firms catered for elite social life, which revolved around the court, and it was widely accepted that, on the whole, they followed Paris trends, as did New York's dressmakers and tailors (figs 144–5). By this date the vogue for flower-decorated apparel was at its peak and the artificial flower trades in Paris, London and New York were flourishing. As the century progressed, and the means of fashion production became established, women became the focus of the new commodity culture as buyers, and sites, of fashionable dress and conspicuous consumption.[14]

Following the opening of Japan's trade ports in 1854, the inter-arts, intercultural phenomenon called Japonisme created a vogue for new fashion flowers: notably, chrysanthemums, hydrangeas, irises, orchids and cherry blossom. But, as ever, the rose remained beloved. In 1876, the *Millinery Trade Review* reported that, 'The object this year seems to be to use the most uncommon flowers – unless it is the rose, and it is always worn and always lovely. A coronet of thick, dark green rose leaves is very beautiful.'[15] The following spring, *Harper's Bazaar* noted the vogue for perfumed flowers in millinery and reported:

...

Everywhere flowers are used: as the corsage, in front, or on the side, in the shape of a half wreath or an elongated tuft; at the belt, on the shoulders, in the hair – everywhere artificial flowers are seen. The simplest fichu, the most unassuming cravat, has at least a rose-bud encircled mignonette to finish the knot in which it is tied.

...

Harper's Bazaar, 1877[16]

By 1860, 89 per cent of Paris-based milliners were women, who headed and managed their own businesses, each meanwhile working as *premierè* (designer) and senior *garnisseuse* (responsible for applying flowers, ribbons, feathers etc.)[17] Caroline Reboux, Maison Virot Mangin Maurice, E. Gauthier, Madame Pouyanne and Maison Camille Marchais were revered internationally for hats decorated with, or seemingly composed entirely from, the most exquisite, naturalistic artificial buds, blooms and foliage.

Artificial flowers are delicate and few nineteenth-century hats with artificial roses survive today (see, however, fig.148), while many museums house examples of haute couture evening gowns, with artificial flower decoration, which may only have been worn once or twice.

....
FOCUS STUDY
....

WORTH EVENING GOWN

....

Charles Frederick Worth was instrumental in setting the template for today's global fashion industry by establishing himself as an arbiter of fashion, who presented seasonal collections of his own, name-labelled designs, some of which he licensed. He conducted himself as artist and dictator of style, rather than a stylist or tradesperson who worked in conjunction with a client. His house was justly famous for, and its product distinguished by, the superlative fabrics that Worth commissioned from specialist silk weavers in Lyon, and by its profusion of exquisite trimmings, including naturalistic silk flowers. His use of roses was so lavish that *Punch* magazine commissioned a satirical cartoon, 'Last Sweet Thing in Toilettes' of a woman wearing a dress with huge applied rose leaves, a bud at each shoulder and an immense bloom as millinery (fig.147). Worth's clientele included international monarchy, aristocracy, those with new industrial fortunes and the demi-monde, for whom his notoriously exorbitant prices rendered the product exclusive and all the more desirable.

Over the course of a day, a fashionable woman might wear *déshabillé* (a night and dressing gown set) a morning dress, an afternoon dress and a tea gown (an at-home garment that was less rigidly boned than outerwear), followed by an evening or ballgown. Evening gowns were divided into two categories, with *demi toilette* being slightly less formal than this gown, which was full *toilette* and would have been worn to attend an official dinner party, a reception, the opera or theatre, or to celebrate a rite of passage. There are several Worth afternoon, evening and ballgowns dating from the 1870s and '80s, now housed in public collections, with designs depicting naturalistic roses with 'thorny' stems and leaves, and embroidered or silk rose decoration.

This arresting rose-themed evening gown, ordered from Paris, was worn by New Yorker Miss Caroline C. 'Daisy' Beard in 1888, when she was a debutante, and exemplifies the house métier. Many of Worth's finest silks were ordered from Tassinari & Chatel, and it is possible that they made this remarkable brocaded silk. Each scattered rose petal is shaded in glistening copper-coloured and pale-pink threads, and the tips are slightly raised and naturalistically curled. A branch of pale-pink muslin roses with leaves trails across the waist and down the left side of the skirt. In 1890, Daisy married John H. Shults, uniting two immensely wealthy Brooklyn families (her father prospered in street and railway construction and his German-born father was proprietor of one of the largest bakeries in the world).

In 1889, one year after this dress was designed, a brilliant-pink, scented, hybrid *rugosa* rose was named 'Madame Charles Frederick Worth', after the couturier's wife and muse, by French rose breeder Madame Veuve Schwartz.

Left
146. House of Worth, evening gown
(and detail), France, 1888.
Brocaded silk satin with rose petals,
lace and silk roses on a trailing stem
with leaves
Museum of the City of New York
Museum of the City of New York. Gift
of Miss Isabel Shults, 1944, 44.197.1A-B

Below
147. 'Last Sweet Thing in Toilettes'
Punch cartoon, 5 July 1879.
Punch Cartoon Library/Top Foto

LAST SWEET THING IN TOILETTES.
(With Punch's Compliments to M. Worth.)

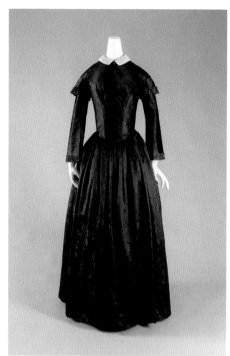

ROSE PERSONIFICATION AND FANCY DRESS

From the 1840s, etiquette writers guided mostly women but also men, and notably those from families with 'new' industrial wealth, on the myriad nuanced social behaviours and appearances deemed correct by polite ('old', landed) society. Within these, flowers – fragile, fragrant, decorative and silent – were presented as exemplars for women, as was Alfred Lord Tennyson's sweet Maud (from the poem of the same name, published in 1855) who was 'Queen rose of the rosebud garden of girls'.[18] The directives extended to posture and movement, with women ideally moving softly like flowers swaying in a gentle breeze. Warning against the vulgarity of 'jerky' movements, the anonymous author of *A Manual of Politeness* (1842) opined, 'The position of the neck is of importance ... quite straight, it wants elegance. It is therefore generally inclined a little to one side, by a gentle and almost imperceptible movement, which gives it a softer character, and a more feminine expression.'[19]

As the century progressed, women increasingly asserted their rights. As indeed did the flowers in *Les Fleurs Animées* ('The Flowers Personified', 1847), by French caricaturist Jean Ignace Isidore Gérard, better known as J. J. Grandville. His protagonists (fig.150) pointed out that, while they provided fragrance and poetic metaphors for humankind, they were rewarded with the florist's knife and left to wilt on a warm breast.

Gendered female, Grandville's flowers reclaimed the meanings bestowed upon them and were given human form, each one costumed in its flower leaves, stems, bud, blooms and thorns. Unusually, in an era when the existence of lesbians was barely acknowledged, Grandville's *femme fleurs* included female lovers 'Tubereuse' and 'Jonquile'. Another radical social commentator, the socialist Arts and Crafts artist Walter Crane, politicised flower personification and illustrated men in flower form (fig.158). These two sources were exceptional amongst the mass of contemporaneous flower personification.

From around 1830 until the outbreak of the Second World War in 1939, fancy dress parties and balls were immensely popular and enjoyed by children and adults in many sections of society. Costumes were made or ordered, and sometimes historical fashion was worn. Even more than fashion, fancy dress can convey – or betray – personal fantasies, aspirations, personality and social status, as well as expressing the broader culture of the time and space in which it is worn. Attending as 'animated flowers' was a non-controversial theme for cis-gendered women and girls. In his top-selling book *Fancy Dresses Described or What to Wear to Fancy Balls* (reprinted six times between 1879 and 1896; see fig.151) Ardern Holt proposed eight different rose costumes, over twice as many as for any other theme. To appear as the 'Queen of the Roses' required a 'White tulle skirt with bouquets of every coloured rose dispersed about it; over-skirt powdered with pink rose-leaves, also the veil, as if a shower of rose-leaves had fallen on them; a wreath of coloured roses; earrings, necklet, and bracelets formed of pink rosebuds.'[20] Alternatively, Holt suggested that 'A fashionable evening dress trimmed with any flower and called after it, is the easiest kind of fancy costume.'[21] Most desirable was a unique costume ordered from a Paris fashion house (haute couture was produced in multiples) and none more so than the creations of Worth, whose costumes reflected father and designer son Jean Philippe's infinitely creative imaginations, vast knowledge of historical fashion and world clothing, and exceptional atelier resources. Charles dressed his most famous client, the Empress Eugénie, wife of Napoleon III, as Marie Antoinette painted by Élisabeth-Louise Vigée Le Brun (see fig.70) – she would, of course, have held a pink rose in one hand. Fancy dress could afford men an opportunity to wear dress that was significantly more elaborate than their daily wear and this was the one area in which the couture houses catered for men. For those with illustrious lineage, wearing ancestral dress was a solution both thrifty and status-driven. Many original eighteenth-century garments now housed in museum collections, some made from silks with rose designs, bear evidence of adaptation for fancy dress.

Opposite left
148. Maison Virot, hat, France, nineteenth century. Plaited straw, silk, velvet with silk roses and leaves
The Fine Arts Museums of San Francisco
This hat has silk roses placed upon the crown and below the brim.
The Fine Arts Museums of San Francisco, gift of Jane Scribner, 49.10.25

Opposite right
149. Day dress, possibly USA, c.1844. Silk satin
This rather modest daytime dress is of a style that might have befitted Charlotte Bronte's fictional heroine Jane Eyre (published 1847): it is made from a jacquard woven silk with a subtle design of roses.
The Museum of FIT, 95.97.1. Museum purchase

Below left
150. J. J. Grandville, 'Eglantine' illustration for *Les Fleurs Animées*, 1847.
In Grandville's narrative the eglantine disputes the universal admiration of the cultivated rose, who Grandville portrayed as the queen of flowers with a flower crown and rosebud sceptre.
© NYPL

Below right
151. Miss Lillian Young, 'Rose Garden', illustration for Ardern Holt, *Fancy Dresses Described or What to Wear to Fancy Balls*, 1879.
This costume illustration depicts a light-green silk-satin gown covered with green tulle and ribbons, over which roses were trailed, and rose-decorated accessories.
Illustration by Miss Lillian Young

Fig. 34.—ROSE GARDEN.

ROSES AND RITES OF PASSAGE

During the nineteenth century, as in ancient Rome, roses were integral to the ceremonies that marked rites of passage. Flowers and buds decorated apparel worn by debutantes, brides and grooms (fig.142), and also the bereaved, often laid out and photographed – Sleeping Beauty-like – surrounded by or holding fresh roses (fig.157). The symbolism of roses and female sexuality has been explored in the introduction and Chapter II of this book. Here it is suffice to recall the widely known associations between the rosebud and white fabrics and female chastity; the open flower and colour red, by contrast, connote passion and sexual consummation. In 1842, the etiquette writer cited above likened the cycle of a woman's life to that of a rose, warning:

...

She has a summer as well as a spring, an autumn and a winter. As the aspect of the earth alters with the changes of the year, so does the appearance of a woman adapt itself to the time which passes over her. Like the rose, she buds, she blooms, she fades, she dies!

...

Anon, 1842 [22]

Some young girls' first experience of a marriage ceremony involved serving as a flower girl, whose role is to strew rose petals, considered symbolic of fertility and heterosexual romantic union, along the bridal path. Elite international society took part in the annual social season, that ran from May to July, with the explicit intention of introducing young women, known as debutantes (from the French, meaning 'to launch'), into polite society in order to meet a suitable husband. In England during Queen Charlotte's reign, the practice of presenting young women of 'noble' birth or diplomatic families to the monarch before making their debut was introduced in 1780 and continued until the mid-twentieth century. For weddings themselves, by the 1830s, the long-standing convention of wearing silver and white bridal gowns had petered out in favour of white alone, with matching flowers; the rose as a symbol of love was a natural choice. Flowers were considered essential to ensure a happy relationship, as the belief that flowers could ward off evil spirits lingered.

A groom often wore uniform or formal tailored daywear; the latter might be enlivened with a white or decorative waistcoat (see fig.153) and a boutonnière. From the 1840s, it was a fashionable and romantic gesture for an affluent groom to express his love by

Above
152. Fashion plate of a woman wearing fashionable bridal dress, in Rudoph Ackermann, *Repository of Arts, Literature, Commerce, Manufactures, Fashion and Politics*, June 1916.
Engraving
Edwina Ehrman's extensive research on the wedding dress has revealed that the earliest known nineteenth-century fashion plate of a bride was published in *Le Journal des dames et des modes* in 1813. This dress, the earliest British one illustrated, was made by Mrs Gill of Cork Street, in the heart of London's elite fashion industry.
© Victoria and Albert Museum, London

Opposite
153. Waistcoat, Britain, 1840s. Embroidered silk with cotton back
Private collection
Decorated with rose flowers, meaning true love; rosebuds, signifying love in its early stages; and blue *Anchusa* (of the borage family), associated with infinite romantic longing, with inducing courage and making a man joyful, this vest lacks provenance but is almost certainly a ceremonial wedding garment.

donning a waistcoat embroidered with a design of flowers rich with symbolic meanings. One example, housed in the collection of the Victoria and Albert Museum, London (museum number T.562–1919) was worn by a Mr Eeles for his wedding in 1848. It is made of white silk decorated with white silk-embroidered lilies of the valley and forget-me-nots – flowers associated with love and purity of heart. He subsequently packed it away as a souvenir and holder of deeply personal memories. But not everyone found love and joy in roses. Charles Baudelaire, widely considered to be the first Modernist poet, lamented in *Les Fleurs du Mal* (1858), 'I could not find amongst such bloodless roses, A flower to match my crimson hued ideal.'[23]

Every culture has its own rituals and customs for mourning the dead, and these often incorporate roses. In ancient Greece and Rome, roses were profoundly significant to funerary rights, often marking an untimely or premature death. The wearing of black mourning dress, which mostly impacted women, was promoted by Napoléon Bonaparte early in the century, partly to boost France's textiles industries, and later by Queen Victoria following the death of her consort Prince Albert in 1861, whereupon it became a major industry. Styles followed fashion but fabrics were black, often matte crape, and decoration was minimal, comprising self-fabric trimmings, black artificial flowers and lace shawls (see fig.156). Jewellery was generally avoided for the first year of mourning; when it was worn it had a black matte surface. Thereafter, roses featured prominently on hair ornaments, necklaces, buttons, rings, brooches and bracelets, made from various black materials: ideally jet, but also black glass, bog oak, gutta percha and vulcanite (fig.155).

In the twilight of the nineteenth century, when women were occupying more active roles in public life and spaces, asserting their suffrage and industrial rights, the divorce rate was rising and birth rates declining; there was a revival in the painting of flower women, most sentimentally by American artist Charles Courtney Curran (see fig.212), whose depictions could not have been further from the tailor-clad, bicycle-riding Gibson Girl. Nor, indeed, from Algernon Swinburne's erotic and masochistic poem about his lover 'Dolores' ('Our Lady of the Pain', from the poem of the same name, published in 1866) for whom men would – in a trice – abandon 'The lilies and languors of virtue, For the raptures and roses of vice.'[24]

Swinburne's poem comprised a prelude to the – shocking, to many – depiction of women as sexually predatory *femmes fatale* by the Symbolists and decadents, who argued that the purpose of art and literature was not to emulate nature, but to negate it. The decadent duc Jean Floressas des Esseintes, the sole character in Joris-Karl Huysmans' cult novel *À Rebours* ('Against Nature', 1884), was modelled on comte Robert de Montesquiou-Fézensac (see fig.137) – a fashionable dandy aristocrat at the heart of Parisian Belle Époque society, who grew 'tired of artificial flowers

aping real ones, he wanted some natural flowers that would look like fakes.'[25] Carl Linnaeus had drawn parallels between 'natural' flowers and human fertility; towards the end of the nineteenth century sexologists exploited botanical references to hermaphrodite plants (including the rose) to explain bisexual and 'invert' sexual activity and it was at this time that gay men came to be abusively referred to as 'pansies' or 'blossoms'.

Where previous analogies had been made, men and male children had been compared to vegetables and trees. By 1889, in *Flora's Feast: A Masque of Flowers*, however, Walter Crane illustrated *fleurs animées* with burly wild-rose male lovers (fig.158). Crane was a champion of the dress reform movement, which advocated the wearing of loose and lightweight clothing in place of cumbersome nineteenth-century fashion, and served as vice president of the Healthy & Artistic Dress Union, established in 1893 by artists, including the Pre-Raphaelites, and writers. He illustrated the organisation's leaflet 'How to Dress Without a Corset', considered radical at the time but presaging a practice that was to become standard for most of the twentieth century. As we have seen, within nineteenth-century fashion, the depiction of the rose remained mostly naturalistic. It was not until the late twentieth century that the transgressive, deathly and decayed rose took stylistic root.

154. Thomas Ralph Spence,
Sleeping Beauty, 1890s.
Oil on canvas
Thomas Ralph Spence draws together
the vogue for fairy tales – such as this
one titled 'Little Briar Rose' – and the
alchemising of women's long hair in
popular culture.
Artepics/Alamy Stock Photo

Above left
155. Expanding mourning bangle,
c.1880s.
Vulcanite with moulded rose
decoration
The Museum at FIT, New York
Vulcanite, made by combining and
heating rubber sap with sulphur, was
cheaper than jet but looked very
similar. The prominent decorative rose
is finely detailed.
The Museum at FIT, 2019.62.1.
Museum purchase

Below left
156. Honiton lace shawl (detail),
probably worn during mourning,
England, mid-to-late nineteenth
century.
Collection of Heather Toomer
© Heather Toomer

Above right
157. Post-mortem portrait,
USA, c.1844.
Hand-tinted Daguerrotype
Far from being considered macabre,
photographs of the deceased at this
time were considered to comprise
vivid remembrances. This deceased
young woman was clothed in a dress
with a rose decoration, which the
photographer has hand-tinted pink.
© Stanley B. Burns, MD & The Burns
Archive

Opposite
158. Walter Crane, illustration for
Flora's Feast: A Masque of Flowers,
1889.
Crane's radical male wild-rose lovers
wear bodices of thorns, petal-like
skirts and rose-hip coloured mules;
what was widely considered as
fantastical has taken form in twenty-
first-century social and fashion
cultures.

Roses
and
violets

CHAPTER VII

THE TWENTIETH CENTURY

...

'A ROSE IS A ROSE IS A ROSE'

AMY DE LA HAYE

...

Rose is a rose is a rose is a rose
Loveliness extreme.
Extra gaiters,
Loveliness extreme.
Sweetest ice-cream.

...

Gertrude Stein, 'Sacred Emily', 1922[1]

This chapter comprises an anthology – borrowed from the Greek *anthologein*, 'to gather flowers' – of work by selected international fashion designers for whom roses had special meaning, became their creative signature or were utilised in one significant design. Roses are a fashion mainstay, especially for summer, but, from 1900 to the late 1930s, during the 1950s, and from the 1980s to the '90s, with a few notable exceptions, rose-themed fashion expression was most bounteous, imaginative and occasionally challenging.

During the eighteenth and nineteenth centuries, fashionable rose depictions were mostly naturalistic; in the twentieth century, the flower was also interpreted in more stylised guise, expressive of movements within art and design. The declaration 'A rose is a rose is a rose' comprises the first line of the Modernist writer and art collector Gertrude Stein's poem 'Sacred Emily' (1913, published 1922, with the title an allusion to the poet Emily Dickinson).[1] It can be interpreted as a demand to see things for what they are: the rose stripped of the mythology and symbolism with which it had become so heavily laden. Having established the narrative of roses within the contexts of rites of passage and fancy dress for the nineteenth century, relevant apparel is, here, integrated within the chronology.

Art Nouveau – an international movement within architecture, the fine and applied arts – was characterised stylistically by a 'whiplash' curve and the sinuous lines of plants and flowing hair. Within fashion, the style was expressed most eloquently within jewellery design (see Chapter IV): decorative metalwork, including belt buckles and buttons, some with enamelled designs, and hair combs carved from horn, all of which featured rose designs. It was within British Art Nouveau that the rose was foregrounded, expressed – unusually, within this movement – as a compact flower form by Glasgow-based Charles Rennie Mackintosh (after whom a lilac-pink English shrub rose was named in 1988), his wife Margaret Macdonald (fig.159), her sister Frances and her future husband Herbert MacNair, all talented artists and multimedia designers. The work of the 'Glasgow Four' was mostly focused upon buildings and interior design, but, from *c*.1910, their distinctive rose motif was appropriated, and further abstracted, within Art Deco design, and featured prominently within fashionable womenswear and illustration (fig.161).

Artificial roses and buds were used most profusely within early twentieth-century fashion: in the early 1900s, the Parisian haute couturier Paul Poiret (see fig.164) recalled looking down in the theatre onto a sea of hats so densely floriated he likened the scene to a 'flower garden'.[2] From 1907, Poiret introduced a leaner, more modern fashion silhouette, which was counterbalanced by immensely wide hats, as popularised by the actress Lily Elsie, who appeared on the London stage as 'The Merry Widow' in an unprecedentedly wide-brimmed hat, designed by Lucile, which was much emulated (and greatly exaggerated and parodied). The new trend further increased the surface area for flower decoration.

159. Margaret Macdonald,
The White Rose and the Red Rose, 1902.
Painted gesso over hessian with glass
beads, 97.8 x 100.3cm
The Hunterian, University of
Glasgow
This panel was hung in the 'Rose
Boudoir' room, designed by Margaret
and Charles Rennie Mackintosh for the
*Prima Esposizione Internazionale d'Arte
Decorativa Moderna* in Turin in 1902.
Margaret depicted women with roses
as isolated and somewhat androgynous
in a lyrical abstracted style.
© The Hunterian, University of Glasgow

Photographer Cecil Beaton, himself a keen gardener, recalled
how his passion for fashion, photography and illustration was
ignited by a pink-tinted picture postcard of Lily Elsie, and later
mused, 'this goddess wrapped the whole of my adolescence in a
haze of roses.'[3]

Lucile was the label of Lucy Christiana Sutherland, who started
dressmaking from home as a divorced single mother; when she
remarried in 1900 and became Lady Duff-Gordon she continued
to work from choice. Tenacious, capricious and infinitely creative,
by 1911 she had become the first woman to head fashion houses
in London, Paris and New York (and another in Chicago). Tiny
pale-pink silk rosebuds or rosebuds embroidered in fine ribbon
work were her hallmark (fig.165). To present her Spring/Summer
1904 collection, Lucile filled her salon with 3,000 scented pink
silk roses; at other summer shows, presented in the garden of
her London house, guests were served tea seated amid planted
roses. Lucile staged lavish fashion shows, presented her models
as personalities (at a time when they were normally rendered
anonymous) and named each of her 'gowns of emotion',
sometimes provocatively. 'Climax' was a blue silk-chiffon gown
decorated with pink silk rosebuds for Autumn/Winter 2005;
'Enrapture' was a ball or opera gown of burnt-pink silk taffeta
ornamented with pink-silver tissue roses. Each Maison Lucile
had an incense-scented 'Rose Room' decorated in the French
Neoclassical style, swathed in filmy fabrics and garlanded with
silk roses, where clients could choose delicate, flower-sprigged
and beribboned silk lingerie, tea gowns and negligees. In 1919
she launched her perfume, called *La Rose*.

Art Deco was an eclectic international style that can be dated
*c.*1910–*c.*1925, and within which the rose was the defining
flower. It was often depicted garlanded, in the style of the
eighteenth century, or as evolved from the Mackintosh rose,
now expressed in a near-rounded form with just a few delineated
petals, sometimes surrounded by curved, partial leaf shapes.

Poiret led the fashion for Orientalism, which drew upon Persian
and Turkish cultures within which the rose was foregrounded.
His 1913 ensemble 'Sorbet' (fig.164) provides an example
of his use of the Art Deco rose. Poiret's own label featured a
more naturalistic rose graphic, illustrated by Paul Iribe; it was
depicted in black for his own models and in pink for authorised
reproductions. Poiret founded an experimental art school
called École Martine (1911–23), which encouraged freedom of
expression among creative working-class women and girls, who
were taken to gardens and the zoo to fire their imaginations.
Surviving fashion textiles designed by the students are vibrant
and modern (fig.162), unhampered by historical art- and textiles-
conventions. To advertise Poiret's perfume *La Rosine* (German for
rose, launched 1911) the school made rose-patterned fans; they
also embroidered, in around 1923, needlepoint roses for shoes
designed by André Perugia for Poiret.

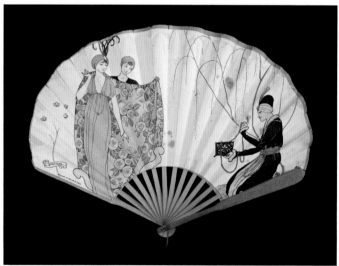

Top
160. Photograph album with design
of a rose with robust, thorny stem,
*c.*1900s.
Private collection
Photography remained popular
throughout the twentieth century and
albums were chosen and assembled
with care.

Above
161. Fan decorated with George
Barbier illustration, France, 1912.
Printed and hand-coloured paper
and wood
George Barbier was a leading
illustrator, who designed fans for
Paul Poiret and Madame Paquin.
This design expresses the prevailing
vogue for Orientalism and the
rose-decorated shawl provides an
early example of the Art Deco-style
rounded rose.
The Royal Pavilion, Art Gallery
and Museums, Brighton.
Photograph by Tessa Hallmann

Top
162. École Martine sample,
Paris, 1915–25.
Printed silk
The Museum at FIT, New York
This silk sample, printed with a design
of roses and wavy lines, was sold at
Paul Poiret's Atelier Martine.
The Museum at FIT, P74.1.13.
Museum purchase

Above
163. Evening dress, USA, c.1926.
Silk with sequins applied in the fish-
scale manner
The Museum at FIT, New York
The Museum at FIT, 2008.78.1.
Gift of Joan Vass

Right
164. Paul Poiret
'Sorbet' evening gown with
lampshade tunic, Paris, 1913.
Beaded silk
The Museum at FIT, New York
Roses, central to many Middle Eastern
cultures, were prominent within the
early-twentieth-century vogue for
'Orientalism', which was fuelled by
the Ballet Russes performance of
Schéhérezade (Paris, 1910). Poiret
combined oriental styling and Art
Deco rose decoration within his
designs for fashion and interiors.
The Museum at FIT, P81.8.1.
Museum purchase

Most women continued to purchase fabrics and trimmings that they made into clothes for themselves or took to a local dressmaker; styles were disseminated and adapted from those presented by the Paris fashion houses. Some women also made their own artificial flowers, working from magazine instructions and manuals. In 1912, in Lawrence, Massachusetts, there was a major strike at the American Woollen Company mills, most of whose 40,000 employees were non-unionised women and child immigrant workers. Among some 25,000 protesters were women bearing placards that read 'We want Bread, but Roses Too!', probably inspired by the final three lines of James Oppenheim's political poem:

...

...Bread and roses! Bread and roses!
Our lives shall not be sweated from birth
until life closes; Hearts starve as well as bodies;
give us bread, but give us roses. [4]

...

James Oppenheim, 'Bread and Roses', 1911 [4]

The international cut-flower trade continued to expand into the twentieth century and female street vendors remained the dominant point of sale. In his political satire *Pygmalion* (1912, adapted for the stage 1913; it was based on *Pygmalion and Galatea* by W. S. Gilbert [1871]), socialist playwright George Bernard Shaw told the story of the beautiful young cockney flower girl, Eliza Doolittle, who, keen to work in the more prestigious environment of a flower shop, agreed to be trained to pass as a lady in fashionable society (later adaptations of the play include the 1965 film musical *My Fair Lady*.)

For men, during the first half of the century, it was the boutonnière that comprised the core form of sartorial rose expression. In Marcel Proust's *À la recherche du temps perdu* ('In Search of Lost Time', 1913–27), the aristocratic homosexual aesthete Palamède, Baron de Charlus – based on Proust's patron, comte Robert de Montesquiou-Fézensac (see fig.137) seductively 'fingered the moss rose in his button-hole' as he watched the narrator. [5]

For over a century, flowers had been associated primarily with the female sex, but this shifted during the First World War, when, amid the terror and brutality of the bloodied battlefields, a few precious flowers continued to grow. Emblematic of the beauty and fragility of life, the flowers – sometimes evoking memories of gardens at home – were picked and dried by the men in honour and memory of the dead; they were tucked into letters sent home and transplanted into pots made from spent artillery shells. Vera Brittain, a Voluntary Aid Detachment nurse,

who became a staunch pacifist, dedicated her poem 'Perhaps' (1915) to her fiancé Roland Aubrey Leighton, killed aged 20 just four months after she had accepted his proposal of marriage:

Perhaps the summer woods will shimmer bright,
And crimson roses once again be fair,
And autumn harvest fields a rich delight,
Although You are not there. [6]

By 1922, flowers (lilac) that grew out of the 'dead land' – in an otherwise flowerless landscape – were evoked by T. S Eliot in his seminal Modernist poem *The Waste Land*, in which he reflected on the harrowed psychological state of post-war society.

From 1918, the fashionable silhouette evolved in two core directions: most practical and popular for day and evening was the short, linear *garçonne* style, which reached its peak in 1926 and continued with little change until 1929; the longer, wide-skirted, historical-revival *robe de style*, by contrast, had petered out by *c.*1926. The Art Deco rose was depicted on *garçonne* style dresses in gleaming sequins, trailing over the right shoulder of a evening dress of 1926, for example (fig.163). Boué Soeurs, the Paris couture house headed by Madame Sylvie Montegut and baronne Jeanne D'Etreillis), was famous for the use of delicate fabrics including flowered laces and rose decoration. Agnes also incorporated rose designs (fig.166), as did Lanvin. In 1923, the British-born socialite Baroness de Meyer commissioned haute couturière Alice Bernard to design a golden rose costume in which she might attend one of comte Etienne de Beaumont's lavish costume balls (fig.171).

Elite fashion in the 1930s revealed influences from multiple sources, including those that indicate a yearning for fantasy and escapism at a time of worldwide economic and political crises. In a bid to moderate their prices, couture houses made extensive use of printed textiles – the cheapest form of ornamentation – and flower designs became the height of chic. Stylistically, fashion was influenced by Modernism (which overlapped with and succeeded Art Deco), Neoclassicism, Surrealism and the Neo-Romantic vogue for mid- to late-nineteenth-century revival styles, also described as neo-Victorian, within which roses were manifest.

Betty Kirke, who studied the context and complexity of the Paris couturière Madeleine Vionnet's innovative designs, has highlighted the significance of the rose within her work and noted that, on a trip to the United States in 1924, the designer had admired and made her exemplar the 'American Beauty' rose (see p.127). [7] Vionnet was a romantic Modernist, who rationalised the use of decorative effects in adherence to the 'truth to materials' mantra by applying delicate appliqué roses crafted from strips of bias-cut fabric that matched each dress, rather than introducing additional elements.

More reductive, still, are the delicate pin-tucked designs of
roses that decorate a 1930 evening dress (fig.168), positioned to
accentuate the contours of the feminine body.

A single, prominent and finely crafted, yellow silk rose with
'woody' stem and leaves complements the printed rose garlands
interspersed with a graphic design of Classical urns on an
unlabelled silk crêpe evening dress dating from c.1935 (fig.169).
The placement of the rose, at the tip of the skirt godet, is
unusual, as is the application of such a robust flower on silk
(see fig.104). The dress was possibly conceived by the Paris- and
London-based couturier Edward Molyneux, who designed
similarly whimsical textiles and was noted for his predilection for
large fashion flowers: a critic for a provincial English newspaper
remarked, with reference to his Autumn/Winter 1938 collection,
'I can't quite agree that chrysanthemums and roses of a size to
create a sensation in a horticultural show are the best things to
decorate an evening dress.'[8] In 1935, the American paper-pattern-
making company McCall offered women an opportunity to make
their own flower-printed dinner gowns designed by Molyneux.

As author Jennifer Potter points out, the rose – 'Virtually
synonymous with bourgeois respectability' – was a 'natural target'
for the Surrealists, who were fascinated by dreams and sexuality.[9]
(It is perhaps surprising that psychoanalyst Sigmund Freud did
not make a single reference to roses in his writings.)[10]

165. Lucile, evening dress, probably
from Lucile's New York branch,
c.1914.
The Museum at FIT, New York
Shot silk with a brocaded design of
rose clusters, lace and silk ribbon,
with self-fabric rose and metal
fringe.
The Museum at FIT, P93.15.1.
Museum purchase

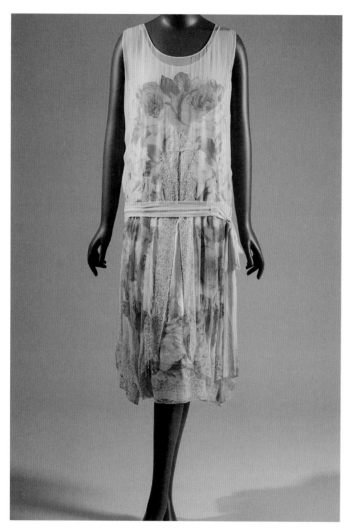

Above left
166. Agnes, evening dress,
Paris, c.1927.
Silk crinkle chiffon, printed silk
chiffon and lace
The Museum at FIT, New York
The Museum at FIT, P83.19.3.
Museum purchase

Above right
167. Wedding dress, USA, 1926.
Silk with a trapunto design of roses
The Museum at FIT, New York
This dress was worn by American
woman Fan Wold for her marriage to
Dr Harry J. Lowen in December 1926.
This interesting, hybrid style comprises
a shortened *robe de style* silhouette
with modern, integral rose decoration.
The Museum at FIT, 91.23.1.
Gift of George and Ann Lowen

Above left
168. Vionnet, evening dress,
France, 1930.
Silk georgette with a pin-tucked
design of roses
The Museum at FIT, New York
The dress has a matching silk crêpe
chemise underdress with scalloped,
petal-like hemline.
The Museum at FIT, P83.39.7.
Museum purchase

Above right
169. Possibly Molyneux, evening
gown, France or Britain, c.1935.
Printed silk crêpe with artificial
rose decoration.
The Museum at FIT, New York
The Museum at FIT, 90.33.6.
Gift of Arne Ekstrom

In a direct affront to romantic flower symbolism, French intellectual Georges Bataille pronounced many flowers were 'unpleasant, if not hideous' and that even the most beautiful blooms were spoiled in their centres by hairy sexual organs. He continued:

Thus the interior of a rose does not at all correspond to its exterior beauty; if one tears off all the corolla's petals, all that remains is a rather sordid tuft ... But even more than the filth of its organs, the flower is betrayed by the fragility of its corolla: thus, far from answering the demands of human ideas, it is the sign of their failure.[11]

Salvador Dalí's painting *Woman with a Head of Roses* (1935) was exhibited at *The International Surrealist Exhibition* at Burlington Galleries, London, in 1936; to mark the launch, performance artist Sheila Legge brought Dalí's canvas 'to life' by posing in Trafalgar Square wearing a shredded white dress and a hood of pink roses commissioned from a Mayfair florist. In one hand she held a prosthetic leg, in the other a lamb chop. These inspired the styling of Paris-based haute couturière Elsa Schiaparelli's 'Tear Dress' (1937) and 'Lamb Cutlet' hat (1937). A photograph of Legge appeared on the cover of the Surrealist journal *Bulletin* in September 1936 and was reworked by Dalí for a cover for *Vogue* (fig.172). Schiaparelli (who designed her own single rose head in the '50s, see fig.174) also collaborated directly with Dalí and Jean Cocteau; the latter designed 'Les Deux Visage' – an illusory decorative graphic showing two face profiles with rosebud lips, which combined to create the silhouette of a roses-topped vase – which was embroidered onto the back of an evening coat for Autumn/Winter 1937 (fig.173).

In 1937, Cecil Beaton hosted a fête champêtre at the Georgian manor house Ashcombe in Wiltshire. A talented costume designer, he donned a surreal rabbit mask and a cream-coloured corduroy jacket decorated with pink muslin roses, clumps of green wool and faux broken egg shells, some with plastic egg content (fig.175).

When the Nazis occupied Paris in June 1940, communications from the fashion French capital were halted; some of the haute couture houses closed, but many remained open to serve the wives and girlfriends of the invading forces, collaborators and wartime profiteers. Designers in London and New York continued to conduct business without Parisian design direction and working within wartime materials restrictions, from which hats were exempt (see fig.180). Mainbocher (Main Rousseau Bocher) started his career in Paris before moving to New York, where, in 1943, he designed a black silk cocktail apron with artificial pink rose decoration and, the following year, a detachable black lace peplum with a posy of pink silk roses and marguerite daisies, with glamour belt in silk satin with beaded and artificial flower decoration (fig.178); such a concentrated decorative could 'lift' an existing or otherwise plain dress.

1. Roses rambling in the flounce of Mainbocher's velvet dress—the shade called "modest violet"
2. Rose-pink—what Schiaparelli calls "cameo-pink"—in a wool jacket with a skunk collar. (Russeks)
3. Roses bunched on the hip of Molyneux's slipper satin dress—the sleeves pure leg-o'-mutton. (Marshall Field)
4. A rose of sequins on the chest of Mainbocher's high-necked, long-sleeved velvet dress. (Bergdorf Goodman)
68

Opposite above
170. Christian Bérard,
'Roses and Violets', American *Vogue*,
1 October 1937.
This rose-themed illustration, with
its fluid, graceful lines and exquisite
use of colour, exemplifies the Neo-
Romantic-style fashion illustrations
provided for leading fashion
magazines by avant-garde artist and
designer Christian Bérard during the
mid- to late 1930s.
Christian Bérard, *Vogue* © Condé Nast

Opposite below
171. Baron de Meyer,
Baroness de Meyer, *Harpers Bazaar*,
September 1923.
Paris haute couture house Alice
Bernard designed this rose costume
for Baroness de Meyer to attend
comte Etienne de Beaumont's 'Fêtes
of Unsurpassed Magnificence',
Published by *Harper's Bazaar*,
September 1923. Photograph by
Baron de Meyer

Right
172. Salvador Dalí, design for the
cover of American *Vogue*,
1 June 1939.
The title page captioned this image,
'Symbols by Salvador Dali, the
fantastic Surrealist: flowers for the
beauty of women, a skipping figure for
the remembrance of her childhood, a
skeleton ship for the sadness of things
past.' It was adapted from his painting
Woman with a Head of Roses (1935).
Salvador Dalí, *Vogue* © Condé Nast

Christian Dior was fashion's floriculturist of the mid-twentieth century. The history of his inaugural 1947 'Corolla' collection – described by the press as the 'New Look', though the name technically refers to the whorling head of flower petals – with its narrow torso, nipped-in waist and immense, flower-like skirts, has been extensively documented, as has the designer's statement that he designed for 'flower-like' women. Dior was born in Normandy, the son of a wealthy fertiliser manufacturer, and from childhood had a love of flowers and gardening. Describing the development of a Spring collection he wrote, 'pieces of material are like young shoots which ripen into a thousand flowery patterns.'[12]

While lily of the valley was Dior's lucky flower, he designed multiple hats with silk roses (see fig.96) and decorated daytime, cocktail and evening dresses (fig.183) with rose designs and flowers. During his brief tenure at the house of Dior, between 1958 and 1960, the young Yves Saint Laurent, who later also became a passionate gardener, designed a silk taffeta *jeune fille* (young woman's) evening dress with a bubble skirt and single, self-fabric rose-and-leaf ornament (fig.179); it is a similar shade of pink to the 'Paris d'Yves Saint Laurent' rose introduced by Alain Meilland in 1994.

Certainly until the mid-1950s, Paris continued to lead international trends, and high-status designers were mostly Caucasian. Ann Cole Lowe was the first African American to become a top-level fashion designer. She came from a family of dressmakers; as a child she made fabric flowers from scraps of leftover fabric. She studied at the S. T. Taylor Design School, New York, where, due to racial segregation, she had to work in a room alone. In 1950, she opened Ann Lowe's Gowns in Harlem, specialising in making formal eveningwear and ceremonial gowns for American socialites; she was noted for her modern, elegant debutante gowns (fig.185) and her most famous commission was to design Jacqueline 'Jackie' Bouvier's dress for her 1963 wedding to Senator J. F. Kennedy.

Above left
173. Schiaparelli, evening coat, Paris, Autumn/Winter 1937. Silk with ribbon roses
Philadelphia Museum of Art
This coat, with a double-faced image, was designed by Jean Cocteau and embroidered by the House of Lesage.
Philadelphia Museum of Art: Gift of Mme Elsa Schiaparelli, 1969-232-7

Above right
174. Schiaparelli, hat, Paris, 1950s. Panne silk velvet, silk organza rose with leaves, feathers and silk veil
The Museum at FIT, New York
The Museum at FIT, 2009.15.6. Museum purchase

Opposite
175. Gordon Anthony, Cecil Beaton in fancy dress with a shadow garland, 1937.
Hulton Deutsch/Contributor/ Getty Images

LA CORSELETTE

The mid- to late-1930s vogue for romantic, neo-Victorian revival styles is epitomised by this evening gown, designed by the Anglo-American couturier Charles James in the year he opened his Paris salon. The neo-Victorian trend was fuelled by the 1937 coronation of George VI and Queen Elizabeth in Britain; by the stage play *Victoria Regina*, which was performed to full houses in London, Paris and New York; and by lavishly costumed Hollywood films set in the period. The sculptural silhouettes of many of James's evening gowns have been likened to flowers, his unusual colour juxtapositions to an orchid-like palette. However, the styling and use of artificial roses on this gown is exceptional within his creative oeuvre.

Variously called 'La Corselette' and 'La Sylphide' – the latter a tribute to the 1932 ballet that ushered in a new era of Romantic dance – this 1937 design comprises a full-length, silk satin gown with an organza off-the-shoulder bodice with twisted shoestring halter-neck. A profusion of artificial roses in pink- and cream-coloured silk sit at the neckline, above a back-laced, boned and quilted, silk satin corselette that is based upon an 1860s design. This dress was ordered and worn by Miss Esme O'Brien for the season she came out as a debutante (fig.177). In March 1942 she married media mogul Robert William Sarnoff; they were divorced in 1947 and two years later she married John Hammond, a Vanderbilt descendant.

'La Corselette' was offered in at least three other colourways. James's friend, the society beauty and campaigner for the conservation of Georgian and Victorian buildings, Anne Parsons, Countess of Rosse, ordered it in white (now perished, private collection). The Victoria and Albert Museum in London houses a model in canary yellow with matching yellow and flesh-pink silk roses (wearer not known). And the New York department store Best & Co. offered a version in pale mauve organza with fewer roses clustered on the right-side bodice. It was the latter that Cecil Beaton, whose romantic aesthetic was so ideally suited to this fashion mood, photographed for American *Vogue* (1 June 1937, p.49). It was worn by a model posed holding a bunch of long-stemmed roses amid a shower of rose leaves.

Roses were not a James signature. It is interesting that in 1984, American photographer Bruce Weber took the photograph *Charles James Dress & Roses, Kent, England*, showing a lustrous off-white silk satin gown, without flower decoration, with the bodice filled with multi-coloured fresh roses.

Left
176. Charles James, 'La Corselette'
evening gown, Paris, 1937.
Silk satin with silk roses
The Museum at FIT, New York
The Museum at FIT, 77.89.3.
Gift of Mrs John Hammond

Above
177. Miss Esme O'Brien as a
debutante wearing Charles James's
'La Corselette' evening gown, 1937.
The Museum at FIT, 77.89.3.
Gift of Mrs John Hammond

New York milliners Lilly Daché (fig.187) and Sally Victor decorated hats with glorious artificial roses and created others formed like the flower, while New York designers James Galanos, Nettie Rosenstein, Pauline Trigère, Norman Norell, Geoffrey Beene and Hattie Carnegie also incorporated the rose into their collections; the latter regularly produced costume jewellery pieces in the form of roses. Los Angeles also became a hub for sportswear and relaxed elegant fashion; occasionally, Hollywood costume designers – including Adrian and Irene, both of whom included roses in their designs – turned their attention to fashion (see fig.181).

If the rose is the queen of flowers, Cristóbal Balenciaga is widely considered the fashion designer's designer. Drawing on his Spanish heritage, the Paris-based haute couturier made extensive use of black lace, which had been worn as an emblem of Spanish national identity by the clergy and monarchy since the late eighteenth century; a cocktail ensemble from c.1963 was made using black Chantilly lace with a design of roses (fig.191). Balenciaga ordered silk roses from the Paris firm Judith Beiber and – unusually, and flatteringly – placed a single rose at the front and back armhole of sleeveless evening dresses. His dramatic and sculptural designs, including 'Black Rose' (1967), were immortalised by, among others, the visionary photographer Irving Penn.

The last season in which (1,400) debutantes were presented to the queen in the UK was March 1958; this was a tradition that had spanned some 200 years and was copied across much of the English-speaking world. London's coterie of couture designers, including Victor Stiebel, Worth, Digby Morton, Rhavis, Norman Hartnell and Hardy Amies, catered for this market, but by the 1950s their industry faced pressure from the reassertion of Paris fashion leadership and a reduction in clientele. This decline was partly due to competition from the cheaper model house designers, such as Susan Small (fig.184), but also reflected the tastes of the new generation of young women, who no longer wanted to dress formally or like their mothers.

Left
178. Mainbocher, glamour belt decorated with artificial flowers including roses, worn with evening dress, New York, 1944.
Silk satin with embroidered and artificial-flower decoration
Museum of the City of New York
Museum of the City of New York, Gift of Mr. Robert Winthrop, 1986.
86.60.43A-C

Above left
179. Christian Dior, designed by
Yves Saint Laurent, evening dress,
Paris, c.1960.
Silk faille
The Museum at FIT, New York
The Museum at FIT, 2017.80.1.
Museum purchase

Above right
180. H. P. Wasson, Hat, USA, c.1943.
Straw, netting, silk and silk velvet
rose, cotton leaves
Museum of the City of New York
The Museum at FIT, 93.169.23.
Gift of Alison Calkins

Right
181. Irene, halter-neck afternoon
dress and dolman-sleeve jacket,
Los Angeles, c.1954.
Printed and plain silk
The Museum at FIT, New York
Irene worked as a costume designer
for MGM before opening her fashion
house in 1950.
The Museum at FIT, P84.17.1.
Museum purchase

Below left
182. Rose-themed issue of *Flair*,
May 1950.
The American magazine *Flair* was
famous for its distinctive die-cut covers
and inspirational graphic design. Artist
Sylvia Braverman was invited to design
this rose personification cover: the
cut-out lifts to reveal a painted portrait
of a young woman with pink roses in
her hair. Balmain and Charles James
designed dresses for the special issue.
Flair, May 1950. Cover art by Sylvia
Braverman

Below right
183. Christian Dior, two-piece
evening dress, Paris, 1950.
Schiffli-embroidered organdie
The Museum at FIT, New York
The Museum at FIT, 68.144.12.
Gift of Miss Adele Simpson

Below
184. Norman Parkinson, Susan
Small evening gown, British *Vogue*,
August 1956.
Anne Gunning models this evening
gown with artificial rose decoration
for British *Vogue*.
Norman Parkinson/Iconic Images

Left
185. Ann Lowe, evening gown,
USA, 1956.
Organza over silk taffeta with silk-
satin decoration
Museum of the City of New York
This dress was designed for a
debutante. The full roses have sheer-
silk-covered petals and jewel-beaded
centres.
Museum of the City of New York.
Gift of Diana Townsend-Butterworth,
2009. 2009.2.1

Above left
186. Henri Cartier-Bresson,
'Easter Sunday in New York', 1947.
Gelatin silver print
French photographer Henri Cartier-
Bresson did much to establish street
photography as a genre; here he
captures a woman wearing a rose-
decorated hat receiving an admiring
glance.
© Henri Cartier-Bresson/
Magnum Photos

Below left
187. Henry Clarke, model wearing
Lilly Daché red rose hat, American
Vogue, September 1960.
Henry Clarke, *Vogue* © Condé Nast

Above
188. Norman Parkinson,
Digby Morton (rose-print shirt)
and Daks (slacks), British *Vogue*,
November 1956.
Ensemble modelled by Barbara Mullen.
Norman Parkinson/Iconic Images

Opposite above
189. Claire McCardell,
shirtwaist dress, New York, 1950.
Printed cotton
The Museum at FIT, New York
The Museum at FIT, 87.51.1.
Gift of Barbie Weinstock

Opposite below
190. Record cover, *The Gilded Palace
of Sin*, The Flying Burrito Brothers,
1969.
Private collection
The male members of the band were
dressed by Nudie Cohn; here, Chris
Ethridge wears a rose-decorated suit.

By the 1950s, New York led the trend for modern sportswear: informal, functional and comfortable separates in practical materials for a young market. Designs by Claire McCardell were instrumental for womenswear, offering stylish wrap-and-tie, buckle- and popper-fastened garments in calico, denim, stretch jerseys and printed cottons. Designing under her own name for the Townley label from 1940, the cotton shirtwaist dress was a mainstay of her collections: an example from 1950 was made using a rose-patterned print (fig.189). Photographer Louise Dahl-Wolfe photographed McCardell's designs on young models in relaxed settings (such as at a diner or the beach). She worked primarily with Diana Vreeland, fashion editor at *Harper's Bazaar*. In 1979, Vreeland ordered a rose-print silk plush top-and-trousers suit by Valentino couture, which could be situated within a trajectory of modern luxury homewear and street style (fig.192).

Roses also fed into subcultural dress – notably in 'western' styling, as exemplified by the fantastical designs of Russian-Jewish émigré Nudie Cohn, founder of 'Nudie's Rodeo Tailors, North Hollywood, California' (see fig.190). Nudie costumed leading country musicians including Tex Williams, Gram Parsons and

Hank Williams for the stage and provided upmarket, 'everyday', western-styled apparel. The 'Texas rose' featured prominently, embroidered onto western-style suits, cowboy hats and boots. In 1957, Nudie created what was to become known as the 'rhinestone cowboy' look, when he was commissioned to tailor a suit for Elvis Presley; it was made from 14-carat gold lamé and tens of thousands of hand-set rhinestones. Meanwhile, loud, wide-cut, hand-painted American ties, some with a design of roses, were being donned by stylish young men, many Afro-Caribbean and Hispanic American, who formed part of the jazz and swing music scenes, teamed with 'sharp' loose-cut, tailored suits.

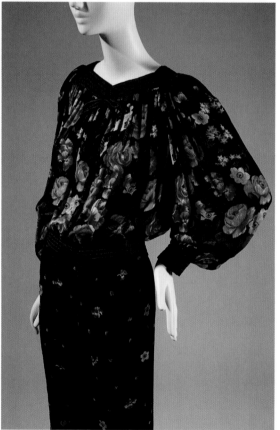

As a teenager, Hiram Maristany started to record everyday life in his Puerto Rican neighbourhood in East Harlem, New York. An exhibition caption for his portrait *Young Man with Roses* (1971, fig.193) read:

…

Who are the flowers for? There are two stories. For his girlfriend, or for his mother. In East Harlem you do not walk around with roses in your hand. If you do, you are a badass. This is no joke of a man. He's a gentle giant who wouldn't harm a fly. I think they were for his girlfriend, but it was easier for him to say they were for his mother.

…

Hiram Maristany, 2017[13]

In spite of strides made by the civil rights movement, racism continued to be rife in mid-century America. In her 'Letter to the Local Police' (published 1980), June Jordan, Jamaican-American bisexual civil rights activist and teacher, used satire and the metaphor of rambling roses to highlight exclusion within communities and the politics of power. Her poem starts 'Dear Sir', and verses 5–6 read as follows:

"I have encountered a regular profusion of certain/unidentified roses, growing to no discernible purpose,/and according to no perceptible control, approximately/one quarter mile west of the Northway, on the southern/side

To be specific, there are practically thousands of/the aforementioned abiding in perpetual near riot/of wild behavior, indiscriminate coloring, and only/the Good Lord Himself can say what diverse soliciting, /of promiscuous cross-fertilization"[14]

Opposite above
191. Balenciaga, cocktail dress with matching jacket, Paris, *c*.1963.
Silk lace and silk satin
The Museum at FIT, New York
The Museum at FIT, 2013.43.4.
Gift of Jo Pulvermacher

Opposite below
192. Valentino couture, plush rose-print top and trousers, Paris, 1979.
Printed cotton and silk velour
The Museum at FIT, New York
The Museum at FIT, 84.40.10.
Gift of Diana Vreeland

Right
193. Hiram Maristany,
Young Man with Roses, 1971.
Gelatin silver print
Smithsonian American Art Museum, Washington D.C.
Smithsonian American Art Museum.
Museum purchase through the Smithsonian Latino Initiatives Pool, Smithsonian Latino Center © 1971 Hiram Maristany

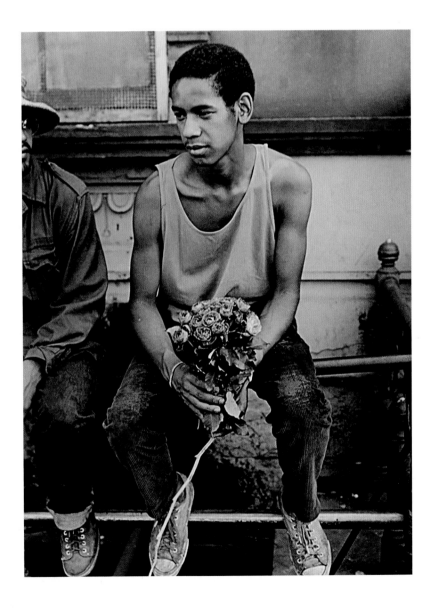

The new youth market in the Western world could shop at boutiques, some of which were opened by art school-trained fashion designers and offered relatively cheap, fun fashion. Disposability became a buzzword in this era, and between 1966 and 1968 there was a trend, particularly in North America, for 'paper' dresses (which were, in fact, made from various bonded fibres) that could be worn just two or three times. Many were brightly coloured and featured abstracted floral, striped, spotted and psychedelic designs, similar to those produced for fashion textiles. American graphic artist Harry Gordon exploited the flat surface planes (the dresses were, necessarily, simple A-line mini shift styles) and paper-like material to design a series of five 'walking-art' poster dresses in 1968. His black-and-white screen-printed designs, taken from blown-up photographs, included the 'Mystic Eye', 'Giant Rocket', 'Pussy Cat', 'Hand' and 'Rose' (fig.194).

From the 1960s, the artificial flower industries fell into steep decline: faux roses did not feed into space-age trends, hippy styles (which favoured wild flowers as an anti-war expression, not garden roses), unisex, punk, 1980s minimalism or '90s deconstructivism. However, there remained a small but continuous demand from milliners, even though far fewer women wore hats, and for luxurious eveningwear, bridal dress, corsages and boutonnières. Paris designers who made lavish use of silk roses included Christian Dior, Guy Laroche, Hubert de Givenchy, Pierre Balmain, Jacques Fath, Emanuel Ungaro, Thierry Mugler (fig.204), Valentino, Nina Ricci and Christian Lacroix. Yves Saint Laurent's scanty bridal outfit, presented at the finale of his Spring/Summer 1999 ready-to-wear show, comprised two garlands of pink silk roses with leaves, made by Paris firm Maison Lemarié (see fig.198). Lemarié worked with feathers until 1946, when André Lemarié joined the company and introduced flowers. In 1996, the firm became a Chanel Métier d'Art, one of a group of haute couture artisanal workshops safeguarded by the house in order to preserve specialist skills.

From the 1980s, handbags became major fashion news. Lulu Guinness introduced a range of stylish flower bucket bags, including the 'Rose Basket' (1993, fig.199). The designer states, 'This design came about as I always wished I could carry my vase of roses around with me and smell the sublime scent they gave off.'[15] She purchased the roses from Dulken & Derrick based in New York and also ordered flowers from Steyer-Kunstblumen in Germany.

London-based milliner Stephen Jones, who established his label in 1980, introduced a new attitude to hat-wearing with his stylish, sometimes radical, and supremely well-crafted headwear, which captured the attention of a new, young and edgy fashion and subcultural clientele, both male and female. He stated that, 'For me flowers are dangerous, because they are such an obvious hat trim, so I tend to use them very sparingly. I love this "Rose Royce"

[fig.195] because it creates a rose in an abstract way. Having said all that, I do want some of my ashes to be sprayed in Queen Mary's rose garden in Regent's Park, because it's one of my favourite places.'[16] When Jones does utilise silk roses, they are made within his atelier. Jones has collaborated with Raf Simons, Lanvin and Balenciaga and has designed millinery for Dior since 1996.

Opposite
194. Harry Gordon, 'Rose' dress,
USA and London, 1968.
Screen-printed rayon-nylon mix
The Museum at FIT, New York
This dress was worn and gifted to FIT
by the American actress and model
Ruth Ford, who, in the 1930s, was a
client of Charles James. She also wore
some of Schiaparelli's most daring,
surreal designs, including the 1938
'Skeleton' dress – a collaboration
with Salvador Dalí.
The Museum at FIT, 86.136.7.
Gift of Ruth Ford

Left
195. Stephen Jones, 'Rose Royce'
spiralled top hat, 'Contours'
collection, Autumn/Winter 1996.
Velvet and satin
Styling by Mattias Karlsson and patent
cotton jacket by Lutz Huelle.
Ben Toms for Luncheon

Below left
196. Halston, 'American Beauty'
evening dress, 'Resort' collection,
New York, 1980.
Organza
The Museum at FIT, New York
The French hybrid rose 'Mme
Ferdinand Janin' was bred by Henri
Lédéchaux in 1875, and renamed
'American Beauty' when it was
imported to America, becoming a
national favourite.

Below right
197. Liberty Studio, 'Carline', 1994.
Printed silk
This top-selling design is part of
the Liberty classic (as opposed to
seasonally changing) range.
Courtesy Liberty Fabric Ltd.

Popstar George O'Dowd – 'Boy George', lead singer of Culture Club – who was among Stephen Jones's clients, has worn screen-printed, rose-patterned apparel designed by Sue Clowes, who juxtaposed large red roses with aeroplanes or religious imagery. Multi-patterned fabrics with roses were also a signature of the Kenzo label, designed by Kenzo Takada. In London, flower-printed cottons were introduced for men by cutting-edge designers Paul Smith, who also made flower-printed boxer shorts and swimwear, and Scott Crolla. London department store Liberty produce fine, flower-printed cottons called 'Tana Lawn' (introduced from c.1918); these, along with their lustrous silks (fig.197), have remained world-famous bestsellers, purchased by designers and home dressmakers.

By the 1980s, roses featured prominently in scores of international collections for men and women. In New York, designers of these collections included Halston (fig.196) and Betsey Johnson. Vivienne Westwood does not often incorporate roses into her designs, but her Spring/Summer 1991 London collection, which referenced eighteenth-century tailored menswear, featured the flower (fig.201).

In Paris, Jean Paul Gaultier designed sheer, tattoo-effect tops that included rose patterns, and sent male models for his Autumn/ Winter 1998 collection down the catwalk, each with a long-stemmed fresh red rose clenched between his teeth. In 1986, Levi Strauss & Co. held a charity benefit with the Downtown branch of Barney's department store in New York to raise money for,

and awareness about, the devastating effects of AIDS: fashion designers and artists, the latter including Andy Warhol and Jean-Michel Basquiat, up-cycled items of Levi's denim. Kenzo re-presented a man's denim jacket as a two-piece: a jacket with puffed sleeves and micro-mini skirt embellished with a vibrant design of sequinned roses (fig.200).

By the late 1980s, the mantle of fashion's floriculturist could fairly be said to have passed to Dries Van Noten; one of the radical 'Antwerp Six' designers, his collections brim with flower-decorated textiles and fabric treatments. He has shown in Paris since 1993; for his Spring/Summer 1993 show he attached multiple and multicoloured long-stemmed fresh roses to cream-coloured jackets and sweaters modelled by men and women. Ann Demeulemeester, another of the Antwerp Six, often utilises a black rose graphic.

Roses were expressed at their most visionary by Rei Kawakubo for Comme des Garçons and John Galliano, who variously suggested the flower by twisting, knotting and otherwise manipulating tailoring and dressmaking materials into rose-like forms; these are techniques the designers have continued to exploit into the twenty-first century. The title of Fashion's Rosarian, however, I hand to Alexander McQueen, whose extraordinary creativity was fuelled primarily by the rose's visceral associations and historical contexts: with blood and battle, dark romance, death and decay (fig.202). His work is explored further in 'The Twenty-First Century: Roses and Cement'.

Opposite left
198. Yves Saint Laurent,
Silk bridal ensemble, Paris,
Spring/Summer 1999.
The Museum at FIT, New York
Modelled by Laetitia Casta, the
ensemble comprised two garlands of
silk roses and leaves made by Lemarié,
with matching bracelet and anklet.
The Museum at FIT, 91.185.2.
Gift of Ms Chris Roger

Opposite right
199. Lulu Guinness,
'Rose Basket' bag, UK, 1993.
Silk satin with silk velvet roses
The Museum at FIT, New York
The Museum at FIT, 2019.61.1.
Gift of Lulu Guinness

Below left
200. Kenzo, repurposed Levis
Strauss & Co. jacket,
Paris and New York, 1986.
Denim with appliqué and sequins
The Museum at FIT, New York
The Museum at FIT, 90.5.4.
Gift of Betsey Johnson

Below right
201. Vivienne Westwood collection
with eighteenth-century menswear
influences and rose decoration,
London, Spring/Summer 1991.
The Museum at FIT, New York
The Museum at FIT, 86.151.1. Gift of
Mr and Mrs Peter Bernstein

Above left
202. Alexander McQueen, trouser
suit embroidered with pink roses
on the jacket, 'Dante' collection,
London, Autumn/Winter 1996.
Acetate and nylon satin with spandex
The Museum at FIT, New York
The Museum at FIT, 2016.110.1.
Museum purchase

Above right
203. Shaun Leane for Alexander
McQueen, silver rose-thorn
jewellery, 'Dante' collection,
London, Autumn/Winter 1996.
FirstView

Opposite
204. Thierry Mugler, haute couture
evening dress, Paris, France, 1994.
Rose-patterned Chantilly lace
over silk
The Museum at FIT, New York
The Museum at FIT, 2016.114.2.
Museum purchase

CHAPTER VIII

SCENT

···

'THE INWARD FRAGRANCE OF EACH OTHER'S HEART'

MAIRI MACKENZIE

...

Parting they seem'd to tread upon the air,
Twin roses by the zephyr blown apart
Only to meet again more close, and share
The inward fragrance of each other's heart.

...

John Keats, 'Isabella: Or, The Pot of Basil', 1818[1]

One does not need to be a perfume connoisseur to recognise the scent of a rose. Its liberal use in modern perfumery, cosmetics, toiletries and the household goods of everyday life has familiarised us with its characteristics, and made the rose a part of our olfactory language. This ubiquity belies, however, the exalted status of the rose and its perfume across many cultures. Throughout history, rose perfumes have been variously used to anoint royalty, cleanse heretics, symbolise Gods, express virginity, cure ailments and flavour celebratory food, but this correlation between the scent, beauty and divinity is not fixed. Rose perfumes have also signified immorality, subversion and death. However, even though the myths, uses, beliefs and connotations associated with the rose are varied, shifting and at times contradictory, they demonstrate the tension that exists between the phenomenological and the culturally constructed in our olfactory preferences, as well as in our persistent, if volatile, relationship with the rose and its perfume.

For the ancient Greeks, roses were bound up with deities and infused their mythology. Aphrodite, the goddess of love, beauty and fertility, was said to smell sweetly of rose, as was Eros. In Homer's *Iliad* (8th century BCE), Aphrodite anoints Hector's body with 'sweet, ambrosial' rose balm, so as to protect him from Achilles's dogs.[2] Greek botanist Theophrastus documented the use of rose oil in perfumery, medicine, food and domestic settings, noting that, 'if one has regard to the virtues of the perfumes in question, one may well be surprised at what happens in the case of rose-perfume: — though it is lighter and less

powerful than any other, if one has first been scented with it, it destroys the odour of the others.'[3] While the Greeks adored the rose, and its scent, it was usually worn as part of an olfactory wardrobe.[4]

Ancient Romans, however, were consumed with thoughts of roses; 'pushing the flower to the limits of debauchery', they used the petals and perfume in all manner of ceremonial, medical, sexual, social, cultural and aesthetic contexts.[5] They used rose perfumes and waters to bathe in; to scent public arenas; to infuse social occasions, from elaborate dinners to orgies; to ward off foul odours and disease; to garland themselves; as a means of keeping cool and abating hangovers; and to flavour their food and wine. The grandest expressions of rose-philia saw the emperor Nero install pipes under plates so that dinner guests could be spritzed between courses; and he once showered guests in so many rose petals that one of them smothered to death. The scent of roses was not confined to special occasions or the upper classes: roses were a part of everyday life, albeit it on a more modest scale, scenting homes, food and even domestic animals.[6]

As the Roman Empire waned, so too did extravagant and dissolute indulgence in perfumes. The Christian West took a very dim view of the licentious behaviour linked with scent, connecting it with pagan idolatry. However, they later unshackled the rose from Roman debauchery and found new meanings for the flower in Christian rituals. The beads of the rosary were, it has been claimed, originally made of 165 rolled and blackened rose leaves;

the symbol of the Virgin Mary was the white rose; rose garlands were worn by priests on feast days; and, in the fight against heresy, forced fumigation was sometimes undertaken with rose and rosemary (as well as the more usual brimstone and sulphur). The 'odour of sanctity', a sweet perfume exhaled by saints upon their death, came to be symbolic of purity and sanctity in the Catholic Church: claims were made in the nineteenth century that St Thérèse of Lisieux gave off a strong scent of roses as she passed. Similarly, Padre Pio has been linked with the smell of roses since his stigmata of 1918 (see also p.39).[7]

The links between the white rose, the Virgin Mary, and the odour of sanctity persist and have been used as a device in literature to symbolise the struggle between purity and the forbidden, in particular, as identified by Laura Frost, in the work of modernist author James Joyce.[8] The protagonist in *A Portrait of the Artist as a Young Man* (1916), Stephen Dedalus, attempts to discipline and mortify his senses – in particular, his sense of smell – to bring his 'unruly body into line' with the will of the Catholic church.[9] The white rose and its scent become emblematic of this struggle for sanctity.[10] However, his sense of smell consistently betrays his endeavours, drawn as he is to the putrid and the bodily. Following a dramatic confession, Stephen kneels in the corner of the nave, where 'his prayers ascended to heaven from his purified heart like perfume streaming upwards from a heart of white rose.'[11] However Stephen still cannot deny himself the smells of the carnal and the animal, and 'reconciles himself to finding pleasure in, what the church would consider an unholy stench, emanating from human bodies, their excreta. In rejecting the pure smell of the white rose, Joyce inverts the sanctity of the flower, and performs an "olfactory revolt" – via Stephen – against Catholic indoctrination.'[12]

In Islam, olfactory codes were also used to separate the sacred from the profane, with bodies of martyrs linked to sweet smells, and those of infidels to a foul stench.[13] In contrast with the puritanical Christian attitude to perfume, genuine pleasure was taken in sweet smells, in particular that of the rose. In turn, it was said by the thirteenth-century Turkish poet and Sufi mystic Yunus Emre that the rose would sigh 'Allah, Allah!' upon being smelled.[14]

The Persian Empire, as noted by many 'dazzled' visitors, was resplendent with roses, the quality of which was far in excess of their European or Indian counterparts. Persian rose water was prized around the world. They had an active perfume industry from the ninth century, which was still thriving at the end of the 1600s, when visiting German traveller and physician Engelbert Kaempfer noted, 'even as the roses in Persia are produced in greater abundance and with finer perfume than those in any other country, so also do those of this particular district in the vicinity of Shiraz, excel in profusion and in fragrance.'[15]

Rosa centifolia

Rosier à cent feuilles

205. Pierre-Joseph Redouté, *Rosa centifolia: Rosier à cent feuilles* Watercolour
Only two species of rose are regularly used in modern perfumery: the *Rosa x centifolia* (pictured here) and *Rosa x damascena* (particularly the damask rose *Kazanlik* of Bulgaria). In 2015 it was announced that the perfumer Francois Kurkdjian and the breeder Fabien Ducher had been working on the cultivation of a new perfume rose named 'Nevarte'.

206. Ibn Sīnā (Avicenna),
nineteenth century.
Print
Ibn Sīnā (c.980–1037) – known in
Europe by his latinised name, Avicenna
– was a Persian polymath and one
of the most important philosophers
and physicians of the pre-modern
period. Ibn Sīnā is often credited with
pioneering the art of steam distillation
to extract the aromatic properties of
plants and flowers, in particular the
rose, from which it was claimed that
he produced the first attar (although
there is now evidence that this was
done much earlier by another Persian
physician, al-Rizi, of c.854–925.)
(Dugan 2011, p.48; Potter 2011, p. 345)
Heritage Images/Contributor/
Getty Images

Fittingly, one of the most celebrated works of Persian literature is a poem named 'Gulistan' ('The Rose Garden'), an ode to the rose by the poet Saadi.[16]

The advances in distillation made by Persian scholar Ibn Sīnā (fig.206), although beneficial to the perfume industry, were actually prompted by the medical and therapeutic benefits of the rose – theories regarding which had been in circulation since ancient Rome and Greece and on which Ibn Sīnā sought to build. Theophrastus considered 'rose-perfume to be excellent for the ears', and Pliny the Elder detailed 32 ailments that the rose could salve, including stomach aches, womb disorders, bowel conditions and insomnia. Amongst the ancient Greeks, Pedanius Dioscorides was hugely important as a pioneer of medical botany, with the rose essential to the remedies detailed in his *De Materia Medica*, said to be the most influential book on herbal pharmacology ever written.[17]

In medieval Europe, rose water was adopted in the fight against the recurring plagues that struck every few years until the end of the seventeenth century. Treated like a hand cleanser, rose water was used, in vain, alongside pomanders, vinegars and other aromatics, to prevent the spread of disease.[18] Elsewhere, rose water was breaking away from its therapeutic uses to become an aesthetic indulgence, used to rinse one's mouth in the French courts or, as detailed in the eighteenth-century novels of Nicolas-Edme Restif (Restif De La Bretonne), to 'ceaselessly [refresh] ... feet and private parts'.[19]

And, far removed from its origins as an exotic aromatic beyond the ken of English chemists, 'by the end of the sixteenth century ... rosewater, was retroactively imagined as a fully English commodity.'[20] This love of rose water and rose essence, particularly in the courts of Henry VIII and Elizabeth I of England, is detailed in Holly Dugan's *The Ephemeral History of Perfume* (2011).

Perfume is not simply a means of enhancing, or masking, our bodily odours; it also operates as a carrier of social mores, particularly in relation to the moral standing of women. The shortcomings of women who wear strong scents has been a recurring theme in medical discourse, particularly throughout the nineteenth century, when the public were warned that, 'The charm of perfumes, the search for "base sensations", symptoms of a "soft, lax" education, increased nervous irritability, led to "feminism", and encouraged debauchery.'[21] While previous cultures had developed codes that held certain smells to be undesirable or improper, the Victorians made the most explicit attempt to codify and inhibit our unruly sense of smell, in what Alison Booth calls 'civilization, as narrated from the habitus of the nineteenth century bourgeois.'[22]

Below left
207. M. V. Dhurandhar, *A Mughal-Style Rose Water Sprinkler*, 1909.
Gouache, 29 x 11cm
Wellcome Collection, London
Rose-water sprinklers, or *gulab pash*, have been in use in the Indian subcontinent since the Mughal period (1526–1857). The first of the Mughal rulers, Babur, is credited with the development of beautiful flower gardens across his empire, but the rose was his particular passion. Rose sprinklers were used to welcome guests, and also during religious and courtly rituals.
Wellcome Collection, London

Below right
208. Women taking roses to make rose water with its petals (folio 93r), *Tacuinum Sanitatis*, fourteenth century.
The *Tacuinum Sanitatis* were health handbooks, popular in Europe from the fourteenth century. They were based upon the eleventh-century treatise on wellbeing by Ibn Butlân of Baghdad, which recommended a life in balance with nature.
PHAS/Contributor/Getty Images

Simple floral perfumes became the new feminine ideal and the perfumers of the nineteenth century attended to these strictures. Rose – along with jasmine, orange blossom, acacia, violet and tuberose – was, according to the London-based perfumer Eugene Rimmel, acceptable. Meanwhile, the Parisian perfumers Debay declared that they had 'banished strong and intoxicating odors that are harmful to the nerves ... and offer only innocent perfumes.'[23]

Twentieth-century articles on perfume in women's magazines often resort to didactic typology, asking their readers what kind of woman they are and, in turn, what kind of perfume would she wear? In these articles, that which was founded in mythology and calcified in nineteenth-century stereotypes is peddled as a guide to finding one's signature scent. In a 1925 issue of *Vogue*, for example, the readers are asked,

...

'What type of women wears rose?', to which the answer comes, 'the woman who draws people to her because of the wholesomeness she radiates.'

...

Vogue, May 1925[24]

By extension, we understand from a young age the relationship between certain types of roses, wholesomeness and appealing beauty. To this end, Mary Pickford, the Hollywood actress, took what seemed like a logical step when, as a child, she ate a rose, hoping that 'the beauty, and the colour and the perfume would somehow get inside me'.[25] I, as a teenage perfume salesgirl in small-town Scotland, was so familiar with these connotations that, by the age of 15, I felt able to identify a person's ideal scent by using my own rudimentary questionnaire.

Modern rose-based perfumes are almost always marketed as being feminine.[26] However, men have always used and enjoyed rose scents. Theophrastus noted that rose perfume was best suited to men.[27] During the reign of Henry VIII in England, the Tudor king capitalised on 'a profound agricultural and technological happenstance': the domestication of the damask rose (*Rosa x damascena*) and the arrival of methods to extract its powerful essence. This 'olfactory breakthrough', and the king's wearing of the strong rose scent, argues Holly Dugan, 'greatly amplified his regal presence at court, just as incense defined the invisible power of transubstantiation in the Catholic Mass'.[28] Napoléon Bonaparte was also well known for his love of scent, and even as he entered his most arduous campaigns, 'he took time his time to choose rose- or violet-scented lotions gloves, and other finery.'[29] The periods in which men were viewed as most foolish for wearing scent have coincided with periods when scent was viewed more generally as an extravagance.[30]

Top
209. Helen Keller smelling a rose, 1900.
At 19 months old, Helen Keller lost her sight and hearing due to illness, and for the rest of life became attuned to the power of and interplay between the senses. Keller considered her sense of smell especially important, describing it as 'a potent wizard that transports us across a thousand miles and all the years we have lived' but noted that 'for some inexplicable reason the sense of smell does not hold the high position it deserves among its sisters. There is something of the fallen angel about it.' (Keller 2013, p.33)
Bettmann/Contributor/Getty Images

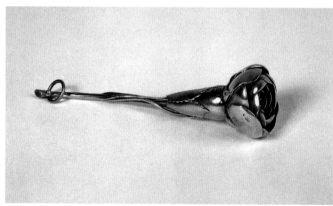

Above
210. Pomander in the form of a rose, Mid-nineteenth century.
Gold
Wellcome Collection, London
Pomanders are small containers filled with scented substances, popular from the late Middle Ages, which were worn to counteract bad smells and to serve as a prophylactic against disease. In keeping with the Victorian love of simple florals, this example takes the form of a stylised rose.
Wellcome Collection, London

12 Pages   **12 Pages**

Le Petit Journal

illustré

HEBDOMADAIRE
61, rue Lafayette, Paris

PRIX : 0 fr. 30
12 Juin 1921

La Récolte des Roses en Bulgarie

Des jeunes filles et des femmes aux costumes pittoresques cueillent ces fleurs merveilleuses dont on fera l'essence parfumée.

Previous spread
211. Bulgarian women picking
roses for the perfume industry,
illustration for *Le Petit Journal Illustré*,
12 June 1921.
Private collection
The *otto* or *attar* of rose produced in
the Kazanlik region of modern Bulgaria
is considered amongst the finest in
the world. It is extracted via distillation
from the *Rosa x damascena* grown
in the region and produces an oil that
has been described as 'warm, deep-
floral, slightly spicy and immensely
rich, truly reminiscent of red roses,
often with nuances in the spicy and
honey like notes.' (Industry chemist
quoted in Potter 2010, p.358)
Leemage/Contributor/Getty Images

Right
212. Charles Courtney Curran,
The Perfume of Roses, 1902.
Oil on canvas, 74.3 x 59.2cm
Smithsonian American Art
Museum, Washington D.C.
Even though we cannot smell the
roses in this painting, we can infer
the experience of the scent via
what Christina Bradstreet identifies
as the semiotics of smell. She
suggests that, 'Curran specifically
intended the soft-tinted lighting
diffused throughout these works
to "suggest the idea of perfume"
and the scented realm within which
the fairies dwell.' She suggests that
there are a number of ways in which
representations of women smelling
flowers can be interpreted; the tilt of
the bloom, distance between nose
and flower, posture, facial expression,
open or closed eyes and context all
contribute to the reading of the image.
(Bradstreet 2019)
Smithsonian American Art Museum

However, even in these moments, the perfume of rose has found a way into the masculine aesthetic. In Victorian Britain, this could be via a buttonhole, or in snuff – sometimes scented with rose oil. The prime minister Benjamin Disraeli (in office 1868; 1874–80) was known to be 'passionately fond of flowers' and noted in his diary that a gift of roses had 'a perfume so exquisite [without whose] latter charm the rarest and the fairest flowers have little spell for me'.[31] *Vogue* magazine, in an article from August 1907, 'The Well Dressed Man', advised on a recipe for a 'delicious perfume and tonic after the bath': 'cover a pint of rose petals with a quart of alcohol, add two grains of musk and bottle. Let stand for a week, then pour off the extract and bottle it. Use for a rub after the bath.'[32]

A beautiful illustration of the tension between the feminine and the masculine rose is expressed in the poetry of Michael Field (a pseudonym used by Katharine Harris Bradley and her niece Edith Emma Cooper). In 'The Grand Mogul' (1894), the death of a rose is described in triumphant and masculine terms, linking the flower with notes that no one would have thought to find in a poem by a Victorian woman. Catherine Maxwell's analysis of this verse states that 'The Grand Mogul' 'forges an identity of masculine command and authority fused with an underlying feminine desire, pleasure, and imaginative inspiration, this is echoed in a ghostly smell-signature, an emancipated fragrance of rose with masculine notes of tobacco, leather, brass ... that is left lingering at the poem's close.'[33]

The smell of roses is not to everyone's taste. In spite of, or perhaps because of, its ubiquity, there are those who find rose perfumes repellent, as is neatly summed up by E. B. White:

...

Madam reeking of the rose,
Red of hair and pearl of earring,
I came not to try my nose,
I was there to try my hearing.
Lost on me the whole darn concert.

...

E. B. White, 'To a Perfumed Lady at the Concert', 1932[34]

Also, because perfume, as a tool of adornment, *is* fashion, and not just an adjunct to the business of fashion, fragrant liquids are subject to the same vagaries as clothing, hairstyles and other forms of modish accoutrements. In December 1930, the British edition of *Vogue* instructs that if you 'say to a woman, "My dear, what a heavenly perfume! Just like a rose," she won't thank you in the least.' The writer goes on to reassure us that it is okay if roses are part of a perfume but only 'so long as nobody could be quite certain they were there.'[35]

Sometimes the reactions to rose perfume are more visceral than fickle, the blame being placed at the door of the devil. At the 1630s demon possession trials in Loudun, a small town in France, it was claimed that 'the odour of musk roses brought on hysterical attacks among the victims and their exorcists to the vast delights of assembled spectators.'[36] In a more modern tale, 2001 saw a Detroit radio DJ successfully sue her employer, Infinity Broadcasting, after exposure in the workplace to the rose-heavy perfume, *Trésor*, caused her to 'lose her voice, to miss work, to depend heavily on medication and ... her doctor warned that extended exposure to the fragrance could end in her death.'[37]

Aversion to the rose's sweet scent can also be prompted by perversion or rebellion. Reacting against 'the nineteenth century repression of smell', which relegated the sense of smell to the concern of the savage, 'the acknowledgment of smell and its complex, dark and sensual effect' can be seen in the work of Charles Baudelaire, Oscar Wilde and Joris-Karl Huysmans (see also chapter IV).[38] Huysmans' novel *À Rebours* ('Against Nature', first published in 1884) articulates this revulsion for the scent of roses and other 'bourgeois blooms' via the protagonist, the duc Jean Floressas des Esseintes – a man whose 'love of flowers had rid itself of residuum, its lees had been clarified, so to speak, and purified'.[39] Unsurprisingly, the rose comes in for harsh criticism, singled out as one of the 'pretentious, conventional, stupid flowers', the type 'whose proper place is in pots concealed inside porcelain vases painted by nice young ladies'.[40]

While many uses of the rose and its perfume detailed in this chapter are now a distant memory, their semiotic imprint has persisted.[41] The rose as a cultural text is a complex matter, and modernity – with its related development of perfume as industry, economy and culture – has not been able to drive out the myths that surround the rose and perfumes more generally. Instead, contemporary rose-based perfumes, and the ways in which they are advertised, are just as contradictory and fanciful as their predecessors, painting the wearers as either temptresses or ingénues. The 1761 treatise on perfume *Le Parfumeur royal* intimated we were about to enter a period of perfumes enjoyed purely for pleasure, yet this era has never fully come to pass and now, as ever, we remain subject to the rich signification of rose and its sweet scent.[42]

Above left
213. Jacques Boyer, workshop where roses are sorted out for the perfume industry, Grasse, France, c.1900.
Photograph
Originally a centre for leather tanning and, later, perfumed gloves, Grasse is now a source of the flowers, aromatics and raw materials required to sustain and develop the perfume industry in France. By the end of the nineteenth century, an estimated six tons of flowers, including roses, were being processed through the town annually (Stamelman 2006, p.96).
Boyer/Contributor/Getty Images

Below left
214. Julio Donoso, two Berber men packing rose petals during the rose harvest, Dades Valley, Morocco, 1989.
Photograph
The village of El Kelaa M'Gouna, in Morocco's 'Valley of Roses', marks its harvest of Rosa x damascena with an annual rose festival. This is a three-day event that celebrates all aspects of the rose, from its cultivation through to its use in cosmetics, toiletries and food. Festivities culminate in the crowning of a Rose Queen, who reigns over the year's scented crop.

Below left
215. *Les Parfums de Rosine*, catalogue,
early 1920s.
Founded by the couturier Paul Poiret
in 1911, Les Parfums de Rosine was
a stand-alone perfume, toiletry
and cosmetics company – the first
established by a fashion designer.
Although not all fragrances produced
under this house were based on the
rose, the flower was an important
ingredient in many of their scents and
also a recurring visual motif.
Image courtesy of Fashion Institute of
Technology | SUNY, FIT Library Unit
of Special Collections and College
Archives

Below right
216. *Outlook*,
Avon campaign magazine, 1972.
The cover and opening pages of this
in-house marketing pamphlet are
dedicated to the launch of Avon's
latest perfume. It reads, 'Roses, Roses
is romance … the rush of a blush to
the cheek of a woman who thinks
one rose is the most romantic gesture
a man can make … the caress of
dew-touched petals in the bath of
Cleopatra, a young Egyptian Queen.'
Courtesy of New Avon and Hagley
Museum and Library

UNE ROSE

. . . .

Une Rose by Edouard Fléchier is an exemplary modern rose perfume. It is a vivid, earthy and 'complete' rose, taking in the petals, the stem and the earth. The scent pairs a new Turkish rose absolute, extracted by molecular distillation by the laboratories of Mane, and wine dregs (a pairing redolent of Roman banquets and the poetry of Edmund Gosse), with a base note of truffle accord (a blend of two or more fragrances, creating a new and unique odour).[1] Monsieur Malle explains:

Perfumer Edouard Fléchier received a challenge from a cooking magazine called La Truffe to reproduce the odor of a Perigord truffle 'by nose' while stripping away its garlicky smell.[2] He did that by jotting down raw materials on paper, like an artist making a sketch. He suggested that it could be an interesting base note. This dark, woodsy, animal-like mix was best suited to masculine fragrances, but a paradoxical idea arose of pairing it with the most feminine of notes: the rose.

Une Rose is one of three rose-dominant perfumes produced by Editions de Parfums Frédéric Malle (EDPFM), the others being *Portrait of a Lady* and *Lipstick Rose*. When asked how he would characterise the rose contained in each perfume and how – if at all – they relate to one another, M. Malle responded:

The rose plays significant roles in each perfume, but to different ends. Portrait of a Lady is a rose Oriental. The base notes are the key elements, they generate the character: patchouli, frankincense, musk, sandalwood. Damascena roses produce Turkish rose absolute and essence. It's sourced from IFF-LMR in Isparta Turkey. The absolute smells sweet, sensual, almost honeyed, and the essence smells fresher and petal-like. Dominique Ropion [the perfumer] adds blackcurrant and clove to rose – these facets are native to some roses and contribute to the rosy effect. Its character is voluptuous and deep. For Lipstick Rose, rose is in an accord that is reminiscent of the smell of lipstick (rose, iris, raspberry and vanilla). It's set against violet and aldehydes for a soft, vintage Hollywood glamour. The rose effect is tender, soft and powdered.[3]

Notes

[1] Maxwell 2017 discusses the 'olfactory language of Romanticism' and the relationship between wine and roses in 'Perfume' by Edmund Gosse, as well as the links of that to the work of John Keats and Percy Bysshe Shelley. She explains, 'scent that provokes dreams and wine that inspires poetry or reverie are thus Romantic precursors for the poet's "thoughts and fancies mingled with perfume."'(p.58); Mane, founded in 1946 by Victor Mane, is a flavour and perfume laboratory based in Le Bar-sur-Loup, just outside Grasse, in southeastern France.

[2] Edouard Fléchier is one of the most successful perfumers of his generation, responsible for some outstanding scents. These include *Davidoff* (Davidoff, 1984); *Poison* (Dior, 1985); *Parfum de Peau* (Montana, 1986); *C'est la Vie* (Christian Lacroix, 1990); *Acqua di Gio* (Giorgio Armani, 1995); and *Michael Kors* (Michael Kors, 2000). *Une Rose* is his very first rose-dominant perfume.

[3] M. Frédéric Malle, correspondence with author, 20 November 2019. Note that the naturally occurring aroma chemicals found in rose are also found in rose geranium, which was the catalyst for *Portrait of a Lady*, inspired as it was by the rosy part of *Geranium pour Monsieur*, another EDPFM perfume.

Above left
217. *Une Rose*, launched 2003, Edouard Fléchier for Editions de Parfums Frédéric Malle
© Frédéric Malle

Above right
218. Konstantin Kakanias, *Une Rose* illustration, for Editions de Parfums Frédéric Malle, c.2011.
© Konstantin Kakanias for Editions de Parfums Frédéric Malle

FOCUS STUDY

OSMOTHÈQUE

The Osmothèque (from the Greek *osme*, meaning smell or scent) is the world's largest repository of perfumes. Founded in 1990 by Jean Kerléo, it is based in Versailles and is responsible for the authentication, documentation, preservation and reproduction of more than 4,000 perfumes, 400 of which are no longer in production. It is also entitled to hold the formula of every new perfume marketed in France. Their charter prevents them from ever using any of these formulas for commercial use.[1]

These scents demonstrate the myriad possibilities available to the perfumer when formulating scents with rose as a central ingredient. Rose perfume, in the commercial sector, is rarely made solely of rose, and blended perfumes, which are often referred to in symphonic or linguistic terms, can be harmonious or discordant, depending on the marriage of notes.[2] All perfumes detailed here are blends, drawing upon a range of notes in their composition.

Le Parfum Idéal, Paul Parquet for Houbigant, 1896[3]
Houbigant, founded in 1775, launched this perfume at the 1900 Exposition Universelle in Paris. As it is a composition of many floral notes – including rose and ylang-ylang – and some recently discovered synthetic ingredients, it was difficult to pinpoint exactly which flower it smelled of. This, however, was the point, the aim being to create the perfect flower, though not one that was recognisable in nature.

La Rose Jacqueminot, François Coty for Coty, 1906
It is said that Coty dropped a bottle of this on the counter of the Grand Magasin de Louvre, a Parisian department store, and created a furore when women wishing to buy it ran towards him (it is most likely that those women were his wife's friends). He was promptly asked to leave the premises. By that evening, however, he had an order for 12 bottles. Named after a breed of cabbage rose, it was an innovative soliflore (focused on a single flower) that used the synthetic materials rhodinol and ionone.

La Rose France, Paul Parquet for Houbigant, 1911
Another rose perfume based around synthetic notes. The posters for this fragrance were designed by Alphonse Mucha and the original bottle was made by crystal manufacturer Baccarat.

N'Aimez Que Moi, Ernest Daltroff for Caron, 1916
The name translates as 'don't love anyone but me', and it was conceived as an olfactory forget-me-not – a means of remembering soldiers who were fighting in the First World War. The Bulgarian rose is balanced with sandalwood, violets and resinous oakmoss notes.

Rose Brumaire, René Duval for Volnay, 1922
Presented in a bottle designed by André Jolivet and made by René Lalique et Cie., this perfume features Bulgarian rose and jasmine with powdery and woody notes.

Joy, Henri Alméras for Jean Patou, 1930
Renowned for being one of the most expensive perfumes in
the world – it is said that 28 dozen roses and 10,600 jasmine
flowers go into every ounce of *extrait* – launching *Joy* one year
after the Wall Street Crash and the onset of the Great Depression
was a bold move. The *Rose de Mai* (*centifolia*) does not take centre
stage but provides a robust core, supporting the jasmine and
ylang-ylang alongside aldehydes, which dominate the opening.

Nahema, Jean-Paul Guerlain for Guerlain, 1979
Described as an homage to the rose, this is not a quiet expression
of the flower. As the name suggests and the advertisement
(fig.219) underlines, *Nahema* is named for the story of
'Scheherezade' in *One Thousand and One Nights*. The scent is
sweet, full and luscious, with notes of ripe peaches (which add
a honeyed quality to the composition), hyacinth, ylang-ylang,
jasmine, sandalwood, balsamic and green notes. *Nahema* was not
a success when launched but is today considered an exemplar
of rose Oriental perfumes. This fragrance is also noteworthy
because it was the first time that a large amount of α-damascone
(an element derived from *Rosa x damascena*) was used in a
commercial perfume.[4]

Paris, Sophia Grojsman for Yves Saint Laurent, 1983
Created by Sophia Grojsman, a perfumer renowned for her rose-
based creations, *Paris* is a bright, vibrant and youthful iteration
of the flower. It contains *Rose de Mai* (*centifolia*) and *Rosa x
damascena*, alongside violet, mimosa and bergamot, with a
base of sandalwood.

Trésor, Sophia Grojsman for Lancôme, 1990
Another Grojsman creation, *Trésor*, meaning treasure, is a big
perfume, with notes of peaches and apricots alongside the rose,
giving it a powdery, full character. Amber and sandalwood notes
in the base give it a balsamic, sweet quality. This is one of the
biggest-selling perfumes of all time.

Sa Majeste la Rose, Christopher Sheldrake for Serge Lutens, 2000
Opens with green, fresh notes, bright fresh Moroccan rose and
geranium but develops into a slightly honeyed rose, with spice.

Notes
[1] The author visited the
Osmothèque in February 2019 to
sample some of the most important
rose perfumes of the modern era.
With thanks to the guide for this,
Isabelle Reynaud-Chazot, board
member in charge of relations with
researchers and academics at the
Osmothèque.

[2] The notion of a perfume organ
was conceived by Septimus Piesse,
a chemist and perfumer who, along
with Eugene Rimmel, was central
to the development of perfumes
and their retail in Victorian Britain.
Convinced that certain notes in
perfume could work harmoniously
as scented chords, he developed the
idea for an organ that would blend
balanced scents. See Maxwell 2017,
pp.23–5.

[3] When a year is given, the
scent tested is the same as the
composition from that year and
not a modern version.

[4] Yudov, 'Her Majesty The Rose'.

219. Advertisement for *Nahema*,
Vogue, December 1820.
© Guerlain

CHAPTER IX

THE TWENTY-FIRST CENTURY

...

ROSES AND CONCRETE

AMY DE LA HAYE

...

Did you hear about the rose that grew
from a crack in the concrete?
Proving nature's law is wrong it
learned to walk with out having feet.
Funny it seems, but by keeping its dreams,
it learned to breathe fresh air.
Long live the rose that grew from concrete
when no one else ever cared.

...

Tupac Shakur, *The Rose That Grew From Concrete*, 1991
(New York: Pocket Books)

In the twenty-first century, the exquisite fragility and paradoxical
beauty of the rose, with its potential to rupture and draw blood,
has been harnessed by an unprecedentedly politicised global
fashion industry. Fashion has a broad reach and the people
working within its creative industries, their social media followers
and consumers have contributed actively to the growing awareness
about racism; sexism; LGBTQI rights; body, skin (colour and
pigmentation) and age diversity; mental health issues; labour
rights; and global sustainability. The rose remains an immensely
popular tattoo design; a number of women who have had
mastectomies have had roses inked where their breasts once
were. This chapter examines fashionable rose expression within
these critical contexts and explores the extraordinary innovation,
imagination and craft skills of designers who have drawn upon
the rose to flatter, adorn and provoke. The vogue for fresh roses
on the catwalk is referenced and parallels are drawn between
farmed roses and fast fashion. A handful of artisanal flower
makers continue to serve the demand for roses and rosebud
decoration on hats, luxury eveningwear and wedding gowns, and
their work is touched upon.

In the new millennium, multiple trends continue to coexist
and are available at all market levels within an industry that has
become ever more global in its reach and representation and
which produces collections with rose-inspired designs year-round.

Opposite
220. Marc Jacobs, New York,
Spring/Summer 2019.
Adwoa Aboah, also a mental health
campaigner, wears a blouse with self-
fabric rose detail in the season's 'blush
pink', from a collection characterised
by fabric rose clusters.
Pietro D'Aprano/Contributor/
Getty Images

Left
221. Jun Takahashi for Undercover,
'But Beautiful II' collection, Paris,
Spring/Summer 2005.
Modelled by Victoria (Nathalie), with
flower headdress by Katsuya Kamo.
FirstView

ALEXANDER MCQUEEN: FASHION'S ROSARION

Lee Alexander McQueen continued to interpreted roses in the contexts of deathliness and decay in the new century, but he also found joy and respite in nature, especially in his own Sussex garden (see also figs 202, 203). For the 'Sarabande' collection of Spring/Summer 2007 (fig.223) – his most floriate collection – masses of dusty mauve tea roses, lilacs and hydrangeas, rendered in silk within McQueen's atelier, sprung from décolletages and the fluted cuffs of hourglass silhouettes with padded hips. His 'Flower dress' was seemingly composed entirely of rose petals, each one individually ombré-dyed in various tea-rose, calico, powder-pink, nude and burgundy tints. For the show finale, the designer crafted a skeletal dress structure which, one hour before the show, was packed with fresh roses and hydrangeas supplied by florists Phyllida Holbeach and Heinz-Josef Brüls; subsequently, it was meticulously reassembled, flower by flower, and rendered in silk by the German firm Blumen. The models wore striking faux-rose headdresses designed by Philip Treacy: these were executed in nature's mixed colours, on long stems, and in solid black, trailing round the neck and on to the bra-top bodices (fig.222).

In an infinitely romantic gesture, when his close friend and patron Isabella Blow took her own life, McQueen entwined their names forever by selecting a pink floribunda rose and naming it 'Alexander's Issie' (introduced by Dickson Nurseries Ltd in 2009). Tragically, in 2010, he followed in her wake; his signature twinning of the skull and rose, which symbolised the fragility of life in vanitas paintings, was all too prescient. Sarah Burton, a core team member, for whom the rose also holds special meaning, took the creative helm after the designer's death. She recalls:

...

The rose represented something in my childhood in the North, as well. I remembered the Rose Queen ceremony from being very young, the summer street procession through villages. Young children were chosen to be the rosebud, and an older girl became the rose queen every year. The rosebud would wear white and the rose queen would wear pink or red, so there was a symbolism of colour. [1]

...

Above
222. Philip Treacy, black-silk rose headdress, for Alexander McQueen, 'Sarabande' collection, Paris, Spring/Summer 2007.
Treacy started collaborating with McQueen from 1992, following an introduction by Isabella Blow. He often worked closely with stylist Katy England to realise McQueen's vision, here modelled by Rachel Alexander.
FirstView

Opposite
223. Alexander McQueen, 'Flower Cage' dress, 'Sarabande' collection, Paris, Spring/Summer 2007.
Fresh dusty-mauve roses and hydrangea flowers seemingly cascade down the dress modelled by Tanya Dziahileva to form a bulbous hemline.
FirstView

Visits by Burton and her team to the informal gardens planted
at Sissinghurst Castle, Kent, and to Great Dixter, East Sussex,
inspired coarse hessian garments decorated with bold, pink
woollen tapestry roses with saddle-leather trim for Spring/
Summer 2018. A modernistic, fractured blue rose print was
developed for Autumn/Winter 2019, and strikingly original
accessories have included the rose knuckleduster clutch (fig.226).
Variations of dresses that resemble rose formations run through
the collections. With reference to the red rose dress for Autumn/
Winter 2019 (fig.227), Burton describes how she wanted it 'to
grow from the body ... almost as if the pleats and the fabric
embrace the female form on the bust and around the waist, to
halo the face ... I wanted her to be a rose, but not a rose that
dominated her.'[2] From the same collection, tailored trouser suits
decorated with clusters of petals on the sleeves and peplums were
described as 'Hybrid Roses'.

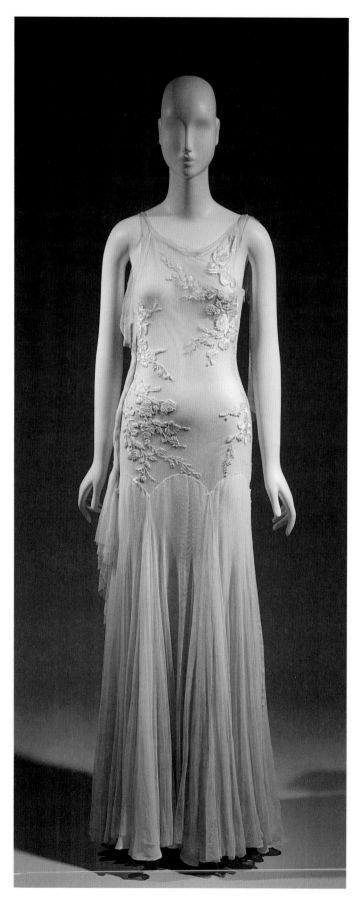

Right and detail opposite
224. Alexander McQueen,
dress with embroidered rose design,
from 'Sarabande' collection, shown
Paris, Spring/Summer 2007.
Silk
The Museum at FIT, New York
The Museum at FIT, 2018.6.1.
Gift of Julie Macklowe

225. Alexander McQueen,
Silk bolero and ballerina dress
embroidered with ruby-red
stones, 'Girl Who Lived in a Tree'
collection, Paris, Autumn/Winter
2008.
This bolero is one of the most
structurally complex rose-themed
garments McQueen envisaged and
has inspired many subsequent designs
by the house.
FirstView

226. Alexander McQueen,
designed by Sarah Burton, 'Roses'
knuckleduster hard-shell evening
bag, 2017.
Silk satin with lace overlay, lacquered
metal knuckleduster handle
The Museum at FIT, New York
The Museum at FIT, 2019.20.1.
Museum purchase

227. Alexander McQueen, designed
by Sarah Burton, 'Red Rose' dress,
Paris, Autumn/Winter 2019.
Silk taffeta
The fashion house refers to this colour
as 'lust red'. The dress, modelled by
Anok Yai, was created by working
directly onto the body, skilfully pin-
tucking and gathering whorls of fabric
to create volume.
FirstView

Above left
228. Rodarte, rose headdresses,
New York, Spring/Summer 2019.
This show was presented in a New
York graveyard in the pouring rain.
Leading hair stylist Odile Gilbert
created unique hair ornaments,
combining fresh roses with Art Deco-
style crowns, some veiled in tulle,
for each model.
Slaven Vlasic/Stringer/Getty Images

Above right
229. Obi Somto, Adebayo Oke-
Lawal for Orange Culture, 'The
Feeling' collection, Lagos, Autumn/
Winter 2013.
This ensemble, modelled by Yemi
Torresma, was styled by Terence
Sambo, who started the 'One Nigerian
Boy' fashion blog for Africans to
engage with African fashion and style.
With permission from Orange Culture

ROSES AND IDENTITY

As growing numbers of people refuse to identify according to the binary male/female, and a broader spectrum of identities is recognised, there has come to be a demand for all types of fashion apparel to be offered in sizes to accommodate all bodies. Gender-neutral fashion is also becoming a significant growth area. Lagos-based designer Adebayo Oke-Lawal, working as Orange Culture, challenges traditional visions of manhood in Nigeria, a country where same-sex relationships are still criminalised. Using local textiles, he combines elements of African and Western clothing styles prescribed male or female. Today, Nigeria and Kenya are among the world's largest exporters of roses although, as Jack Goody explores in his study *The Culture of Flowers* (1993), historically there was a general absence of flowers within African culture. Roses do not appear in Orange Culture's designs, but fresh roses were used strategically to style 'The Feeling' collection (Autumn/Winter 2013; fig.229). Oke-Lawal advised, 'The roses on the head are crowns of vulnerability! It is about exploring the idea that men need to be more in touch with their emotional side and the beauty that comes with that!'[3] For Spring/Summer 2019, Lagos Fashion Design Week presented collections that were overtly political, engaging with issues of gender fluidity, identity and heritage.

Nihl is the New York label of Neil Grotzinger, whose gender-neutral collections convey the designer's preoccupations with masculinity, queerness, power and sensuality. Having worked as a womenswear embroidery designer for Marc Jacobs, Prabal Gurung and Diane von Furstenberg, Grotzinger formed his own label to combine conventionally feminine fabrics and treatments with American hyper-masculine clothing tropes. With reference to the look shown overleaf (fig.231), he stated:

I consistently try to find aspects of the gendered grey area within my designs. I find the rose to be a very empowering flower, it is symbolic of strength and virility. When I was making the pants out of embroidered guipure, I applied a very rushed, haphazard treatment to the surface to juxtapose the intricacy of the floral, which was why I chose to spray paint over the most delicate parts of each flower. My process often involves finding something which is either iconically masculine or iconically feminine, and then negating its gendered qualities to a certain degree so that it no longer sits within either sphere.[4]

Prabal Gurung studied and started his fashion career working in Delhi; when he moved to New York he studied and worked with Donna Karan, Cynthia Rowley and Bill Blass. He presented his own-label collection in New York in February 2009. His references are truly wide-ranging, drawing upon his childhood in Nepal, cross-cultural clothing traditions and migration, modern sportswear and haute couture glamour. He is preoccupied with feminism and powerful women. He regularly includes designs

featuring roses in his collections (fig.230) and, for the finale of his Autumn/Winter 2018 show, the models walked in silence, each carrying the white rose that has become the symbol of the #MeToo movement.

Simone Rocha, whose label was established in 2010, finds the term 'feminist' divisive (fig.250). As a woman designing for women, she creates ethereal feminine clothing, sometimes with a dark undercurrent. She often uses rose designs and sheer fabrics, which she presents in the context of female empowerment. For Autumn/Winter 2019, 1950s-style bra tops and glimpses of silk bloomers were teamed with rose-design chiné weaves.

Ashish Gupta highlights issues surrounding multiculturalism and inclusivity (he has made his work accessible by designing 10 collections for the high-street chain Topshop). He creates gender-fluid collections that combine Indian fabrics and ornamentation with western clothing silhouettes. The designer's 'Bollywood Bloodbath' collection (Spring/Summer 2017) celebrated Indian culture in the UK and included sheer silk shirts embroidered with red roses and sportswear-style sequinned trousers in azure blue with a design of red roses (fig.233). To protest the British exit from the EU, Gupta took his catwalk bow wearing a T-shirt emblazoned with the word 'IMMIGRANT'.

Charles Jeffrey's LOVERBOY brand encompasses a fashion label and cult club night; his runway shows have revived the performativity of London's 1980s queer club scene. The 'Rose scribble' print (fig.234) is characteristic of his use of bold colour and graphic designs, but the rose is not a signature. A member of his press team stated, 'I have to say I don't believe the rose holds a special symbolism for Charles – the design is purely an aesthetic choice in this case, an illustration of his which turned out beautifully and became a print.'[5]

In the twenty-first century, and most notably since the 2010s, trans activists have drawn attention to the lives and rights of trans people. Writer Trace Peterson drew upon the symbolism of roses and violets (the latter associated with everlasting affection, death and rebirth) in 'Exclusively on Venus' (2016), a trans woman's love poem to a cis woman: 'Roses are born this way/ violets have a lesbian streak ... Roses are trochaic/violets have their original plumbing.'[6] The first openly trans model to be signed by top American agency IMG was Hari Nef – signed as the face of Gucci's perfume *Bloom* (launched May 2017) and cast under the creative direction of Alessandro Michele. Michele has led a trend for maximalism, in which seemingly mismatched colours, patterns – including masses of roses – textures and layers are combined. Michele has done much to popularise the vogue for roses by decorating evening gowns, rocker-style leather jackets, bags, shoes and louche smoking slippers, and – most accessible of all – iron-on embroidered patches, with the flower.

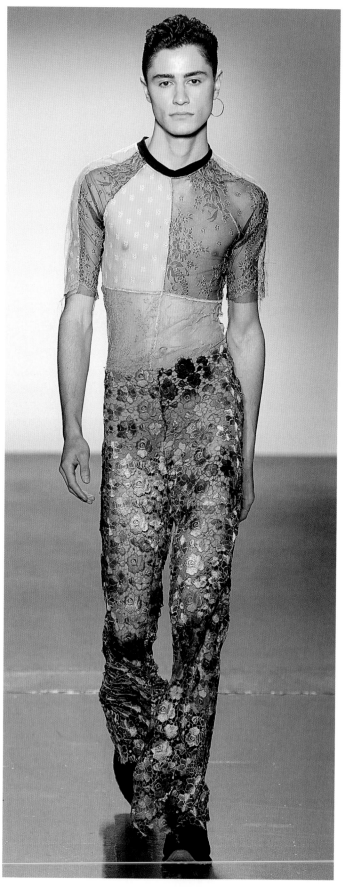

Opposite left
230. Prabal Gurung, sportswear
with tie-dye and Pop Art rose-print
designs, accessorised with a rose-
decorated bag, New York,
Spring/Summer 2020.
FirstView

Opposite right
231. Nihl, lace and embroidered
outfit, New York,
Autumn/Winter 2019.
Five different Chantilly laces are
patchworked together to create the
shape of a raglan-sleeved racer's
top; the trousers are made from
embroidered guipure lace. The rose
appliqués were cut from the lace itself
and spray-painted in shades of black,
bronze and silver.
FirstView

Right
232. Jourdan Dunn dressed as a rose
at the Met Gala to mark the opening
of the exhibition *Camp*, New York,
2019.
This costume was designed by Zac
Posen, an avid gardener. It comprises
21 unique, overlapping, glossy plastic
petals (each weighing 450 grams) that
were 3D printed using a precision
stereolithographic process (SLA) by
Protolabs. The dress frame, fitted
to Dunn's body, was 3D printed in
titanium using electric beam melting
(EBM) technology at GE Additive.
It took 700 hours of print time and
400 hours to construct.
Kevin Tachman/MG19/Contributor/
Getty Images

RADICAL ROSES

Textiles and fashion designer Richard Quinn encases the body – head, face, torso, arms, legs and feet – in fabrics digitally printed with rose designs, in muted and livid colourways (fig.236). Roses supplant black rubber and leather in fetish-style face masks to create a modern rendition of the tradition of engulfment by roses (see fig.41). The juxtaposition is provocative, even surreal, yet the designer's perspective on the rose is near universal: 'The rose is the most traditional and timeless icon of the floral themes in fashion and the arts, as well as being an inherently British symbol. I have used it in all of my collections – it is as romantic as it is dark and mysterious.'[7] Quinn works in partnership with cutting-edge textiles printing firm Epson; he can customise his orders and – exceptionally – opens his studio to other designers. For Spring/Summer 2020, Quinn designed a black, short-sleeved shirt with a brilliant blue-rose print. In spite of the real-world introduction of genetically engineered blue roses, the flower retains its otherworldly and decadent allure.

Jun Takahashi started his Undercover label selling deconstructed leather jackets and denim jeans. While retaining his edgy, street-style savvy clientele, and with the invaluable mentorship of Rei Kawakubo, he staged Undercover's first Paris show in October 2002. Takahashi's garments, and the way they are styled, can be simultaneously macabre and sublimely beautiful, or sometimes pagan or humorous. The designer exploits the ambiguity and richness of the rose. For Spring/Summer 2005, his 'But Beautiful ll' collection of surreal, doll-like ensembles, with models walking in deconstructed tailoring and lace slip dresses, with silk-flower headdresses made by Katsuya Kamo, was redolent of Salvador Dali's painting *Woman with a Head of Roses* (1935, see fig.172).

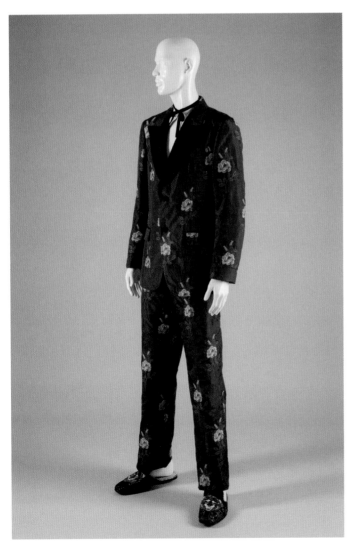

Opposite left
233. Ashish,
'Bollywood Bloodbath' collection,
London, Spring/Summer 2017.
Sportswear styles are combined
with ornate Indian fabrics and
embellishments. Here the model
carries a bunch of individually
cellophane-wrapped red roses.
FirstView

Opposite right
234. Charles Jeffrey ensemble,
London, Spring/Summer 2019.
This 'Rose-scribble' linen coat with
'puritan collar' is styled with a belt and
worn with matching trousers.
Image courtesy of Charles Jeffrey

Left
235. Gucci, designed by Alessandro
Michele, suit, shown Milan, Spring/
Summer 2017.
Embroidered silk
The Museum at FIT, New York
On the catwalk, this was worn with a
black-velvet bow choker and beaded
evening slippers. It was Michele's
last 'menswear' show; subsequent
collections – often androgyne –
have been presented without
gender distinctions.
The Museum at FIT, 2017.18.1.
Gift of Gucci

ROSES AND STREET STYLE

Roses are not a Raf Simons signature but, like Takahashi, the designer has featured them on garments including T-shirts with printed rose designs. For Spring/Summer 2014, his menswear jackets were styled with safety-pinned, fresh red rose corsages, and he has offered blue ceramic rose pendants and brooches. In 2003, he started a collaboration with art director and graphic designer Peter Saville, co-founder of Factory Records, reproducing his record cover graphics on apparel that has become as iconic in its own right as the original graphics. Most unusual and memorable is the record sleeve design for New Order's *Power, Corruption & Lies* (1983), for which Saville reproduced Henri Fantin-Latour's painting *A Basket of Roses* (1890), housed in London's National Gallery. It was a chance encounter that sparked the design decision, as Saville's girlfriend had bought the postcard and joked about him using it in his work. In their first collaboration, Simons applied the rose design to garments including fin-tailed parkas (fig.237), hooded sweatshirts and T-shirts.

Supreme, established by James Jebbia in 1994 in Soho, New York, quickly gained a cult following among skaters and those interested in streetwear. The brand became known for appropriating imagery from popular culture and incorporating it into designs, accompanied by the globally recognisable 'Supreme' box logo. For Autumn/Winter 2012, Supreme produced a range of sweaters knitted with a repeat rose pattern, and, in Autumn/Winter 2016, made thick fleece sweatshirts and Sherpa-style hats with a pattern of roses (fig.238). Supreme produce limited-quantity ranges that, when dropped (released), generate consumer frenzy, with items resold for many times the retail price.

In London, a brand called Aries (established by Sofia Prantera) started, like Supreme, as a skate shop. Prantera works closely with graphic designer Fergus Percell, who designed the cult Palace skateboard logo. For Spring/Summer 2019, Aries produced unisex Harrington jackets, bowling shirts (green printed on black, and black on pink), chinos (red on ecru ground), and skirts and shorts in cotton twill with an all-over 'techno pagan rose' print.

Some of the Paris haute couture houses have also introduced sportswear: for Spring/Summer 2014, Givenchy's rose-camouflage print was used on sweatshirts, T-shirts and backpacks, and the Valentino x Undercover collaboration for Autumn/Winter 2019 saw a design of chained red roses on trainers, T-shirts and metal-studded, high-heeled sandals.

Top
237. Raf Simons, parka with roses design, 'Closer' collection, New York, Autumn/Winter 2003.
© Fashion Museum Hasselt/ Kristof Vrancken

Above
238. Supreme, Sherpa cap with roses design, New York, Autumn/Winter 2016.
Fleece
The Museum at FIT, New York
The Museum at FIT, 2019.81.1.
Museum purchase

COMME DES GARÇONS:
'ROSES AND BLOOD'

In November 2014 – on the centenary of the start of the First
World War, and during the month in which peace was declared,
four devastating years later – Comme des Garçons presented the
'Roses and Blood' collection for Spring/Summer 2015 (fig.240);
it was one of Rei Kawakubo's most hauntingly beautiful and
disturbing to date. While the designer asserts that she does
not want to overtly convey ideas and frustrations about socio-
political issues within her work, her profound designs are widely
interpreted within political contexts, and for this collection she
uncharacteristically acknowledged references to political and
religious conflicts, war and blood.

With the exception of a few black-and-white painterly splashes,
fabrics and shiny resins were uniformly poppy/blood red.
Garment forms were inflated and sculptural – some padded and
almost intestinal in appearance – and tattered in places, with a
profusion of the designer's signature self-fabric rose and rosette
decorations, some cascading down trailing ribbons. In a very
different vein, for Autumn/Winter 2016, Kawakubo imagined
how punks might have looked had they lived in the eighteenth
century – another period of tumultuous change – and sourced
the finest silks woven with patterns of roses from Lyon to create
disrupted, armour-like silhouettes and hugely inflated flower-like
shapes in pink vinyl.

NOIR KEI NINOMIYA

Futuristic and fantastical, wild yet cultivated, Noir Kei Ninomiya's *fleurs animées* march in fashion's vanguard, expressing a new organic modernism. The formation of the striking garment shown here can be likened to a head-on view of an old garden rose (fig.243), with its irregularly clustered mass of petals, or even a single petal, which contains individual cells so loosely packed that air pockets form between them. However, the designer rebuffs any notion of fragility – floral or feminine. Ninomiya's fashion rose is subversive and armoured, in the manner of the somewhat surreal 'Habit de Bouquetiere' ('Attire of the flower seller'), from Nicolas ll de Larmessin's seventeeth-century engraving series of *Les costumes grotesques et les métiers* ('Costumes of the Trades'; fig.241). This outfit, in particular (fig.242), comprises a dress-like form in two pieces made from polyester organdie, padding and a sleeve with integral gloves made from a stretched satin woven from 68 per cent rayon, 30 per cent wool and 2 per cent polyurethane. Entirely conspicuous, yet masked for anonymity, the model dons insectile short black gloves that are integral to the sleeves, ankle socks and sturdy leather oxfords in order to stride through this world. This is candy floss-coloured fashionable flower personification at its most militant.

Ninomiya studied French literature at Aoyama University in Tokyo before enrolling to study fashion at the Royal Academy of Fine Arts Antwerp, but left once he had secured a job as pattern cutter for Comme des Garçons. In 2012, Rei Kawakubo proposed he create his own label under the Comme des Garçons umbrella. He made his Paris catwalk debut to present the Autumn/Winter

2018 collection, which, along with Spring/Summer 2019, was dedicated to floral themes. The Autumn/Winter 2019 collection, in particular, paid homage to a single flower – the rose. At this show, the scent from hundreds of fresh red roses – made into headdresses by Taka Nukui, working with flower artist and botanical sculptor Azuma Makoto – wafted through the space and the rose experience extended to the olfactory.

Ninomiya's garments are constructed from PVC, leather, organza and polyester, and these materials are laser-cut, pleated, manipulated, riveted, layered, linked and inter-linked, like molecules, on to a poppered faux-leather foundation. Structurally, their closest fashion precedent might be Paco Rabanne's late-1960s chain-mail dresses, although it is cult designers Jean Paul Gaultier and Thierry Mugler who are muses to Ninomiya. As the designer's trade name – 'Noir' – makes explicit, black is the mainstay of his collections. Shown alongside this model were biker styles and dress forms constructed from black PVC rosettes, joined by outward-facing shards of corset boning – protective prickles for the modern woman.

It is indeed rare that fashion takes new forms, and here the rose has inspired an extraordinary manifestation.

Above left
241. Nicolas ll de Larmessin,
'Habit de Bouquetiere', from *Les
costumes grotesques et les métiers*, 1675.
This flower seller is depicted wearing
the attributes of her trade: her bodice
is a flower bucket and the sleeves are
comprised of vases.
Bibliothèque nationale de France

Above middle
242. Noir Kei Ninomiya,
Rose ensemble with headdress of
fresh roses, Paris, Autumn/Winter
2019.
FirstView

Above right
243. *Centifolia muscosa* rose
(also known as 'Mrs William Paul').
Paul Starosta/Getty Images

FRESH ROSES AND SUSTAINABILITY

Over 500 years ago, with characteristic wisdom, William Shakespeare wrote:

…

At Christmas I no more desire a rose
Than wish a snow in May's new-fangled shows,
But like of each thing that in season grows.

…

William Shakespeare, *Love's Labour's Lost*, 1590s[8]

Today, cut roses can be enjoyed by the world's wealthiest communities 365 days a year, supplied by some of the world's poorest people working on plantations in Ecuador, Colombia, Kenya, Nigeria and Ethiopia. Like fast fashion (cheap apparel that is worn barely a handful of times), the rose has fallen victim to standardisation, suffering from the huge demand for bunched buds with straight stems at the expense of diversity. Some sectors of the industry exploit human labour, including child workers, and use hazardous chemicals. In 2003, the International Labor Rights Forum launched its 'Fairness in Flowers' campaign to improve working conditions and provide labelling to identify fair-traded roses. Since the late twentieth century, it is women who have become the major consumers of cut flowers, often buying them for themselves and as gifts for other women.[9]

As we have seen, the aesthetic and spirit of the rose has long fed fashion; in the late 2010s, the rose has literally been incorporated into fashion production, as discarded branches and stems are processed to create a silky, natural (100 per cent rose-fibre) yarn.

Above left
244. Alabama Chanin, jacket with reverse appliqué rose design, New York, 2000.
Cotton jersey
The Museum at FIT, New York
The rose is a signature motif used by American eco-company Alabama Chanin, used for ready-made fashion and D.I.Y sewing kits.
The Museum at FIT, 2016.108.1.
Gift of Nancy Gewirz

Above right
245. 100 per cent rose-fibre yarn developed by Ashleigh Chambers.
Image courtesy of Ashleigh Chambers

(Each autumn, bushes are cut down to make way for new growth but are not composted on the same farms to avoid the possible spread of disease.) Global sustainability and environmental damage have become a major preoccupation, especially among young people and students, who are striving to create innovative and responsible future strategies. At the time of writing, Ashleigh Chambers, a London College of Fashion student, has developed the concept for a biodegradable yarn that is fully sustainable by ensuring a local supply chain from British rose farm to spun yarn (fig.245).

Flowers are inherently ephemeral, but the central principle for sustainable fashion is to create products that consumers value and don't want to throw away. Alabama Chanin is a company that subscribes to the 'slow fashion' movement, creating intricately worked apparel that is made in fair-trade environments with minimal environmental impact (fig.244). Stella McCartney, who established her brand in 2001, has consistently refused to use leather or fur and also campaigns for more sustainable fashion solutions. The rose-printed stretch textiles she uses for her 'Adidas by Stella McCartney' sportswear collaboration are almost 70 per cent recycled.

ROSES ON THE CATWALK

For Autumn/Winter 2013, New York-based designer Thom Browne presented a sensational rose-themed tailored collection (fig.247). The surreal *mise en scène* for the presentation, choreographed by the designer, comprised a dead forest setting within which Thom Browne-clad male models wearing crowns of thorns (associated with mockery) were tied with red-ribbon straps to metal, hospital-style beds. Models with towering beehives and painted rosebud-red lips wandered dreamily through this setting. They wore red, grey and black-and-white tailored suits, dresses and coats in classic menswear wools; the silhouettes merged Dior's 'New Look' with American football uniforms. These were adorned with laser-cut, rose-design lace appliqué cellophane and faux roses with stand-away, trailing green stems. Thom Browne – along with Marc Jacobs, Oscar de la Renta and Ralph Lauren – is among the American fashion designer clients of fourth-generation, New York-based artificial flower-making firm M. & S. Schmalberg.

Erdem Moralioglu is known for his vibrant flower prints and embroideries. From the beginning, his collections have featured roses: from 2007's rose-patterned black lace and the rose-strewn silks and velvets of 2018, to the extravagant, overblown rose prints and embroidered appliqué roses of the 2020 Spring/Summer collections. The designer also applies rose decoration to tailoring: a suit for Autumn/Winter 2019 was liberally decorated with black-sequinned rose clusters (fig.246).

The rose is not a signature theme of Prada but, perhaps not surprisingly, the flower took centre stage in the collection 'Anatomy of Romance' for Autumn/Winter 2019 (fig.251). Miuccia Prada explored the oppositional forces – of beauty and danger, and the pain and joys of romance – for which the rose has, for so long, triumphantly stood. Silk satin and Pop Art-style painted roses and drooping silk artificial roses, in black and unnatural colours, decorated dresses, coats and separates, which were accessorised with leather combat boots. The show notes described 'The interplay between different dichotomies,

between dualities of materials and approaches, natural and man-made, [which] here convey a suggestion of two lovers meeting, two halves to one whole.' Large roses in neon pink with brilliant-blue lightning flashes adorned black knits; a huge bouquet of brilliant yellow, printed roses, supplemented with yellow silk roses, decorated an otherwise understated white coat; and sheer skirts and capes were made in black lace with a rose motif.

Azuma Makoto, Tokyo-based floral artist and botanical sculptor, transformed fashion presentation with his floral ice sculptures – huge blocks of ice encasing flowers – for Dries Van Noten's Spring/Summer 2017 show in Paris, a collection in which the designer foregrounded 'exotic and erotic' blooms. Over the course of his career, Van Noten has increasingly used roses in prints and embroidery. With reference to his Autumn/Winter 2019 collection, 'A rose is a rose is a rose' (fig.248), he stated that, 'The roses were literally from the garden. We made a small video to look at, but it was really the idea of having the right feel of strangeness ... Flowers can be sweet and romantic, but it had

to be a vision of roses from now, not from the past.'[10] On the juxtaposition of brilliant, colour-saturated rose prints and grey tailoring he added, 'For me, you have the masculine side and the extremely feminine side with the roses. The grey outfits were a balance between men and women.'[11] Roses shimmered on sheer, silvery-grey raincoats and were printed on to dresses as inflated, life-like graphics executed in unnatural colours.

Opposite left
248. Dries Van Noten,
'A rose is a rose is a rose' collection,
Paris, Autumn/Winter 2019.
This polo-neck dress with naturalistic print of long-stemmed roses is modelled by Aliet Sarah.
FirstView

Opposite right
249. Moschino, designed by Jeremy Scott, Rose bouquet dress, Milan, Spring/Summer 2018.
Paying homage to the founder's irreverent Pop Art and postmodern aesthetic, Jeremy Scott, creative director at Moschino, presented a collection of flower bouquet dresses, some ribbon-tied. This outfit features an elongated bunch of artificial red roses placed upside down, reversing the symbolic meanings of love, devotion and desire.
FirstView

Left
250. Simone Rocha,
Coat dress ensemble, London, Autumn/Winter 2019.
Printed silk taffeta and silk crystal 'wiggle crown' with beaded pumps
Rocha stated, 'I love the life of a rose, the bud blooming into the flower and then the final decay. The density and fragility, the intoxicating scent of a wild garden rose.' (Livio Damiano, email correspondence with author, 2019)
FirstView

Opposite
251. Prada, dress, 'Anatomy of
Romance' collection, Milan,
Autumn/Winter 2019.
Printed silk, with silk roses
FirstView

Below
252. Stephen Jones, 'Limo' panné
top hat with silk rose, 'Covent
Garden' collection, London,
Autumn/Winter 2008.
Velvet and silk
This collection was a tribute to the film
My Fair Lady (1965) about a flower
seller, played by Audrey Hepburn.
The trim was based on the buttonhole
worn by Professor Higgins, played by
Rex Harrison.
The Museum at FIT, 2020.3.1.
Museum purchase

In 2001, Marc Jacobs (artistic director at Louis Vuitton from 1997 to 2014) invited designer and artist Stephen Sprouse to design a graffiti graphic for 'LV'; the neon rose, Pop Art-cum-punk-aesthetic design was created at this time but was not put into production until 2009, in a collection that paid posthumous tribute to Sprouse (fig.253). The Yoon Ahn Ambush jewellery label, also interpreted roses through the lens of a punk aesthetic: in 2017 the range included a safety pin with rose charm and long-stemmed rose earrings in silver and gold, photographed on men and women. These were marketed as combining 'a repurposing and representation of two key symbols of classic American punk culture'.[12] Ahn was appointed head of Dior Homme's jewellery and made her debut at the Spring/Summer 2019 show, which was staged against a backdrop of a huge bank of fresh pink roses.

Below
253. Philipe Jumin,
Louis Vuitton x Stephen Sprouse, Monogram Roses Speedy 30 bag, USA, Spring/Summer 2009.
Canvas with day-glo-coloured graffiti design, leather handles
© Louis Vuitton/Photographed by Philippe Jumin

Opposite above
254. Rodarte, dress, New York, Spring/Summer 2017.
Organza, silk tulle and feathers
The Museum at FIT, New York
The Museum at FIT, 2007.13.1.
Museum purchase

Opposite below
255. Dior haute couture, designed by John Galliano, Cocktail dress, Paris, Autumn/Winter 2007.
Silk
Galliano suggests rose flowers by clustering fabric, a practice he introduced in the 1980s. Reinforcing the theme of this design, milliner Stephen Jones created the 'artist's palette' hat.
Alamy Stock photo

HAUTE COUTURE AND ARTIFICIAL ROSES

The most exquisite artificial roses continue to be crafted by Maison Legeron and Lemarié, who supply the haute couture houses and luxury brands. In the early 1970s, Bruno Légeron took over the firm his great-grandfather had acquired in 1880, when it was called Guth. In 2019, Légeron employed eight skilled flower makers. The firm makes silk roses and also works with fresh flowers. (When this author visited in May 2019, they were working on a huge order of fresh roses for Louis Vuitton.) Most of their orders are for roses, including black ones for funeral wear, and for camellias (for Chanel). Alexander McQueen both order and make roses in their own atelier and so does Stephen Jones, on the occasions he uses them, as for his 'Limo' hat (fig.252), which formed part of the 'Covent Garden' collection inspired by the film *My Fair Lady* (1965).

The Parisian haute couture industries remain the pinnacle of elite fashion luxury and serve a small, immensely wealthy global clientele of around 4,000 women. The coterie of houses includes Giorgio Armani Privé, Chanel, Dior, Jean Paul Gaultier, Givenchy, Iris Van Herpen, Georges Hobeika, Ziad Nakad, Elie Saab, Saint Laurent, Giambattista Valli, Valentino, Atelier Versace, Ralph & Russo, Vetements and revived houses Schiaparelli, Vionnet and Poiret. Roses remain perennially popular and are especially evident in collections by Dior, Givenchy, Valentino, Elie Saab and Giambattista Valli. Valli's lavish, romantic gowns are decorated with rose prints, pale pink on white. Silk roses decorate one shoulder on white ruffled and frilled gowns; and gauzy tulle headdresses in palest pink are topped with bright pink silk roses.

As creative director at Dior from 1996 to 2011, John Galliano drew on fashion-historical, as well as the house's own archival, references. His Autumn/Winter 2007 'Le Bal des Artistes' collection made reference to the lavish costume balls of the 1930s and the Neo-Romantic movement whose work he reveres; ensembles were inspired by and dedicated to fine artists, photographers and illustrators. A silk cocktail dress with an immense pink rose in a painted fabric clustered on one hip was dedicated to René Gruau, whose elegant, spare lines exemplified Dior's style (fig.255). 'Ligne Floral' for Autumn/Winter 2010 paid homage to Dior's love of flowers and included romantic, corseted evening gowns based on individual flowers, including a rose; the models wore tinted cellophane headdresses and had raffia-tied waists. In the show notes Galliano stated, 'I wanted to bring a bold new bloom into the salon and let the colour, texture and structure of flowers inspire a new beauty.'[13] Galliano took his catwalk bow costumed as a dandy beekeeper.

Pierpaolo Piccioli, creative director at Valentino, has upheld the founder's signature rose within his collections. Stating that, as a designer, it was his responsibility to reflect the times we live in, for the Spring/Summer 2019 haute couture collection, the designer reimagined Cecil Beaton's seminal 1948 photograph of a group of models wearing Charles James's elegant, sculptural evening gowns using models of colour. He also paid homage to the pioneering magazines *Ebony* and *Jet*. In a collection almost exclusively comprising evening gowns dedicated to a floral theme, Adut Akech, the face of Valentino, modelled a dramatic pink silk-satin rose ensemble comprising a headdress-cape with matching long skirt (fig.256). While uncompromisingly modern, it also evoked nineteenth-century flower personifications and Balenciaga's black rose dress, as photographed by Irving Penn in 1967.

Over the centuries, the rose – the most ravishingly beautiful and fragrant of flowers – has become entwined variously with myths and religions, stories of travel and migration, collecting, cross-cultural influences, gardening and interior decoration, politics and shifting perceptions of identity, status, beauty and transgression. During the twenty-first century, more than ever before, fashion creatives inspired by the flower and its associated narratives have utilised the rose – fresh, faux, and in manipulated fabric form – to adorn, provoke and protest. One of the world's oldest and most beloved of flowers has captured the zeitgeist.

256. Valentino haute couture,
designed by Pierpaolo Piccioli,
Rose dress, Paris,
Spring/Summer 2019.
Silk
Modelled by Adut Akech
FirstView

'IT WILL NEVER RAIN ROSES:

WHEN WE WANT TO HAVE MORE ROSES WE MUST PLANT MORE TREES'

GEORGE ELIOT, *THE SPANISH GYPSY*, 1868

Notes

Introduction

1. Eliot 1936, p.178.
2. Seward 1989 [1954], p.1.
3. Potter 2010, p.4.
4. This dating from Cortambert 2010 [1820], pp.x–xi.
5. Quoted in Potter 2010, p.19.
6. Potter 2010, p.21.
7. Ibid., p.20.
8. Many rose-growing countries stage annual festivals dedicated to the flower; these run from one or two days to three weeks and celebrate the rose's flowering, significance to local industries, its history and special applications. There are festivals in the UK, Republic of Ireland, France (Grasse, a perfume-producing capital), the Netherlands, Italy (Busalla, cuisine), Bulgaria, Greece (The Rhodes Medieval Rose Festival), Turkey, Iran (the Kashan Rose Water Festival), India and Pakistan. In the United States, the Portland (Oregon) Rose Festival has been staged since 1907; the festival in Tyler, Texas, has run since 1933.
9. Potter 2010, p.103.
10. Anon 1895, p.236.
11. Nick Knight, email correspondence with Charlotte Knight, 26 November 2019.

Chapter II

1. Zola 1970 [1875], p.122.
2. Deleuze and Guattari 1992, p.21.
3. Zola 1970 [1875], p.133.
4. See Lorris and Meun 1994.
5. Bataille 1993, p.11.
6. Ibid., p.12.
7. As part of his stage act, Max Miller would produce two joke books from the pockets of his floral suits: one white, with innocent jokes, the other blue, containing a selection of sexual verses, puns and one-liners. On asking his audience which they would prefer, Miller invariably received the answer - 'blue'!
8. Zola 1970 [1875], p.136.
9. Ibid., pp.300–301.
10. Deleuze and Guattari 1992, p.320.
11. William Shakespeare, *Henry VI, Part I*, Act 2 Scene 4, in *Norton Shakespeare* 1997, p.464.
12. Bataille 1993, p.12.
13. William Shakespeare's Sonnet 35, published in 1609, contains the lines 'Roses have thorns, and silver fountains mud,/ Clouds and eclipses stain both moon and sun,/ And loathsome canker lives in sweetest bud.' *Shakespeare's Sonnets* 1907, p.22. William Blake's poem 'The Sick Rose' of 1794 also uses the rose as a metaphor for carnal corruption and betrayal.
14. Dialogue from *A Matter of Life and Death*, dirs Michael Powell and Emeric Pressburger, 1946.
15. *Le Spectre de la Rose* was premiered in Monte Carlo as part of the 1911 Ballets Russes season. Based on a verse by Théophile Gautier, with a score by Carl Maria von Weber, the ballet was choreographed by Michel Fokine and designed by Léon Bakst.
16. Zola 1970 [1875], p.135.

17. Kipling 1887.
18. The blue pigmentation of other flowers is caused by delphinidin, which does not occur naturally in the rose. However, after years of research prompted by desire for the mythic blue rose, scientists have finally synthesised delphinidin and the first genetically engineered blue rose was produced in Colombia in 2006.
19. Bataille 1993, p.12.
20. Aragon 1974.
21. Zola 1970 [1875], p.302.

Chapter III

1. Cowper 1959, pp.312–13.
2. Smith 1799 [1738/56]), p.47.
3. Fearrington 2013, p.71.
4. McNeil 2010.
5. Buchmann 2015, p.153.
6. Old garden roses, also referred to as antique or heirloom roses, are types of roses cultivated prior to 1867, the year that the first hybrid tea rose was introduced.
7. Joyaux 2001, p.30. Translation author's own.
8. Printed cottons also featured many floral motifs, but that history is beyond the scope of this study. For an excellent introduction to floral motifs on printed cotton, see McNeil 2010.
9. Brown 1996, p.7.
10. Charmantier 2011, p.365.
11. Anishanslin 2016, p.89.
12. The surviving collection of Mary Delany's cut-paper flowers is housed at the British Museum, London.
13. Miller 2005, p.204.
14. Miller 2014, p.12.
15. Miller 1995, p.81.
16. Ibid.
17. Anishanslin 2016, p.36.
18. See Brown 1996. For a global study of the textile market during this time period, see Peck 2013.
19. Brown 1996, p.8.
20. Kraak 1998, p.842.
21. The collections of The Museum of London, the Museum of Fine Arts Boston, and the Albany County Historical Society (Wyoming) include dresses remade during the nineteenth century from eighteenth-century Spitalfields silks; undoubtedly there are other extant examples.
22. Kaiser 1996, p.1027.
23. Vigée-Lebrun 1986, p.40.
24. Quoted in Ribeiro 1995, p.53. Translation author's own.
25. Miller 2014, p.21.
26. Menkes 2002, p.6
27. Kleeck 1913, p.151.
28. Carr 1803.
29. Reilly 1989, p.15.
30. Potter 2010, p.160.
31. Vigée-Lebrun 1904, p.26.
32. Weber 2006, p.27.
33. Ribeiro 1984, p.118.
34. Cited in Waugh 1968, p.124.
35. Campan 1900.
36. Festa 2019, p.66.

37. Ribeiro 1984, p.113.
38. Walpole 1903, p.264.
39. Buss 1990, p.14.
40. Cited in Langlade 1913, p.47. *Correspondance Secrète* was a covert, weekly publication about French court life by Louis-François Métra that ran from 2 January 1775 to 7 March 1793. Its publication in Germany allowed it to bypass censorship.
41. Chrisman-Campbell 2015, p.100.
42. Sadako Takeda, Durland Spilker and Esguerra 2016, p.212.
43. Scheurer 1983, p.94.
44. Ibid.
45. Saint-Aubin 1983 [1770], p.49.
46. McNeil 2016, p.238.
47. J. J. Grandville's *Les Fleurs Animées* of 1867 remains one of the most famous books centered on this subject.
48. Langhorne 1804 [1771], pp.38–9.

Chapter IV

1. Naiman 2010, p.86.
2. Cooper 1978. See entry 'Rose'.
3. *The Oxford Classical Dictionary* 1970. See entry 'Rosalia'.
4. Cooper 1978.
5. Munn 1993, p.33.
6. Fisher 2011, p.22.
7. Ibid., p.28.
8. Munn 1993, p.33.
9. Mauriés 2002, p.48.
10. Evans 1953, p.149.
11. Gorewa et al. 1991, p.33.
12. Barten 1977.

Chapter V

1. Kleeck 1913, p.156.
2. *Artisans de l'élégance*, 1993
3. Lemercier 2007, p.199.
4. Ibid., p.198.
5. Boxer 1982, p.407.
6. *Millinery Trade Review*, May 1876, p.55.
7. Boxer 1982, p.412.
8. Ibid., pp.405–6.
9. Matthews David 2015, p.86 (quoting from 'Death from Arsenic', *The Times*, 20 October 1862).
10. Kleeck 1913, pp.153–4.
11. Ibid., p.154.
12. Ibid.
13. Ibid.
14. Ibid., p.156.
15. 'Royal and Sun Alliance Insurance Group', 1557–2007, London Metropolitan Archives, CLC/B/192.
16. Booth 1969 [1889], p.294.
17. Lord 1865, p.109.
18. Ibid., p.114.
19. Ibid., p.110.
20. Ibid., p.115.
21. Booth 1969 [1889], pp.303, 59.
22. Ibid., p.58.
23. Ibid., p.60.
24. Ibid., p.296.

25. Ibid., p.321.
26. Zola 2009 [1877], p.315.
27. Oakeshott 1903, p.129.
28. Ibid., pp.129–30.
29. Ibid., p.127.
30. Ibid., p.124.
31. Ibid., p.128.
32. Ibid., p.131.
33. I would like to thank curator Dr Miles Lambert, Platt Hall, Manchester Art Gallery. The hats referenced here are 1959: 262 and 1947: 4533 in that collection.
34. Lord 1865, p.119.
35. Ibid., p.119.
36. Ibid., p.43.
37. Kleeck 1913, p.13.
38. Ibid., p.20.
39. Wharton 2008.
40. Kleeck 1913, p.3.
41. Ibid., p.144.
42. Ibid., p.43.
43. Ibid., p.44.
44. Richards O'Hare 1904, p.2.
45. Kleeck 1913, p.90.
46. Ibid.

Chapter VI

1. Attributed to Richard Brinsley Sheridan in *Oxford Dictionary of Quotations* 1999, p.716.
2. [Attrib.] Cortambert 2010 [1820], pp.59–60. (Beverly Seaton's extensive research on semiology and the language of flowers has revealed this, and the author challenges the widespread belief that this book was written by Louise Cortambert.)
3. Cortambert 2010 [1820], pp.x–xi.
4. See Looby 1995. Looby offers alternative readings of floriculture with regards to race, racial eroticisation and sexuality, which is fascinating but does not directly relate to this floral discourse.
5. Beaujot 2012, p.77.
6. Ibid., pp.776; 65.
7. *Harper's Bazaar*, 24 June 1882, p.394.
8. Mayhew 1851, p.135.
9. Ibid., p.137.
10. Haweis 1878, pp.167–8.
11. *Harper's Bazaar*, 14 June 1884, p.242.
12. Cunnington and Lucas 1972, p.70.
13. *Harper's Bazaar*, 19 April 1884, p.370.
14. Veblen 1899.
15. 'Notes from Paris', *Millinery Trade Review*, June 1876, p.62.
16. *Harper's Bazaar*, 3 March 1877, p.138.
17. Hiner 2017, p.52.
18. Tennyson 1855.
19. Anon 1842, p.56.
20. Holt 1896 [1879], p.223.
21. Ibid., p.57.
22. Anon 1842, p.199.
23. Charles Baudelaire, 'The Ideal' [1857], lines 7–8 in Baudelaire 1952.
24. Algernon Swinburne, 'Our Lady of the Pain' [1866], verse 9, lines 3–4, in Swinburne 1866.
25. Huysmans 1956 [1884], p.83.

Chapter VII

1. Stein 1922.
2. Poiret 1931, p.26.
3. Beaton 1965, p.110.
4. Oppenheim 1911.
5. Proust 1981, p.807.
6. Vera Brittain, 'Perhaps', verse 3, Brittain 1918.
7. Kirke 1998, p.186.
8. *Devon & Exeter Gazette*, 2 December 1938, p.3, quoted in Taylor 2015, p.107.
9. Potter 2010, p.429.
10. Bataille 1993.
11. I thank Adam Philips and Judith Clark for providing this information.
12. Dior 1957, p.64.
13. Hiram Mirastany, exhibition note, *What Hiram Maristany Saw Through the Lens at El Barrio*, Smithsonian American Art Museum, 2017.
14. June Jordan, 'Letter to the Local Police', verses 5–6, in Jordan 1980.
15. Lulu Guinness, email correspondence with author, August 2019.
16. Annika Lievesley, email correspondence with author, Press & Communications Manager, Stephen Jones Millinery, 10 October 2019.

Chapter VIII

1. J. Keats, 'Isabella; or, The Pot of Basil. A Story from Boccaccio' (1818) in Strachan 2003, p.86.
2. Potter 2010, pp.18–28; Classen 1993, p.19.
3. Theophrastus 1926.
4. Classen, Howes and Synott 1994, p.17.
5. Potter 2010, pp.29–51.
6. For further reading on the Roman relationship with roses, and sources for the above, see Ackerman 1991, p.36; Classen 1993, pp.17–19; Lilja 1972; and Potter 2010, pp.29–51.
7. Ackerman 1991, pp.36–7; Classen 1993, pp.19–22; Potter 2010, pp.73–91; Harvey 2006.
8. Frost 2013.
9. Ibid., p.44.
10. Joyce again employs the device of the white rose in *Ulysses* to symbolise the devout and pure nature of Gerty. Ibid., p.49.
11. Ibid., p.44.
12. Aside from rejecting Catholic doctrine, Joyce is also subverting the sensual imperatives of smell-averse philosophers and thinkers including Plato, Immanuel Kant and Sigmund Freud. See also Douglas 1966.
13. D. Cook, *Martyrdom in Islam* (Cambridge University Press, 2007), quoted in Reinarz 2014, p.38.
14. Ackerman 1991, p.36.
15. Potter 2010, pp.248–50, 346–7. Vita-Sackville West visited Persia in 1926 and also wrote of their roses; ibid., p.252.
16. The complete poem can be found at http://classics.mit.edu/Sadi/gulistan.html (accessed 10 January 2019). There is much evidence of vibrant perfume cultures in other ancient and pre-modern societies but the focus of this essay is upon the rose and not perfume more generally, so they have been omitted.
17. Theophrastus on the medicinal properties of certain perfumes (Theophrastus 1926); Potter 2010 on Pliny, pp.35–6; Potter 2010 on Dioscordes, pp.293–7.
18. Classen, Howes and Synott 1994, pp.58–62.
19. Corbin 1996, p.75; the London perfumery Floris still produces a rose mouthwash.
20. Dugan 2011, p.49.
21. Ibid., p.184.
22. Booth 2000, p.6.
23. Corbin 1996, p.184.
24. Strakosh 1925. In a more recent edition of *Vogue* (September 2019) these other 'types of roses' are touched upon when Chloe Sevigny discusses her new rose-based perfume and describes it as a 'city rose'; Singer 2019, pp.320–21.
25. Mary Pickford in Dyhouse 2011, p.53.
26. There are many examples of scents marketed as masculine or unisex that contain rose – for example *Aramis 900* (Aramis, 1973), *Égoiste* (Chanel, 1990), *Twill Rose* (Les Parfums de Rosine, 2006), *Noir de Noir* (Tom Ford, 2007), *Amouage* (Lyric Man, 2008) and *Declaration d'Un Soir* (Cartier, 2012) – but the rose content is underplayed or not mentioned
27. Theophrastus 1926.
28. Dugan 2011, p.45.
29. Ackerman 1991, p.62.
30. Classen, Howes and Synott 1994, p.83.
31. William Kuhn, *The Politics of Pleasure: A Portrait of Benjamin Disraeli* (London: Free Press, 2006), quoted in Maxwell 2017, pp.43–4.
32. 'The Well Dressed Man', p.212.
33. Maxwell 2017, pp.232–9. Maxwell points out that this poem anticipated the forthcoming use of tobacco and leather notes in perfumes of the early twentieth century including Caron's *Tabac Blond* (1919), Molinard's *Habanita* (1921), Chanel's *Cuir de Russie* (1925) and Robert Piguet's *Bandit* (1944).
34. E. B. White, 'To a Perfumed Lady at the Concert' [1932], in Remnick and Finder 2001.
35. 'French Fragrance' 1930.
36. Reinarz 2014, p.124.
37. Stamelman 2006, p.25.
38. Booth 2000, p.6.
39. This new-found discernment reflects a similar shift in Des Esseintes's literary and artistic preferences, towards the work of only 'subtle and tormented minds'.
40. Huysmans 2005 [1884], p.82.
41. Fashion houses and perfumers still draw upon and reconfigure the contradictory connotations of the rose in the development and marketing of their perfumes today.
42. From *Le Parfumeur royal* (1761) in Corbin 1996, p.76.

Chapter IX

1. 'Roses' 2019.
2. Ibid.
3. Adebayo Oke-Lawal, email correspondence with author, 29 October 2019.
4. Neil Grotzinger, email correspondence with author, 31 October 2019.
5. Katy Guyan for Charles Jeffrey, email correspondence with Cicely Rose-Proctor, 10 August 2019.
6. Peterson 2016, verses 7 and 10.
7. Jessica Sherman for Richard Quinn, email correspondence with author, 5 December 2019.
8. *Love's Labour's Lost*, Act 1, Scene 1, lines 105–107, in *Norton Shakespeare* 1997, p.743.
9. Goody 1993, p.313.
10. Menkes 2019.
11. Ibid.
12 /017.shop.ca.
13. Taylor 2019, p.36.

Bibliography

A

Abrevaya Stein, Sarah, *Plumes: Ostrich Feathers, Jews, and a Lost World of Global Commerce* (New Haven and London: Yale University Press, 2008).

Ackerman, Diane, *A Natural History of the Senses* (New York: Vintage Books, 1991).

Anishanslin, Zara, *Portrait of a Woman in Silk: Hidden Histories of the British Atlantic World* (New Haven, CT, and London: Yale University Press, 2016).

Anon, *A Manual of Politeness* (Philadelphia, PA: J. B. Lippincott & Co., 1842).

Anon, *Vocabula Amatoria: A French–English Glossary of Words, Phrases and Allusions Occurring in the Works of Rabelais, Voltaire, Molière, Rousseau, Béranag, Zola and Others* (London: privately printed in 1895).

Aragon, Louis, 'I'll Reinvent the Rose for You', in *The Poetry of Surrealism: An Anthology*, Michael Benedikt (ed.) (New York: Little Brown & Co., 1974).

Artisans de l'élégance, exh. cat. (Paris: RMN, 1993).

B

Barten, Sigrid, *René Lalique: Schmuck und Objets d'Art 1890–1910* (Munich: Prestel, 1977).

Bataille, Georges, 'The Language of Flowers' (1929), in Georges Bataille, *Visions of Excess: Selected Writings 1927–1939*, ed. by Allan Stoekl, trans. by Allan Stoekl with Carl R. Lovitt and Donald M. Leslie, Jr (Minneapolis, MN: University of Minnesota Press, 1993), pp.10–14.

Baudelaire, Charles, *Poems of Baudelaire: A Translation of Les Fleurs du mal by Roy Campbell* (London: Harvill Press, 1952).

Beaton, Cecil, *The Years Between: Diaries, 1939–44* (London: Weidenfeld & Nicolson, 1965).

Beaujot, Ariel, *Victorian Fashion Acessories* (London: Bloomsbury, 2012).

Booth, Alison, 'The Scent of a Narrative: Rank Discourse in "Flush" and "Written on the Body"', *Narrative*, vol.8, no.1 (January 2000), pp.3–22.

Booth, Charles, *The Life and Labour of the People in London: First Series: Poverty*, rev. edn (New York: A. M. Kelley Press, 1969 [1889]).

Boxer, Marilyn J., 'Women in Industrial Homework: the Flowermakers of Paris in The Belle Epoque', *French Historical Studies*, vol.12, no.3 (Spring 1982), pp.401–23.

Bradstreet, Christina, '"Wicked with Roses": Floral Femininity and the Erotics of Scent', *Nineteenth-Century Art Worldwide*, vol.18, issue 2 (Autumn 2019), https://www.19thc-artworldwide.org/46-spring07/spring07article/144-qwicked-with-rosesq-floral-femininity-and-the-erotics-of-scent, accessed 10 January 2019.

Brittain, Vera, *Verses of a V. A. D.* (London: Erskine MacDonald, 1918).

Brown, Clare, *Silk Designs of the Eighteenth Century from the Victoria and Albert Museum, London* (London: Thames & Hudson, 1996).

Buchmann, Stephen, *The Reason for Flowers: Their History, Culture, Biology, and How They Change Our Lives* (New York: Scribner, 2015).

Buss, Chiara, *The Meandering Pattern in Brocaded Silks, 1745–1775* (Milan: Ermenegildo Zegna, 1990).

C

Campan, Madame [Henriette], *Memoirs of the Court of Marie Antoinette, Queen of France* (Boston, MA: L. C. Page, pub. 1900). Digitised by Project Gutenberg, https://www.gutenberg.org/files/3891/3891-h/3891-h.htm, accessed 5 December 2019.

Carr, John, *The Stranger in France* (London: J. Johnson, 1803). Digitised by Project Gutenberg, http://www.gutenberg.org/files/20296/20296-h/20296-h.htm, accessed 5 December 2019.

Casini, Silvia, 'Synesthesia, Transformation and Synthesis: Toward a Multi-Sensory Pedagogy of the Image', *The Senses and Society*, vol.12, issue 1 (2017), pp.1–17.

Charmantier, Isabelle, 'Carl Linnaeus and the Visual Representation of Nature', *Historical Studies in the Natural Sciences*, vol.41, no.4 (2011), pp.365–404.

Chrisman-Campbell, Kimberly, *Fashion Victims: Dress at the Court of Louis XVI and Marie Antoinette* (New Haven, CT, and London: Yale University Press, 2015).

Christopher, F. J., *Artificial Flowers, Craft for All* (London: Pitman, 1957).

Classen, Constance, *Worlds of Sense: Exploring the Senses in History and Across Cultures* (London: Routledge, 1993).

Classen, Constance, Howes, David and Synnott, Anthony, *Aroma: The Cultural History of Smell* (London: Routledge, 1994).

'Coloring Artificial Flowers', *Harper's Bazaar*, 1 July 1871, pp.401–2.

Cooper, J. C., *An Illustrated Encyclopaedia of Traditional Symbols* (London: Thames & Hudson, 1978). See entry 'Rose'.

Corbin, Alain, *The Foul and The Fragrant: Odour and the Social Imagination* (London: Berg, 1996).

Cortambert, Louise [attrib.], *The Language of Flowers*, trans. by Frederic Shoberl (Charleston, SC: Nabu Press, 2010 [1820]).

Cowper, William, *The Poetical Works of William Cowper*, H. S. Milford (ed.), 4th edn (London: Oxford University Press, 1959).

Cunnington, C. Willett, *Handbook of English Costume in the Eighteenth Century* (London: Faber and Faber, 1972).

Cunnington, Phillis, and Lucas, Catherine, *Costumes for Births, Marriages and Deaths* (London: A. & C. Black, 1972).

D

Deleuze, Gilles, and Guattari, Félix, *A Thousand Plateaus: Capitalism and Schizophrenia*, trans. by Brian Massumi (London: Athlone Press, 1992).

Diderot, Denis, and Le Rond d'Alembert, Jean (eds), *Encyclopédie, ou dictionnaire raisonné des sciences, des arts et des métiers* (Paris, Neufchastel: 1751–72).

Dior, Christian, *Dior by Dior: The Autobiography of Christian Dior*, trans. by Antonia Fraser (London: Weidenfeld & Nicolson, 1957).

Douglas, Mary, *Purity and Danger: An Analysis of Concepts of Pollution and Taboo* (London: Penguin, 1966).

Dugan, Holly, *The Ephemeral History of Perfume: Scent and Sense in Early Modern England* (Baltimore, MA: The Johns Hopkins University Press, 2011).

Dyhouse, Carol, *Glamour: Women, History, Feminism* (London: Zed Books, 2011).

E

Ehrman, Edwina, *The Wedding Dress: 300 Years of Bridal Fashion* (London: V&A Publishing, 2011).

Eliot, George, *The Works of George Eliot: The Spanish Gypsy* (London: Virtue and Co., 1868).

Eliot, T. S., 'Burnt Norton', in *Collected Poems 1909–1935* (London: Faber and Faber, 1936).

Evans, Joan, *A History of Jewellery, 1100–1870* (London: Faber and Faber, 1953).

F

Fearrington, Florence, *From Wunderkammer to the Modern Museum, 1606–1884: An Exhibition Drawn from the Collection of Florence Fearrington*, exh. cat. (Grinnell, IA: Bucksbaum Center for the Arts, 2013).

Festa, Lynn, 'Fashion and Adornment', in *A Cultural History of Hair in the Age of Enlightenment*, vol.4, Margaret K. Powell and Joseph Roach (eds) (London: Bloomsbury, 2019).

Fisher, Celia, *Flowers of the Renaissance* (London: Frances Lincoln, 2011).

'French Fragrance: On the Scent of New Perfume Mysteries', *Vogue*, 8 December 1930, p.77.

Frost, Laura, 'James Joyce and The Scent of Modernity', in Laura Frost, *The Problem with Pleasure: Modernism and Its Discontents* (New York: Columbia University Press, 2013), pp.33–62.

G

Geczy, Adam, '1690–1815: Chinoiserie, Indiennerie, Turquerie and Egyptomania', in Adam Geczy, *Fashion and Orientalism: Dress, Textiles and Culture from the 17th to the 21st Century* (London: Bloomsbury Academic, 2013), pp.41–84. See http://dx.doi.org/10.2752/9781474235280/Geczy0004, accessed 5 December 2019.

'German Artificial Flower Industry', *Journal of the Royal Society of Arts*, vol.70, no.3644 (22 September 1922), p.767.

Goody, Jack, *The Culture of Flowers* (Cambridge and New York: Cambridge University Press, 1993).

Gorewa, Olga W. et al., *Joyaux du Trésor de Russie* (Paris: Bibliothèque des arts, 1991).

H

Harvey, Susan A., *Scenting Salvation: Ancient Christianity and the Olfactory Imagination* (Berkeley, CA: University of California Press, 2006).

Haweis, Mary Eliza, *The Art of Beauty* (London: Chatto & Windus, 1878).

Haye, Amy de la, and Ehrman, Edwina (eds) *London Couture 1923–1975: British Luxury* (London: V&A Publishing, 2015).

Higgins, R. A., *Greek and Roman Jewellery* (London: Methuen & Co., 1961).

Hiner, Susan, 'The Modiste's Palette and the Artist's Hat', in Simon Kelly and Esther Bell, *Degas, Impressionism, and the Paris Millinery Trade*, exh. cat.(San Francisco, CA: Fine Arts Museums of San Francisco-Legion of Honor, 2017).

Hoffman, Herbert, and Davidson, Patricia F., *Greek Gold: Jewellery from the Age of Alexander*, exh. cat. (Mainz/Rhein: von Zabern, 1965).

Holt, Ardern, *Fancy Dresses Described or What to Wear to Fancy Balls* (London: Debenham & Freebody, 1896 [1879]).

Huysmans, Joris-Karl, *Against Nature: A New Translation*, trans. by Robert Baldick (Harmondsworth: Penguin Books, 1956, 2005 [1884]).

J

Jordan, June, *Passion: New Poems, 1977–1980* (Boston, MA: Beacon, 1980).

Joyaux, François, *La rose, une passion française (1778–1914)* (Paris: Éditions Complexe, 2001).

Joyce, James, *A Portrait of the Artist as a Young Man* (London: Penguin, 2011).

K

Kaiser, Thomas E., 'Madame de Pompadour and the Theaters of Power', *French Historical Studies*, vol.19, no.4 (Autumn 1996), pp.1025–44.
Keats, John, *Poetical Works* (London: Macmillan, 1884).

Keller, Helen, *The World I Live In* (The Floating Press [ebook], 2013).

Kelly, Simon and Bell, Esther, *Degas, Impressionism, and the Paris Millinery Trade*, exh.cat. (San Francisco, CA: Fine Arts Museums of San Francisco-Legion of Honor, 2017).

Kipling, Rudyard, 'Blue Roses', published in *Military Gazette*, vol.6, 16 August 1887, p.5185.

Kirke, Betty, *Madeleine Vionnet* (San Francisco: Chronicle Books, 1998).

Kleeck, Mary Van ['Secretary Committee on Women's Work, Russell Sage Foundation'], *Artificial Flower Makers* (New York: Russell Sage Foundation, 1913).

Knight, Nick, and Knapp, Sandra, *Flora* (Munich: Schirmer/Mosel, 2004).

Kraak, Deborah E., 'Eighteenth-Century English Floral Silks', *The Magazine Antiques*, vol.153, no.6 (June 1998), pp.842–49.

L

Lang, Evelyn M., 'Artificial Flower-Making in Paris', *Lady's Realm*, vol.XII (1902), pp.555–8.

Langhorne, John, *The Fables of Flora* (London: B. Crosby, 1804 [1771]).

Langlade, Émile, *Rose Bertin: Creator of Fashion at the Court of Marie Antoinette*, adapted from the French by Angelo S. Rappoport (New York: Charles Scribner's Sons, 1913).

Lemercier, Claire, '"Articles de Paris": fabriques et institutions économiques à Paris au XIXème siècle', in *Les territoires de l'industrie en Europe (1750–2000): Entreprises, régulations et trajectoires*, Jean-Claude Daumas, Pierre Lamard and Laurent Tissot (eds) (Besançon: Presses universitaires de Franche-Comté, 2007), pp.191–206.

Lightbown, Ronald W., *Mediaeval European Jewellery: With a Catalogue of the Collection in the Victoria and Albert Museum* (London: Victoria and Albert Museum, 1992).

Lilja, Saara, *The Treatment of Odours in the Poetry of Antiquity* (Helsinki: Societas Scientiarum Fennica, 1972).

Lodia, W., 'The Manufacture of Artificial Flowers on the Riviera', *Decorator and Furnisher*, vol.20, no.6 (September 1892), pp.210–12.

Looby, Christopher, 'Flowers of Manhood: Race, Sex and Floriculture from Thomas Wentworth Higginson to Robert Mapplethorpe', *Criticism*, vol.37, no.1 (Winter 1995), pp.109–56.

Lord, W. H., *Report on Artificial Flower and Ostrich Feather Makers* (London: Children's Employment Commission, 1865).

Lorris, Guillaume de, and Meun, Jean de, *The Romance of the Rose*, Oxford World's Classics, trans. by Frances Horgan (Oxford: Oxford University Press, 1994).

M

Mahieu, Kathleen, 'Painted Silk Costume: A Closer Look', in *The Conservation of 18th-Century Painted Silk Dress*, Chris Paulocik and Sean Flaherty (eds) (New York: Costume Institute, Metropolitan Museum of Art, and New York University, 1995), pp.69–77.

Matthews David, Alison, *Fashion Victims: The Dangers of Dress Past and Present* (London: Bloomsbury Visual Arts, 2015).

Mauriès, Patrick, *Cabinets of Curiosities* (London: Thames & Hudson, 2002).

Maxwell, Catherine, *Scents and Sensibility: Perfume in Victorian Literary Culture* (Oxford: Oxford University Press, 2017).

Mayhew, Henry, *London Labour and The London Poor: A Cyclopaedia of the Condition and Earnings of Those that Will Work, Those that Cannot Work, and Those that Will Not Work* (London, 1851).

McNeil, Peter, 'Flowers in the Art of Dress across the World', in *Berg Encyclopedia of World Dress and Fashion: Global Perspectives*, Joanne B. Eicher and Phyllis G. Tortora (eds) (Oxford: Berg, 2010), pp.146–56. Bloomsbury Fashion Central, http://dx.doi.org/10.2752/BEWDF/EDch10019, accessed 5 December 2019.

–'Despots of Elegance', in *Reigning Men: Fashion in Menswear, 1715–2015*, Sharon Sadako Takeda, Kaye Durland Spilker and Clarissa M. Esguerra (eds), exh. cat. (London: DelMonico Books, 2016), p.238.

Menkes, Suzy, 'The Faces of Madame de Pompadour', *Herald Tribune*, 3 December 2002, p.6.

–'#SuzyPFW: Melancholic Beauty from Dries Van Noten', *Vogue*, 28 February 2019, https://www.vogue.co.uk/article/suzypfw-melancholic-beauty-from-dries-van-noten, accessed 14 January 2020.

Miller, Lesley Ellis, 'Jean Revel: Silk Designer, Fine Artist, or Entrepreneur?', *Journal of Design History*, vol.8, no.2 (1995), pp.79–96.

–'The Marriage of Art and Commerce: Philippe de Lasalle's Success in Silk', *Art History*, vol.28, no.2 (April 2005), pp.200–26.

–*Selling Silks: A Merchant's Sample Book 1764* (London: V&A Publishing, 2014).

Munn, Geoffrey C., *The Triumph of Love: Jewellery 1530–1930* (London: Thames & Hudson, 1993). Murphy, Sophia, *The Duchess of Devonshire's Ball* (London: Sidgwick & Jackson, 1984).

N

Naiman, Eric, *Nabokov, Perversely* (Ithaca, N.Y., and London: Cornell University Press, 2010).

Norton Shakespeare: Based on the Oxford Edition, Stephen Greenblatt et al. (eds) (New York: W. W. Norton & Company, 1997).

O

Oakeshott, Grace M., 'Artificial Flower-Making: An Account of the Trade, and a Plea for Municipal Training', *Economic Journal*, vol.13, no.49 (March 1903), pp.123–31.

Oppenheim, James, 'Bread and Roses', *American Magazine*, December 1911, p.619.

The Oxford Classical Dictionary, N. G. L. Hammond and H. H. Scullard (eds) (Oxford: Clarendon Press, 1970). See entry 'Rosalia'.

The Oxford Dictionary of Quotations, Elizabeth Knowles (ed.), 5th edn (Oxford: Oxford University Press, 1999).

P

Peck, Amelia (ed.), *Interwoven Globe: The Worldwide Textile Trade, 1500–1800*, exh. cat. (London: Thames & Hudson, 2013).

Peterson, Trace, 'Exclusively on Venus', *Brooklyn Rail*, October 2016.

Pipelet, Constance, *Rapport sur les fleurs artificielles de la citoyenne Roux-Montagnac* (Paris: Lycée des Arts, 1798).

Poiret, Paul, *My First Fifty Years*, trans. by Stephen Haden (London: Victor Gollancz, 1931).

Potter, Jennifer, *The Rose: A True History* (London: Atlantic Books, 2010).

Proust, Marcel, *Within a Budding Grove, Remembrance of Things Past: Volume II*, trans. by C. K. Scott Moncrieff and Terence Kilmartin (New York: Random House, 1981).

Reilly, Ann, *The Rose* (New York: Portland House, 1989).

R

Reinarz, Jonathan, *Past Scents: Historical Perspectives on Smell* (Chicago: University of Illinois Press, 2014).

Remnick, David, and Finder, Henry (eds), *Fierce Pajamas: An Anthology of Humor Writing from The New Yorker* (New York: Random House, 2001).

Reusch, Glad, and Noble, Mary, *Corsage Craft* (Toronto, New York and London: D. Van Nostrand Company Inc., 1951).

Ribeiro, Aileen, *Dress in Eighteenth-Century Europe: 1715–1789* (London: B. T. Batsford, 1984).

–*The Art of Dress: Fashion in England and France, 1750 to 1820* (New Haven, CT, and London: Yale University Press, 1995).

Richards O'Hare, Kate, 'He Counteth the Sparrow's Fall', *Appeal to Reason*, 19 November 1904.

Rindisbacher, Hans J., *The Smell of Books: A Cultural-Historical Study of Olfactory Perception in Literature* (Ann Arbor, MI: University of Michigan Press, 1992).

'Roses', limited-edition booklet for Alexander McQueen, for the exhibition *Roses*, staged in the Bond Street store, London, November 2019.

S

Sadako Takeda, Sharon, Durland Spilker, Kaye, and Esguerra, Clarissa M. (eds), *Reigning Men: Fashion in Menswear, 1715–2015* exh. cat. (London: DelMonico Books, 2016).

Saint-Aubin, Charles Germain de, *Art of the Embroiderer*, trans. and annotated by Nikki Scheurer (Los Angeles, CA: Los Angeles County Museum of Art, 1983 [1770]).

Scheurer, Nikki, 'The Elegant Art of Embroidery', in *An Elegant Art: Fashion and Fantasy in the Eighteenth Century*, Edward Maeder (ed.), exh. cat. (New York: H. N. Abrams, 1983), pp.89–105.

Seward, Barbara, *The Symbolic Rose* (Dallas, TX: Spring Publications, 1989 [1954]).

Shakespeare, William, *Shakespeare's Sonnets and A Lover's Complaint* (Oxford: Clarendon Press, 1907).

Singer, Maya, 'Petal Pusher', *Vogue*, vol.209, no.9 (September 2019), pp.320–21.

Smith, Godfrey, *The Laboratory; or, School of Arts*, 6th edn (London: C. Whittingham, 1799 [1738?/56]).

Stamelman, Richard, *Perfume: Joy, Obsession, Scandal, Sin, A Cultural History of Fragrance from 1750 to the Present* (New York: Rizzoli, 2006).

Stein, Gertrude, *Geography and Plays* (Boston, MA: Four Seas Co., 1922).

Strachan, John R. (ed.), *A Routledge Literary Sourcebook on the Poems of John Keats* (London: Routledge, 2003).

Strakosh, Avery, 'What's in a Perfume', *Vogue*, 1 May 1925, p.104.

Swinburne, Algernon, 'Our Lady of the Pain' (1866), in *Poems & Ballads* (London: Edward Moxon & Co., 1866).

Syme, Alison, *A Touch of Blossom: John Singer Sargent and the Queer Flora of Fin-de-Siècle Art* (University Park, PA: The Pennsylvania State University Press, 2010).

T

Taylor, Kerry, *Galliano: Spectacular Fashion* (London: Bloomsbury Visual Arts, 2019).

Taylor, Neil, 'Molyneux', in *London Couture 1923–1975: British Luxury*, Amy de la Haye and Edwina Ehrman (eds) (London: V&A Publishing, 2015).

Tennyson, Alfred, *Maud and Other Poems* (London: Tickner & Fields, 1855).

Theophrastus, 'De odoribus', *Enquiry into Plants*, vol.II, Loeb Classical Library (1926), http://

penelope.uchicago.edu/Thayer/E/Roman/Texts/
Theophrastus/De_odoribus*.html, accessed 10
January 2019.

Turin, Luca, *The Secret of Scent: Adventures in
Perfume and the Science of Smell* (London: Faber
and Faber, 2006).

V

Veblen, Thorstein, *The Theory of the Leisure Class:
An Economy Study in the Evolution of Institutions*
(New York: Macmillan Co., 1899).

Vigée-Lebrun [Le Brun], Mary Louise Élisabeth
[Élisabeth-Louise], *Souvenirs: Une édition féministe
de Claudine Herrmann*, 2 vols (Paris: Éditions des
femmes, 1986).

—*Memoirs of Madame Vigée-Lebrun*, trans. by Lionel
Strachey (London: Grant Richards, 1904).

W

Walpole, Horace, *The Letters of Horace Walpole,
Fourth Earl of Orford*, Paget Toynbee (ed.) (Oxford:
Clarendon Press, 1903).

Waugh, Norah, *The Cut of Women's Clothes,
1600–1930* (New York: Routledge, 1968).

Weber, Caroline, *The Queen of Fashion: What Marie
Antoinette Wore to the Revolution* (New York: H. Holt,
2006).

'The Well Dressed Man', *Vogue* (New York), vol.30,
no.1 (22 August 1907), p.212.

Wharton, Edith, *Ethan Frome; Summer; Bunner
Sisters* (London: Everyman, 2008).

Y

Yudov, Matvey, 'Her Majesty The Rose: Raw
Materials', *Fragrantica*, https://www.fragrantica.
com/news/Her-Majesty-the-Rose-10905.html,
accessed 10 January 2020.

Z

Zola, Émile, *The Abbé Mouret's Sin*, trans. by Alex
Brown (London: Elek Books, 1970 [1875])

—*L'Assommoir*, trans. by Margaret Mauldon (Oxford:
Oxford University Press, 2009 [1877])

Biographies

Jonathan Faiers is Professor of Fashion Thinking at the University of Southampton, UK, and he lectures internationally on the interface between popular culture, textiles and dress. His publications include *Tartan* (Berg, 2008), *Dressing Dangerously*, *Fur: A Sensitive History* (both Yale University Press, 2013 and 2020) and essays for *Alexander McQueen, London Couture* (both V&A, 2015) and *Expedition: Fashion from the Extreme* (F.I.T./Thames & Hudson, 2017).

Amy de la Haye is Professor of Dress History & Curatorship and joint director, with Judith Clark, of the Research Centre for Fashion Curation at London College of Fashion, University of the Arts London. From 1991 to 1999 she was Curator of Twentieth Century Dress at the V&A. Her major exhibitions include *Streetstyle: From Sidewalk to Catwalk* (V&A, 1994), *The Cutting Edge: Fifty Years of British Fashion 1947–97* (V&A, 1997), *The Landgirls: Cinderellas of the Soil* (Brighton Museum, 2009) and *Gluck: Art & Identity* (Brighton Museum, 2017). She has published extensively on fashion, museology and collecting.

Colleen Hill is Curator of Costume and Accessories at The Museum at FIT. She has curated more than a dozen exhibitions, including *Paris Refashioned, 1957–1968* (2017), *Fairy Tale Fashion* (2016), and *Exposed: A History of Lingerie* (2014). She has also published several books on fashion.

Nick Knight OBE is one of the world's most visionary, innovative and creative image makers. Working primarily in the realms of fashion and style, his award winning images have been instrumental in challenging conventional notions of beauty and identity. In order to champion fashion film and develop a forum to explore experimental technologies, he launched what was to become the award-winning SHOWStudio website in 2000. He has developed his passion for posting i-Phone photographs of 'Roses from my Garden' on Instagram to create major unique art works that exploit AI.

Mairi MacKenzie is Research Fellow in Fashion and Textiles at Glasgow School of Art and a visiting lecturer at Glasgow University. Her current research is concerned with the relationship between popular music and fashion and social histories of perfume. She is author of *Dream Suits: The Wonderful World of Nudie Cohn* (Lannoo, 2011), *Isms: Understanding Fashion* (A&C Black, 2009), and *Perfume and Fantasy: Scent in Popular Culture and Everyday Life* (Bloomsbury, forthcoming).

Geoffrey Munn OBE, MVO is a jewellery specialist, television presenter, writer and historian. He has published a number of books on precious metalwork and has also contributed to the specialist press on the subject of Nicholas Hilliard, J. M.W. Turner, Dante Gabriel Rossetti and Edward Lear. Geoffrey is a Fellow of both the Linnean Society and the Society of Antiquaries.

Valerie Steele is Director and Chief Curator of The Museum at FIT, where she has curated more than 25 exhibitions, including *Japan Fashion Now* (2010–11) and *A Queer History of Fashion* (2013–14). A prolific author, she is also founder and editor in chief of *Fashion Theory: The Journal of Dress, Body & Culture*.

Acknowledgements

Ravishing: The Rose in Fashion accompanies an exhibition of the same title at The Museum at the Fashion Institute of Technology, New York (MFIT), which is inspirationally directed by Dr Valerie Steele. Many of the garments and accessories featured are drawn from the museum's superlative collection, of which Colleen Hill, with whom I have enjoyed working closely, is Curator of Costume and Accessories. Emma McClendon, Associate Curator of Costume, coordinated the considerable task of picture clearances for this book and liaised with the publisher. The stunning images of objects from MFIT are the results of the skills and creative eyes of Fred Dennis, Senior Curator of Costume, Museum Installation Assistant Thomas Synnamon and Museum Photographer Eileen Costa. Object conservation was provided by the expert Senior Conservator Ann Coppinger, with the help of Associate Conservator Alison Casteneda, and Assistant Conservator Marjorie Jonas. Michelle McVicker, Education and Collections Assistant, helped to organise objects for research appointments and highlighted works by global designers; Tanya Melendez-Escalante, Senior Curator of Education and Public Programs, also advised on the latter and introduced me to curatorial colleagues regarding photography. Sonia Dingilian, Senior Registrar, and Jill Hemingway, Associate Registrar, were instrumental in coordinating new acquisitions and objects for loan. April Calahan, Special Collections Associate at The Gladys Marcus Library at FIT, provided access and valuable direction to fashion plates and journals. I also thank Patricia Mears and Elizabeth Way. It has been a privilege and a lot of fun working with this team of highly talented professionals. I thank them all for their vital contributions and for making me feel so welcome.

My own team at London College of Fashion (LCF), University of the Arts London, is based at the research Centre for Fashion Curation, of which I am co-director with Professor Judith Clark. They have been variously instrumental in the successful completion of this book. I would like to acknowledge Cicely-Rose Proctor and Laura Thornley, who provided research and administrative support; (as ever) my friend and respected colleague Judith Clark; Dr Ben Whyman, Dr Jeffrey Horsley and Bre Stitt. LCF Librarians Dr Christen Ericsson and Marta Cassaro were very generous with their knowledge and expertise. Without the support of Professor Frances Corner, former Vice Chancellor of UAL and Head of LCF, this – for me, dream – project would not have been possible. I would also like to thank Professor Felicity Colman, recently appointed Associate Dean of Research at LCF.

I am immensely grateful to Charlotte and Nick Knight for agreeing to my request to capture in print a conversation on roses, a shared love of which Nick and I have discussed over the years, and for providing the staggeringly beautiful images that have so greatly enhanced this book. I also offer my gratitude and respect to my esteemed co-authors for their fascinating specialist contributions: Professor Jonathan Faiers, Colleen Hill, Mairi MacKenzie and Geoffrey Munn. Dr Philip Sykas generously directed me to sources for nineteenth-century menswear with rose decoration that I would not have found independently. My former MA Fashion Curation students Wen Bi and Hayley Edwards-Dujardin, respectively, undertook detailed research on roses in fashion in the 1980s and '90s and the artificial flower industry in Paris, and Susanna Shubin provided several references. Miriam Veil-Powley worked with me on placement and undertook wide-ranging and self-directed research that was an immense help, as were the literary references provided by Caroline Nunneley. Valerie D. and Peter Mendes provided specialist advice. Helen Tyas helped me with the final twenty-first-century section edit; Martin Pel advised on twentieth-century menswear and my son Felix Reitze de la Haye provided me with research and insights into contemporary fashion.

I also thank those without whom the more contemporary component of this book would simply not have been possible: the many designers and their representatives, archivists and picture librarians. Many other people have also provided references, furnished introductions, shared their collections knowledge and provided support. I thank the following: Alex Antony, Charles Bordin, Ellie Brown, Elizabeth Burns, Anna Buruma, Susanna Cordner, Antonis Daikos, William DiGregorio, Martin Kamer, Dr Miles Lambert, Bruno Legeron, Phylis Magidson, Jacob Moss, Marie Olivier, Adam Phillips, Riccardo Pillon, Scott Schiavone, June Swan, Kerry Taylor, Neil Taylor, Susanna Temkin, Heather Toomer, Igor Uria, Harriet Welty Rochefort and Dilys Williams.

Finally, I have once again thoroughly enjoyed working with Yale University Press: Editorial Director of Art & Architecture Mark Eastment, who has consistently championed my various projects; Anjali Bulley, amazing project manager and Managing Editor, and Marina Asenjo, Production Manager. Faye Robson remains my editor of choice: she subtly but vitally enhances the writing and book content. Charlie Smith and Ben White at Charlie Smith Design have created a graphic concept that conveys so eloquently and with such elegance the juxtaposition of fashion and the rose, the beauty and the pain.

Index